Gold and World Power

GOLD

and World Power

The Dollar, the Pound, and the Plans for Reform

BY SIDNEY E. ROLFE

With the assistance of ROBERT G. HAWKINS

HARPER & ROW, PUBLISHERS, NEW YORK

To Maria

Chapter VII of this book was originally published in the November 1965 issue of *The Bulletin*, a publication of New York University Graduate School of Business Administration, under the title "A Critical Survey of Plans for International Monetary Reform." Copyright © 1965 by Robert G. Hawkins and Sidney E. Rolfe.

FIRST EDITION

LIBRARY OF CONGRESS CATALOG CARD NUMBER:66–10658

C-Q

Contents

Acknowledgments

The assistance of some of the many people who were helpful in the writing of this book is acknowledged with the usual caveat: Any quirks which remain or the ultimate views expressed may in no way be pinned on those to be thanked.

At various stages the manuscript was very kindly read by Professor John Gurley at Stanford, Professor Alan Day of the London School of Economics, and, in part, by Professor Leon Schur at Wisconsin. William Butler, vice president of the Chase Manhattan Bank, gave generously of this time and was most helpful. Certain sections of the manuscript were aided by the comments of John McCloy and Winthrop Knowlton, deputy assistant secretary of the U.S. Treasury. Professor Ben Roberts, Maurice Macmillan, former economic secretary of H. M. Treasury, and Costa Carras were disputants and contributors, particularly to the British section.

Chapter VII appeared in slightly altered form as Bulletin No. 36 of the C. J. Devine Institute of Finance of New York University, with Robert G. Hawkins as coauthor. Professor Arnold Sametz of the Institute was largely responsible for editing an earlier draft, and many of his valuable contributions remain in the chapter.

Robert Hawkins actively assisted throughout the writing of the book, and his comments and contributions to successive steps of the draft were most helpful. Frank W. Scott is responsible for the execution of charts in Chapters V and VI.

John Macrae and Elizabeth Pace Barnes at Harper & Row have

consistently provided sympathetic and understanding editorial assistance.

To Mrs. Thelma Nirou, who has been at all times patient and industrious, thanks are due for her secretarial and ministerial services.

S.E.R.

New York City
February 1966

Gold and World Power

CHAPTER I

Whose Problem?

OURS is a generation which has learned to live with paradox. It has learned to treat sizes with a fine sense of relativity. Something as tiny as an atom when split releases energy capable of destroying at once millions of people. Something as small as a cell when dividing too rapidly in the body produces a cancer, and in too short a time kills the organism.

In the area of the balance of payments we are also confronted by paradoxes. On February 10, 1965, President Johnson sent a special message to Congress on the balance-of-payments problem. In it he rightly emphasized that our over-all economic position is one of great strength. Yet the very facts that a special message on the subject is required, that it is coupled with callings-to-Washington of businessmen and bankers, that the meetings are followed by a panoply of "voluntary" restrictions on the economic activity of the business community with respect to their foreign operations, that the balance-of-payments problem has come front and center in every economic discussion and is the subject of a thousand journalistic alarums, all betray a basic and justified fear. Can one small component of the American economy, an international deficit which totaled $2.8 billion in 1964—or about ½ of 1 per cent of our gross national product, 5 per cent of our international trade, and less than one year's foreign aid program—carry the destructive potential of a cancerous cell or unstable atom? The nation's response makes it appear so.

Indeed, the American economy has never been stronger. By every measure of economic activity the United States is at the zenith of its power. Gross national product (GNP) exceeds $650 billion a year. Over 8 million cars per year are sold. The stock market has, at least temporarily, pierced the Dow-Jones average of 900. Prices have been stable, and taxes were reduced in 1964, with proposals for a further reduction in 1965. There are rockets on the moon and nearly 75 million people are employed. The pundits write with mixed awe and contempt of "the affluent society," and the phrase has become a household word.

Yet within this strength lies a paradoxical weakness. At the zenith of power we find a persistent problem in the international balance of payments. Over the past seven years we have spent or sent abroad roughly $24 billion more than we have taken in; technically, we have incurred a deficit in the international balance. This has led to a loss in gold of nearly $8 billion. It has also led to the creation of IOU's against the United States. If these were exchanged for gold—a definite theoretical possibility—the further outflow of gold would exhaust the U.S. gold stock. But to state a paradox does not imply that the nation should tolerate it, and certainly implies even less that the nation should leave it unsolved.

The United States has had a balance-of-payments deficit for fourteen of the fifteen years since 1950, and there has been, both in the United States and abroad, a willingness to tolerate it for eight or nine of those years. Every deficit implies a surplus in other countries, and the American deficits corresponded to gains or surpluses which, after 1958, accrued primarily to the nations of continental Europe. The change in their attitude and policy by the 1960s took the form of occasional "cashing in" of their American IOU's—dollar obligations given to cover the American deficits—for gold. Into the 1960s the conversions became larger and the gold drain more severe and alarming for the United States. In addition, there has been consistent pressure on Americans to exercise financial discipline.

SOME FACTS

Just what is the balance of payments? A brief preview of the statistics—holding in abeyance until Chapter II a more sophisticated analysis of its derivation—should focus on both the U.S. and U.K. deficits and the reasons therefor. Since both the dollar and the British pound are the "reserve" currencies of the free world, it is necessary for Americans to take the British position into cognizance.

Table 1 summarizes the American and British positions from 1958 through 1964. The salient conclusion from Table 1 is that the *nature* of the American and British deficits is very different.

Balance-of-payments figures, as presented above or elsewhere, show the residue—the net result—of inflows and outflows of money resulting from various transactions between the United States (and United Kingdom in the above table) and the rest of the world. The first column in Table 1, the "visible trade balance," sometimes called the "merchandise account," shows the result of imports and exports of goods. Thus, when an American imports a Volkswagen, the American account chalks up a negative $1,700; when Germans or other Europeans buy wheat or Fords or machinery or other American exports, the account chalks up a positive amount of whatever was sold. Netting all the pluses and minuses, we arrive at Column 1.

In the aggregate, these figures show the fundamental difference between the U.S. and U.K. positions. For to sell $6.7 billion more in goods to the world than we buy from it is no mean accomplishment. In this category the British did badly, importing $1.5 billion more than they sold. They did much better in prior years; one result of the 1964 runaway of imports was the imposition by the United Kingdom of the 15 per cent import "surcharge" (tax); another was the sterling crisis and the "rescue operation"; and, all in all, this performance and the British determination to "save the pound" set the background for the 1965–1966 British budget which is highly restrictive at best.

Both the United States and the United Kingdom show strength in Column 2, the "current balance." The items which make up this column, in addition to the "visible trade balance" (carried cumulatively from Column 1), include dividend and other earnings from past long-term overseas investments. American citizens own net over $40 billion in foreign investment and earned over $4.5 billion on them in 1964; the United Kingdom owns net about £5.2 billion of such foreign investments, and earned over £750 million. Because of these holdings, both the United States and the United Kingdom

TABLE 1. THE BALANCE OF PAYMENTS IN SUMMARY [a]
UNITED STATES AND UNITED KINGDOM, 1958–1964
(billions of dollars)

Year	Visible Trade Balance		Current Balance		Basic Balance		Other Transactions		Monetary Balance	
	U.S.	U.K.	U.S.	U.K.	U.S.	U.K.	U.S.	U.K.	U.S.	U.K.
1958	+3.3	+0.1	+2.2	+1.0	-3.7	+0.5	+0.2	+0.1	-3.5	+0.6
1959	+1.0	-0.3	+0.1	+0.4	-4.2	-0.3	+0.5	-0.2	-3.7	-0.5
1960	+4.7	-1.1	+4.1	-0.8	-1.5	-1.3	-2.4	+0.8	-3.9	-0.5
1961	+5.4	-0.4	+5.6	-0.1	-0.6	+0.1	-1.8	neg.	-2.4	+0.1
1962	+4.4	-0.3	+5.1	+0.3	-1.6	-0.1	-0.6	+0.3	-2.2	+0.2
1963	+5.1	-0.2	+5.9	+0.3	-2.0	-0.2	-0.7	-0.2	-2.7	-0.4
1964	+6.7	-1.5	+8.6	-1.0	-0.1	-2.1	-2.7	neg.	-2.8	-2.1

SOURCE: *The Economist*, April 3–9, 1965, p. 70; and U.S. Department of Commerce, *Survey of Current Business*.
[a] The figures are to be read cumulatively.

are said to be "solvent but illiquid." But short of massive nationalization of these assets, which occurred in Britain in 1939 but never before or since, such assets are likely to remain in private hands, unavailable to government to solve current problems. This column also adds in and subtracts out income from transportation, insurance, banking services, military expenditures, etc., as well as the enormous U.S. and British expenditures on foreign travel. Still, the net total of these items which are added to the Column 1 totals gives the United States a net surplus of over $8 billion in 1964 and reduces the U.K. deficit on merchandise trade by about one-half billion dollars.

By Column 3, the "basic balance," we find that the U.S. surplus of over $8 billion has vanished into a deficit, and the U.K. deficit has doubled. What is added to, or subtracted from, the "current balance" (Column 2) to dissipate such large sums? Hitting the highlights, the "basic balance" adds net long-term lending and foreign aid to the "current balance." American private long-term (repayment maturity in excess of one year) investment abroad was $2.4 billion in 1964. This means simply that U.S. corporations and banks invested or loaned this amount of their dollars abroad at long term, in excess of what U.S. private borrowers got from foreign sources. In the case of Britain, long-term capital outflow was $1 billion (£371 million, more than double the £174 million in 1963), and this accounts for nearly the entire increase in the U.K. deficit appearing in Column 3. But the United States still has more to account for to dissipate the $8 billion surplus. Two types of government expenditures loom large: Government long-term capital loans, which are mainly AID loans to developing countries, were $2.4 billion, but some $800 million of past loans was repaid, so the net outflow here was $1.6 billion; and unilateral transfers, which means government AID payments and *grants* (as opposed to loans), cost $2.7 billion. Trading, buying, and selling of U.S. and foreign securities account for the bulk of the balance of the deficit appearing in Column 3.

Column 4, "other transactions," is mainly short-term capital outflows—net U.S. loans to foreigners with a maturity of less than one year; some of this came from banks, some from corporate or personal investment sources. The figure for the United States, $2.7

billion, is equal to 90 per cent of the final U.S. deficit of $2.8 billion, appearing in Column 5 as "monetary balance." The short-term capital figure for the United Kingdom is negligible.

How did the United States pay for its $2.8 billion deficit? First, it sold some gold, about $171 million, and issued some $375 million in IOU's in the form of "Roosa bonds"—guaranteed U.S. obligations to foreign countries. Other U.S. obligations in the form of government securities, time deposits, etc. acquired by foreign nations and individuals, "paid for" the rest of the deficit. This raised the total of American short-term obligations in the hands of other nations to over $23 billion. We owe other nations this much, and to this extent they are financing our deficits. If these countries wish to, they can convert their holdings of U.S. paper obligations into gold, which would pose an interesting problem since we have only about $15 billion of gold left. In the case of the United Kingdom, its deficit of $2.1 billion was financed by selling $342 million (£122 million) of reserves (gold and dollars), and by borrowing from the International Monetary Fund (IMF) $1 billion (£357 million) and from foreign central banks (the "rescue operation") $605 million (£216 million). The remainder was financed by an increase in liabilities (IOU's) to private foreigners.

SOME QUESTIONS

This preliminary view of the balance-of-payments data occasions several equally preliminary questions about the whole matter of deficits; to whether or not the deficit currencies are overvalued; and what can be done about it all.

First, it is the established fashion, of mercantilist origin, to refer to the acquisition of gold or currency as "surplus," and to the acquisition of goods, services, or ownership of interest or dividend-paying paper as "deficits." Clearly, there is little intrinsic value to gold per se; once teeth are filled it can simply be held in the ground as "reserves" to ship to someone else. The real value of any goods or commodity should lie in their usefulness, and one could well look upon a deficit as good. Nevertheless, so long as all the world uses this language, no writer can part from it except at the risk of confusing his readers.

A far more important question, and one to which we will return at length later, is whether or not both the dollar and the pound are overvalued. Stated differently, if the dollar were worth, say, three German marks instead of four, American exports would be cheaper for Germans to buy, German exports more expensive for Americans to buy, and the United States would presumably earn even more than the $8 billion it does on "current balance." If the Americans earned enough more here, then they could aid, invest, militarize, and do all the other things they wish to do without running deficits. If the British pound were cheaper, i.e., if it were not overvalued, then the United Kingdom could export more, import less, and earn its way without periodic sterling crises. If the deficits continue, and other nations refuse to finance them as they are now threatening to do, the dollar and more likely the pound could perforce be devalued, a turn of events the leaders of these nations consider catastrophic.

Actually, most economists agree that to do all the things the United States is doing now, the dollar is overvalued. Thus Paul Samuelson has written:

The dollar has been somewhat overvalued in this last decade. This does not imply that we should depreciate. It does imply that economists everywhere would prefer, if they could rerun history, that the 1949 depreciations [of foreign currencies] had been somewhat less sharp.[1]

He goes on to point out that overvaluation has hampered a high employment policy at home; has limited America's freedom to spend abroad *in an efficient manner*; has kept pressure on our price levels, but this benefit has been dearly bought in terms of unemployment, excess capacity, slow growth, and low domestic profits; has pushed American capital abroad which, in turn, reduces the technological gap between the United States and other nations; and has helped to redistribute gold and liquid reserves abroad, "providing the miracle nations of Europe and Japan with a needed secular increase of liquidity."

In the currency devaluations of 1948–1949, the Germans depreciated their currency by 93 per cent, the French by over 50 per cent (and by another 20 per cent in 1957 and 1958), and other currencies

[1] "Theoretical Notes on Trade Problems," *Review of Economics and Statistics*, May 1964, p. 153.

have followed the same pattern. But the British devalued only about 30 per cent, and the United States not at all.

The British, subsequent to 1949, and the Americans have resisted devaluation, even though it is permitted under the IMF rules for currencies in fundamental disequilibrium, which these surely are. By this ostensibly magnificent display of social responsibility two governmental authorities see themselves as the benevolent protectors of the international financial system. (This is an argument which ramifies broadly, and we shall return to it in detail later.)

SOME VIEWS

What is to be done? This is, of course, the key question, the full answers to which constitute the bulk of this book. But in a preliminary way, it is clear from Table 1 that the origin of the problem is quite different in the United States and the United Kingdom. For the United States, there is one school of thought that holds that not much need be done. Voluntary devaluation is ruled out officially, and to prevent involuntary devaluation, temporary restrictions will suffice. The London *Economist* [2] cited Walter Salant in concluding that the major source of the U.S. deficit is in short-term capital movements (Column 5) which our rising short-term interest rates have been designed to alleviate. The Brookings Institution in its famous study [3] predicts that, under certain assumptions, European inflation may solve the problem by 1968, as the United States inflates less rapidly and thus gains price advantages. But the Brookings study explicitly recognizes that part of the price the United States is paying for this type of adjustment is underemployment.

The failure to reduce unemployment, even to a 4 per cent level, has cost the United States $30 to $40 billion *per year* in lost jobs, production, and income. It was first Lord Keynes who pointed out that it is not only prices which equilibrate balance-of-payments deficits and surpluses, but also the level of employment. [4] Once hotly

[2] *The Economist*, April 3–9, 1965, p. 70.
[3] Walter Salant, et al., *The United States Balance of Payments in 1968* (Washington, D.C.: The Brookings Institution, 1963).
[4] There were precursors of this argument, from the eighteenth century on, but the position is today considered "Keynesian" and Keynes's contribution; cf. Lloyd Metzler, "The Theory of International Trade," *A Survey of Contemporary Economics* (Philadelphia: Blakiston Co., 1949).

contested, this contribution is now so widely accepted that even so classic a free marketeer as Milton Friedman has written one of the most lucid statements of the Keynesian position:

Wage rates tend to be among the least flexible prices. In consequence, an incipient deficit that is countered by a policy of permitting or forcing prices to decline is likely to produce unemployment rather than, or in addition to, wage decreases. . . . This is clearly a highly inefficient method of adjusting to external changes.[5]

Others have wondered why government spending, particularly for AID and military purposes, is not cut to overcome the deficit. It was once the style of economists to accept these expenditures as "given," or "politically determined exogenous variables," or some such semantic of acquiescence. Still ineffective, many voices have been raised now to this point. Senator William Fulbright and others have questioned our AID program. Senator George McGovern and others have questioned our military expenditure policy, particularly in Vietnam which promises now to become very costly, to the detriment of our balance-of-payments position. J. K. Galbraith has written:

Military obligations must always be examined in the full context of other policy. We cannot do abroad what we do not have the external resources to pay for; the price of present military outlays could always be a more severe contraction later on . . . (troop) deployment must also be examined in the light of modern technical developments in air transport and long-range fighter aircraft. These now give the option of deploying troops so as to minimize foreign exchange cost without lessening their real as distinct from symbolic effectiveness.[6]

Some observers, including Galbraith, point to our large long-term private capital outflows as the cause of the deficit and are willing to impose restrictions on these as the lesser of evils necessary to provide a cure.[7] The U.S. government has heeded this advice with President Kennedy's "interest equalization tax" and President Johnson's "voluntary restraints," both aimed at cutting private investment abroad.

[5] *Essays in Positive Economics* (Chicago: University of Chicago Press, 1953), p. 165.
[6] "The Balance of Payments: A Political and Administrative View," *Review of Economics and Statistics*, May 1964, p. 120.
[7] *Ibid.*; see also D. A. Snider, "Capital Controls and the U.S. Balance of Payments," *American Economic Review*, June 1964, pp. 346–357.

A deeper point emerges from this preliminary discussion of what to do. It is that, in the absence of an operative equilibrating mechanism which automatically solves balance-of-payments deficits, the nation must make a choice between internal and external needs. The necessity to resort to one or more of the items mentioned—underemployment of labor and other resources, controls of investments, cutting aid and military budgets, or failure to grow—results from overvaluation of the American currency, and the U.S. choice to keep the dollar at its present value. There is no such thing as something for nothing, and the United States has paid in internal adjustment for this external rigidity.

The United States is by no means the first country to face this conflict between internal needs and external rigidity—the "defense of the currency" vs. domestic needs. Great Britain faces the problem today and also faced it in the 1920s. The British had permitted the pound to float, i.e., to seek its own level in terms of other currencies, in the early 1920s, but in 1925 they went back to a fixed price pound at the prewar level. The results were horrendous. They deepened the internal depression. Internal acrimony of the worst type resulted, in the course of which Lord Keynes wrote his famous polemic, "The Economic Consequences of Mr. Churchill," who, as Chancellor of the Exchequer, had made the move to fix the price of sterling.

How do the overvaluation of the American and British currencies and the consequent effects appear from a European point of view? It has been pointed out that the unwillingness of the European central bankers to continue to accumulate dollar deficit obligations has been the precipitant of both the gold outflow and the American restrictions, not to mention the British crisis. Yet the fact is, as Samuelson pointed out above, that the very outflow of American currency has contributed to the growth of European industry. Therefore, there are some Europeans who are fearful that this outflow of American dollars will stop. Others, notably President Charles de Gaulle and his advisers, have argued that the outpouring of American capital tends to "export inflation" and, more important, to seize control of European industry by purchasing, takeover, competition, etc. The Europeans demand that the Americans "discipline" themselves is partially a reaction to American foreign investment.

Obviously, there is no single Europe, even within the Common

Market, and thus there is ambivalence in the European response. Some would stanch the flow of American deficits, including the flow of capital investment; others fear this stanching. Two articles almost side by side in the *New York Times* of February 15, 1965, illustrate the point. First:

President Johnson's proposals for reducing the persistent deficit in the nation's balance of payments represent merely the latest attempt to solve the problem . . . but if the results are disappointing, European governments will promptly demand tougher action in return for agreeing to continue to finance the U.S. deficit.

Then the other side of the coin:

A weekend survey of economists and bankers in the six nation . . . Common Market has elicited the unanimous view that if the inflow of American dollars to the trade group is substantially curtailed, the European bloc will have a serious payments problem of its own that could have disastrous consequences.

The American reaction to this state of affairs has been complex and deserves fuller analysis, which Chapter VI provides. Briefly, it has been chagrin; the United States is amazed that its friends and allies, who without its help from 1945 on would never have gained the strength they have, should be so "ungrateful" and balk at further financing its deficits. But, *more important, the response has been to impose restrictions on itself* in response to European complaints.

To date, activity has been restricted in three major ways which touch the life of almost every citizen. First, tourist expenditures have been reduced to discourage Americans from going abroad; second, American individuals and corporations have been restricted from investing in or acquiring foreign assets, despite the fact that dividends on these investments come back quickly; third, and, perhaps most important, internal policies have been adjusted to the external position which may have diminished the rate of growth and investment and helped to perpetuate the relatively high level of American unemployment. Failure to achieve full employment has cost the United States $30 to $50 billion *per year* in lost output since 1958, some of which may be the result of its concern with the balance-of-payments problem.

In any appraisal of the problem, there must be heavy interplay between political and economic considerations. That foreign nations can impose their will on the United States by virtue of their surplus position is a sign of their political strength and its political shrinkage. That the United States must go to the Western European nations with offers of guarantees and pleas for mercy, that the United States must go to Japan and even Hong Kong and ask that they voluntarily restrict their exports to the United States, are further humiliating signs of weakness. Galbraith has summarized the relation:

A strong balance of payments is a factor of major importance in national position and leadership. In the past our force commitment to France and Germany has poured dollars into these countries and, by weakening our balance of payments, weakened our bargaining position vis-à-vis these countries.[8]

Indeed, at present the United States has been forced by its deficits to play a waiting game, because it cannot open needed discussion on the whole question with the Europeans from its present position of weakness. Thus the United States waits, hoping that the restrictions it has imposed on itself will alleviate, at least temporarily, its present weakness by reducing its deficit so that it can negotiate from a position of strength certain fundamental changes in the system it feels necessary.

To the American citizen, therefore, it must by now be all too apparent that the balance-of-payments problem is real, and that it affects him deeply and personally. It affects his pride and his self-esteem as an American. It affects his pocket in many and unsuspected ways.

As an investor, he may wonder why he must pay a special tax if he wants to invest abroad. As a stockholder or a corporate executive, he may be willing to go along with the President's voluntary restriction on overseas investment, implying as it does a voluntary diminution of his dividends. (Why invest at all unless there are profits to be earned?) But in going along, he may also realize that failure to invest now will diminish his stake in large and growing markets abroad in the future. And the rules of patriotism do not preclude logical wonder about whether or not this is a wise course,

[8] *Op. cit.*, p. 120.

or whether the government's judgment as a restrictor is better than his as an investor.

If the citizen has a speculative turn of mind, he will certainly wonder how much more of the same medicine is in store in the future. "Temporary" restrictions, however well meant, have a testy way of becoming permanent, particularly when the problem is not solved at its root. If the problem cannot be solved now, at the peak of America's internal prosperity, when can it be solved?

If he probes more deeply, the citizen may wonder how much of the lost output of $30 to $50 billion a year was a result of policies to improve the balance of payments, and what his share of this would have been. He may well wonder why, with the present state of economic sophistication, such losses have continued to be allowed. This game gets costly. Is it really necessary?

SOME DEFINITIONS

There is no paucity of literature about the balance-of-payments problem. Quite naturally, every piece written starts with some sort of definition of the problem. But this is a heuristic exercise. The questions one asks determine the answers one gets. Of course, if short-term capital flight were stopped, the U.S. deficit (or the bulk of it) would vanish; the same may be said of foreign aid; or capital investment; or tourism; or virtually any component of the balance which happens to approximate in magnitude (or in some combination) the $2.8 billion deficit.

Since most of the writing is done by economists, the solutions proffered are usually of a purely economic nature; that is, they rely on the use of one or another economic mechanism, and the basic historical and political substructure on which economics rests is sometimes ignored.

Which item is selected for reduction or suppression actually reflects the hierarchy of social priorities of the selector. Those who prefer a maximum reliance on free markets (and, incidentally, a maximum of free trade) will select a changed or a free exchange rate; the burden of adjustment will thus fall on the exchange rate. Among those who favor internal controls or restrictions there is also a hierarchy of importance. At the extremes, if the economist is of a "classical" bent, he will usually advocate higher interest rates within the United States, to depress the American economy further and make exports still cheaper. If he is of the more modern or "control" mold, he will usually advocate some form of direct controls over investment, tourism, or other economic activity for the sake of ending the U.S. deficit and keeping the dollar (or pound) strong. Between the extremes lie a variety of views.

This, then, begins to define the problem. The United States and consequently the whole free world, for which the U.S. economy is still the linchpin, have a problem. Stated briefly, it is that if the quantity of monetary reserves available to the world is adequate, its quality is questionable. When there is an abundance of dollars in the tills of the Western central banks and governments, the till-keepers object, preferring gold, of which there is no abundance and little available additional supply. When there is a shortage of dollars, the other countries suffer a liquidity or reserve shortage which hampers their operation and could cripple their growth.

But neither the United States nor the tillkeepers abroad have much freedom to alter the course of events because the game is played according to certain rules which were set up during World War II, and which the United States virtually dictated since it was the dominant political power. Two new dimensions of definition emerge. The first is the rules which are: (1) The foreign exchange value of currencies is set in price and, within very narrow bands, must remain rigid; and (2) the price of gold, to which currency prices in turn are related, is also rigid at $35 per troy ounce.

The second dimension is political. The rules were established in a political conclave where give-and-take prevail. When the current rules were established in 1944, in effect only the United States did the giving and taking, the main parties concerned being the Treasury and the Congress. True, the British were there, but they were soon overruled because political power and economic rule-making were one, even then. The Russians were also there, but they soon withdrew and never entered the game. Other representatives provided Bretton Woods with an international flavor, but the domination of the United States was complete.

Now, it is thought that the rules must be changed. There is wide consensus that they have outlived their usefulness. A new conference will not be so easy for the United States. Clearly, the currently strong economic parties, particularly France, Germany, and other Common Market nations, will be more reluctant to take their lead from the United States. The embarrassment and, if possible, removal of the United States as the sole Western leader is clearly de Gaulle's prime international motive. A major purpose of the temporary restrictions placed on the American economy by three successive administrations of both political parties is to strengthen the American balance-of-payments position in order to strengthen the American hand at the forthcoming rule-making negotiations.

Negotiations to what end? A variety of reforms of the international monetary system have been proposed. While each of them is couched in economic language, and each proclaims its superiority and the inferiority of the alternatives in economic terms, the fact is that behind each plan lies a different vision of power, a different political scheme favoring someone at someone else's cost.

The layman, and particularly the businessman, is often impressed with the disagreements among economists as much as or more than with the value of their advice. When rational men disagree, there can basically be two reasons. The first is ignorance of the facts. For past and present periods this ignorance can be rectified by research and fact-finding. With reference to the future, facts are necessarily conjectures. Disagreements may be quite honestly reached, and only time—the working of one type of variable as opposed to another—will tell the tale. But a second and more important type of disagreement reflects the political preference or the relative social valuations of the economist. These preferences are not always made explicit; indeed, the holder is usually not able to state them because they are often subconsciously held. To look behind economic plans and preferences to their political or ideological roots is part of the elucidating game. In analyzing the various plans for reform put forward, we will attempt to understand in political terms what each plan is really designed to achieve.

These rather extended remarks about the definition of the problem, then, constitute the *raison d'etre* and the plan of this book. First, the data constituting balance-of-payments statistics will be examined. What are their components, how do they arise in the economy, and what do they mean? Next, the various possible types of equilibrating adjustments to changes in the balance of payments will be examined. Here it is hoped to provide an analytic framework of the prototypes of adjustment mechanisms available to free nations, and the cost and benefits of each type. Next, the roots of the current system are examined: the historic and political mechanisms by which it arose, what it tried to solve, and what seeds of fruition or destruction it carried at birth. Doubtless, attempted solutions at new conferences to be held will face many of the same problems.

The revelation of inherent weaknesses of the present system is nowhere better documented than in the plight of the United States and the United Kingdom, which is next analyzed. For better or worse, the United States and the United Kingdom are in the same boat in this matter. In the light of current resurgence of economic and even regional nationalism in Europe—in which de Gaulle is only today's protagonist and will quite probably be followed by others tomorrow, because the disease is social and not personal—a happy conclusion to monetary reform is not likely. Nevertheless, the various proposals for reform are next analyzed, in terms of both their explicit economic propositions and their implicit political goals, as we are able to understand the latter.

CHAPTER II

The Balance of Payments:
Basic Accounting* and Concepts

In the simplest terms, the "balance of payments" is the difference between a country's payments to foreigners and its receipts (of payments) from foreigners. Thus, net *money* flows are the raw materials of balance-of-payments accounting. This is true whether the entire payments position or any component of it is being analyzed.

The major component of the total balance of payments for most countries measures payments and receipts from the sale of goods, i.e., the merchandise or "visible trade balance." Referring back to our Table 1 in Chapter I (p. 4), it is seen that the United States had a "visible trade balance" of +$6.7 billion dollars in 1964. Actually, this figure is the net result of two much larger figures, the values of goods exported and imported. Thus, the value of U.S. exports in 1964 was $25.3 billion [1] while U.S. imports from all countries amounted to $18.6 billion. Subtracting the latter (payments for imports) from the former (receipts from exports) gives the net positive $6.7 billion "visible trade balance."

But a country's foreign trade does not consist of goods alone. It also includes the purchase and sale of services. Among these services,

* This section is intended for readers interested in accounting detail; others should skip to "Concepts" on p. 28 or to Chapter III.

[1] This export figure excludes the value of military goods sent to foreign governments under U.S. military grants. This procedure is followed consistently throughout this book.

freight and shipping charges for the transport of goods, travel expenditures of tourists, and interest and dividend payments on foreign capital are obvious examples. Thus, if an exporter ships his exports on a ship of another country, the payment of the charges is part of total payments to foreigners; so, too, with tourist expenditures abroad and payments of income on foreign-owned investments.

On these nonvisible trade items, the United States earned *net* an additional $1.9 billion in 1964. The following table illustrates the exports (receipts) and imports (expenditures) and net balance for these services in 1964. These data make quite clear why tourism and military expenditures are such an inviting target for control.

The sums of the payments and receipts for "visible trade" and all services, as shown in the totals of Table 1, are generally called current payments and receipts, or receipts and payments on goods and services. The net (receipts minus payments) figure is commonly called the "current account balance," for which the United States had a positive $8.6 billion figure (surplus) in 1964.

TABLE 1. U.S. RECEIPTS AND PAYMENTS
FOR GOODS AND SERVICES, 1964 [a]
(*billions of dollars*)

	Receipts	Payments	Net Receipts or Payments (−)
Visible trade [b]	25.3	18.6	6.7
Transportation	2.3	2.5	−0.2
Travel	1.1	2.2	−1.1
Income on foreign investments	5.4	1.3	4.1
Miscellaneous services	2.0	0.9	1.1
Military expenditures and transactions	0.8	2.8	−2.0
CURRENT ACCOUNT BALANCE	36.9	28.3	8.6

SOURCE: U.S. Department of Commerce, *Survey of Current Business*, March 1965, Table 3, p. 14.

[a] Detail may not add to total because of rounding.
[b] Excludes exports given under military grants.

Another large category of payments and receipts is *private foreign investments*, i.e., international capital movements. The importance of international capital flows has increased greatly in the postwar period and has become a major balance-of-payments consideration for a number of countries, not least the United States, in the last decade. Stated simply, when an American buys a foreign bond or stock, or purchases a foreign firm, his payment for the purchase must be included in total payments to foreigners. Similarly, if a foreigner makes such purchases of U.S. capital instruments, his payment represents a receipt in the balance of payments. For example, in 1964 U.S. citizens and corporations made direct investments in foreign firms and subsidiaries, purchased foreign stocks, bonds, and other capital assets, in the amount of $6.4 billion. In the same period, private foreigners (excluding governments and central banks) purchased U.S. capital assets of only about $0.5 billion. However, an essential distinction is made, for balance-of-payments purposes, between long-term investments abroad and short-term capital. This will be discussed in detail below.

We have thus far isolated two major categories of payments and receipts. First, the balance of payments *measures* payments and receipts arising from trade—in both goods and services—and second, it *measures* the private capital flows between the country and the outside world.

Three other categories of payments and receipts may be identified before we proceed. First, the *government* may make foreign payments in ways other than the purchase of foreign services shown in Table 1. It may make a loan to a foreign country (invest abroad) or perhaps give money to a country (make a grant). In 1964, the United States made loans of $2.4 billion to foreign countries (mostly under the foreign aid program) and money grants of $1.9 billion. Second, a private individual or company may transfer money to a foreigner for which nothing is received in return (for example, an immigrant remits a gift to his family or friends in another country), i.e., make a *unilateral transfer* of money to a foreigner. These payments totaled over $0.5 billion in 1964. Finally, a country may sell (or buy) *gold or foreign currency* to (or from) another country. The payment for the sale is included in total receipts (or payments) from abroad. Gold and foreign currency sales to foreigners (or purchases from foreigners) are included as a separate balance-of-payments category because these items are the *international reserves* of a country. They are of such importance in the existing international monetary system that they merit a special place in the balance of payments. (More will be said of their role in following chapters.)

Table 2 below presents a scheme of the balance of payments which summarizes the major components and the main subcomponents of each. More detail is shown in the capital and official reserves accounts than has thus far been discussed. The significance of this detail will emerge in what follows; what is important now are the broad categories of payments and receipts.

Before we turn to more intricate questions of balance-of-payments accounting, a bothersome question should be considered. Why is it that the *international* balance of payments is deemed of such importance, while those of various areas within a nation are usually ignored? Surely, total payments by Chicago or Texas to the rest of the United States do not always equal receipts from the rest of the United States. In fact, it would be purely accidental if they were ever equal. A seemingly plausible answer might lie in the importance of the political boundary involved. Although the city limits of Chicago and the state limits of Texas can be specifically defined, they are not as important as the boundary of the United States.

But this is only a half-truth. It is evident that any arbitrarily chosen geographical area has a balance of payments with the rest of the world, yet we chose to ignore, and usually not even measure, these balances, except for those between one nation-state and the rest of the nation-states. The real answer lies in the use of *national currencies*. Most foreign transactions must involve an exchange of one national currency for another. In the case of an import, the importer wants to pay for the foreign goods in his domestic currency, while the foreign exporter wants to be paid in his domestic currency. This exchange of currencies occurs in the *foreign exchange market*. This is a market between large domestic and foreign banks and other institutions in which various national currencies are bought and sold. A country's balance of payments is therefore directly related to the foreign exchange market, and directly affects the supply of its currency to foreigners and the demand for its national currency by foreigners.

Returning to the example of Chicago and Texas, there is no foreign exchange market since only one national currency is involved, the U.S. dollar. Thus, the balance of payments of Chicago or Texas

TABLE 2. SCHEME OF THE BALANCE OF PAYMENTS

Receipts from Foreigners (credits)	Payments to Foreigners (debits)

Current account
1. Sale of goods (exports)
2. Sale of services
  a. Travel and tourist expenditures by foreigners in U.S.
  b. Transportation, freight, and insurance expenditures in U.S.
  c. Miscellaneous services sold
  d. Income on investments in foreign countries
	Current account
	1. Purchase of goods (imports)
	2. Purchase of services
	  a. Travel and tourist expenditures abroad
	  b. Transportation, freight, and insurance expenditures to foreigners
	  c. Miscellaneous foreign services purchased
	  d. Income paid on foreign investments in U.S.

Unilateral transfers from abroad
  a. Private
  b. Government grants to U.S.
	Unilateral transfers to foreigners
	  a. Private
	  b. Government grants to foreigners

Capital account
1. Long-term investment in U.S.
  a. Direct investment
  b. Foreign purchase of U.S. stocks and bonds, minus redemptions
  c. Foreign government loans to U.S. (less repayments)
2. Short-term capital (including deposit balances)
  a. Increase in short-term liabilities to foreigners, i.e., an increase in foreigners' holdings of short-term dollar assets
	Capital account
	1. Long-term investment abroad
	  a. Direct investment
	  b. Purchase of foreign stocks and bonds, minus redemption
	  c. Government loans to foreigners (less repayments)
	2. Short-term capital (including deposit balances)
	  a. Increase in short-term foreign assets held by Americans

Official reserves account
  a. Sale of gold to foreigners
  b. Sale of foreign currency reserves to foreigners
	Official reserves account
	  a. Purchase of gold from foreigners
	  b. Purchase of foreign currency to hold as official reserves

TOTAL RECEIPTS (+)	= TOTAL PAYMENTS (−)

takes care of itself. Chicago may spend more in the rest of the United States than it receives from the rest of the United States (run a balance-of-payments deficit) as long as any dollars remain in Chicago; but the act of running a deficit automatically produces forces which will correct it. Thus, if money is leaving Chicago, the mere action of supply and demand will cause incomes, wages, employment, and prices of goods and services in Chicago to fall relative to those outside, and interest rates to rise. Thus, Chicagoans will tend to emigrate, to buy more at home than outside, and to invest in Chicago at higher interest rates. Likewise, outsiders will spend more in Chicago due to the falling prices, and invest more there because of higher interest rates. Therefore, the loss of dollars due to the deficit changes economic conditions in Chicago or Texas vis-à-vis the rest of the United States so that payments to the outside are reduced and receipts from the outside are increased. The deficit is eliminated.

The question arises as to why this automatic mechanism does not also operate internationally. In part, this reflects (1) separate national currencies and (2) different national policies. This will be taken up more fully in the next chapter, but for the moment it suffices to reiterate that balance-of-payments problems revolve around the fact that national currencies must be exchanged for international transactions to take place. It then follows that the balance of payments is a *monetary* phenomenon; it is concerned only with money flows reflecting the flows of physical goods and services.

The Logic of Balance-of-Payments Accounts

The foregoing section isolated a number of categories of foreign payments and receipts according to the reason for or cause of the transaction. In this section, balance-of-payments accounting will be dealt with in somewhat more detail, to show the interconnections between various categories of payments and receipts.

Balance-of-payments accounting (or measurement) is based upon the familiar concept of double entry bookkeeping. For every transaction, there are conceptually two entries. In more familiar terms, there is a debit (−) and there is a credit (+) for every transaction, and if one adds up the totals, debits must equal credits (or total payments must equal total receipts).

The two sides of each transaction may be most effectively looked at as (1) recording the *value* of whatever is purchased from or sold to foreigners, and (2) recording the actual means by which the payment is made or the debt arising from the purchase or sale is extinguished. Each side of the transaction must be expressed in the currency of the country under consideration even though payment may be made in foreign currency. This is accomplished by converting the foreign currency figure into the comparable amount of domestic currency.

Let us look more closely at (1) above, the *value* of what is purchased or sold. If something is purchased from foreigners, its value in domestic currency is entered as a debit (minus) in the appropriate category. As we have seen, the purchase may be of (a) foreign goods (imports), (b) foreign services, or (c) a foreign capital asset (a foreign stock, bond, company, plant, etc.). A credit (plus) is entered for the value of sales in these categories to foreigners. Items in (a) and (b) are current payments and receipts, as opposed to capital transactions, and are therefore shown in the *Current account* of the balance of payments. Item (c) is shown in the *Capital account*. (See Table 2, p. 21).

It was mentioned above that there are some foreign payments and receipts for which there is nothing bought or sold, i.e., gifts, remittances, and unrequited payments of any kind. A separate category was shown in Table 2 for these items under the head *Unilateral transfers*. A unilateral transfer to a foreigner is a debit (minus), while a unilateral transfer from abroad is a credit (plus). It is also common to break down unilateral transfers into private gifts (including pensions, etc.) and government grants.

As noted earlier, government payments and receipts may arise for various reasons. The value of government *grants* (gifts) is included in the unilateral transfers account. Government lending abroad is actually the purchase of a foreign debt instrument, and its value is shown as a debit (minus) in the capital account.

This leaves us with one final category in recording the *value* of total foreign purchases and sales. This is the value of gold or foreign currencies (official reserves) purchased or sold. Like the other items, a purchase is recorded as a debit (minus) and a sale as a credit (plus).

So much for the one side of each transaction. We have isolated four accounts in which the *value* of every foreign purchase and unilateral transfer is a debit (minus), and every sale to foreigners and unilateral transfer from foreigners is a credit (plus). These are the current account, unilateral transfers account, capital account, and official reserves account.

Let us now look at the second entry for each transaction, i.e., the actual money payment or settlement of the debt arising from the purchase or sale.

This does not allow such a straightforward examination as the first entry. At the outset, we know that if the first entry is a credit, the second must be a debit, and vice versa. How the settlement (the actual payment or receipt) is made dictates how the second entry for a transaction is recorded. Take as an example a purchase abroad (either of goods, services, capital instruments, or unilateral transfer to foreigners). We may settle our debt to the foreign seller by either (1) transferring money in the form of bank balances to him or (2) by giving him a promise to pay money at some future time. The latter, of course, means that we have incurred a continuing debt to the foreign seller. Or, in other words, he has extended credit to us to make the purchase. The domestic currency equivalent of either of these actions must be entered as a credit (plus) in the balance of payments, not simply to offset the debit entry of the value of the purchase but also because conceptually the foreigner has given us credit.

In the case of our giving him our promise to pay, the credit granted is clear. We should, therefore, record this as a credit (plus) entry in the capital account since, in fact, a foreigner has purchased one of our debt instruments. If the payment is made by the transfer of a bank balance it is not so clearly an extension of credit to us. In this case, we must look at our country's total international creditor-debtor position. When we transfer a bank balance to a foreigner to pay for a purchase, there are two possible ways the transfer may be made. Each results in recording the transfer as a credit (plus) in the capital account in the balance of payments. First, we may draw a domestic currency check on our bank which is then deposited by the foreign seller in his account in one of our domestic banks. In this case, our total of liabilities to foreigners has increased (i.e., our capital indebtedness to foreigners is now greater) and this must be recorded as a credit (plus) in the capital account. Second, we may purchase a bank check from our local bank denominated in the foreign seller's currency which he, in turn, deposits in his local bank. Here, our total foreign assets (our banks' deposit holdings of foreign currency) have declined. Thus our *net* foreign currency assets relative to foreigners' assets in our currency (our foreign liabilities) have declined, and this can be looked upon as a capital inflow. Indeed, it is recorded as such, i.e., a credit (plus) in the capital account.

To summarize, then, regardless of how we pay for our foreign purchase, conceptually, there is a capital inflow which is recorded as an offsetting credit (plus) in the balance of payments. The essence of the matter revolves around the fact that in international credit and capital flows, cash, or bank balances, are treated no differently from actual short-term credit instruments such as notes, bankers' acceptances, etc. Thus any increase in foreign holdings of domestic currency assets is a capital inflow (credit), and any decrease in our holdings of foreign currency assets is likewise a capital inflow. This mechanical procedure allows the *payment* for each domestic purchase from abroad to be recorded as a credit in the balance of payments, while the *value* of the purchase is recorded as a debit.

It is not necessary to go through the generation of the offsetting debit entry for a domestic sale to foreigners in detail. We know that the values of the sales (of goods, services, capital assets, or unilateral transfers from abroad) are entered as credits (plus) in the appropriate accounts. The actual payment is made in either the transference of a bank balance to our seller or his accepting an IOU from the foreign buyer. In either case there is generated a debit (minus) entry in the capital account, because our foreign currency assets have increased (either bank deposits or IOU's) or our foreign currency liabilities have decreased (when the foreign buyer has purchased a bank draft denominated in our currency). In each case, there has been an offsetting debit (minus) entry in the capital account.

It is evident that at least one entry for any foreign transaction is made in the capital account: the entry which represents the actual discharge of the debt. If the transaction originates as a purchase or sale of a capital instrument, the offsetting entry also arises in the capital account. The net result is, of course, that total payments must equal total receipts in the balance of payments. The capital account records both the value of the initiating capital transaction and the actual payment for or settlement of *all* transactions.

The capital account is generally broken down into two separate categories: long-term capital, which includes those capital instruments of one year or over to maturity, and short-term capital for instruments of less than a year to maturity. Money on deposit or bank balances fall in the latter category. Although it is by no means completely correct, one can view the long-term capital account as that which records the value of capital instruments bought and sold while the short-term capital account records the actual settlement of all purchases and sales abroad. In this view, all other accounts cause the changes in the short-term capital account. But in practice, there are many transactions which originate within the short-term capital account, and thus are offset by another entry in the same account. The recent discussion of short-term capital movements and "hot" money reflects the importance of this.

To illustrate the type of accounting discussed above, a few hypothetical transactions may be examined. We assume that these transactions apply to the U.S. balance of payments, and hence all entries will be in U.S. dollars regardless of the currency of actual payment.

1. A U.S. exporter sells goods to a foreign importer and accepts a note due in 90 days in payment: The value of the export is a credit (plus) in the current account (exports); the amount of the note is a debit (minus) in the short-term capital account (short-term capital outflow).

2. A U.S. tourist spends foreign currency, which he acquired for dollars from a French bank, for a hotel in France: The value of the hotel services is debited (minus) in the current account (tourists or travel); the increase in the dollar assets of the French bank is a credit (plus) in the short-term capital account.

3. The United States gives (not lends) dollars to a foreign country under the foreign aid program: The amount of the grant is a debit (minus) in the unilateral transfer (government) account; the increase in the dollar holdings of the foreign country is a credit (plus) in the short-term capital account (short-term capital inflow).

4. A U.S. bank purchases British Treasury bills (90 days) with its

pound deposit in a British bank: The value of the bills is recorded as a debit (minus) in the short-term capital account (capital outflow, since America's ownership of foreign assets has increased); the reduction in pound deposits is a credit (plus) in the short-term capital account (capital inflow, since our foreign assets have decreased); thus, there are offsetting short-term capital movements.

5. The United States sells gold to France for dollars: The value of the gold is a credit (plus) in the *official reserves* account; the reduction in French dollar deposits in U.S. banks is a debit (minus) since our liabilities to foreigners have declined (a short-term capital outflow).

If total payments to foreigners must equal total receipts from foreigners over any given period, why are we concerned with balance-of-payments problems? The answer is that only part of total payments and receipts are included in the "balance." While the totals in the scheme shown in Table 2 above must be equal because everything has been entered twice, this will not be the case for any particular item or group of items. Hence, *the* balance of international payments must consider only a part of the total; that is, a line must be drawn through our table and a balance struck on everything above the line, which will give as a net credit (receipts) or net debit (payments) balance that will be equal (but with opposite sign) to the total of everything below the line.

We have already seen two examples of this earlier in examining the favorable "visible trade balance" and "current account balance" of the United States. We obtained the former by subtracting the value of imports from the value of exports to arrive at a positive (plus) trade surplus. But it must be true that the sum of all other items will give a net excess of payments (minus) over receipts (plus) of an exactly equal amount. The same is true of the "balance on current account." [2] This is the sum of the net receipts on current

---

[2] The current account is an important balance for certain economic matters. It essentially involves the amount of current domestic production sold to foreigners and the amount of current domestic demand which is satisfied by foreign goods and services. Thus, this balance, with only minor adjustments, is the net foreign balance to be found in the national income accounts and represents the difference between domestic production of output and domestic consumption, investment expenditures, and government expenditures.

account less the net payments on current account items. Here again the United States had a positive (favorable) balance but, again, all noncurrent account items must have given an equal negative balance.

CONCEPTS OF DEFICIT AND SURPLUS

What is the appropriate balance to concern ourselves with in the study of balance-of-payments problems and international financial arrangements? There are three basic concepts of balance which merit brief discussion. We shall define these in terms of Table 2 (p. 21).[3] The first concept has been popularized by the U.S. Council of Economic Advisers in its annual reports and is known as the "basic balance." [4] The idea that it is "basic" revolves around the fact that only those items which arise as a result of "basic" economic considerations are included. Those items which occur as a *result* of the behavior of the basic items are excluded. This concept draws the balance line under the long-term capital account, and everything else is treated as if it results from the balance above the line. Thus, the "basic balance" is:

1. Current account balance
2. Unilateral transfer balance
3. Long-term capital account balance
   which equals
1. The net official reserves balance, *plus*
2. The increase in short-term liabilities to foreigners, *minus*
3. Increase of foreign short-term assets of the United States

The essential value of this "basic balance" is that it includes those major items which are indicative of the long-run balance-of-payments position of a country. Thus, it assumes that long-term foreign investments more closely reflect the underlying economic conditions than do short-term investments (capital movements), which, on balance, may well be true.

The second major balance, which we will call the "over-all bal-

---

[3] For discussion of these and additional concepts using recent U.S. balance-of-payments statistics, see Peter B. Kenen, "Measuring the United States Balance of Payments," *Review of Economics and Statistics*, May 1964, pp. 139–144.
[4] *The Economic Report of the President*, 1962, (Washington, D.C.: U.S.G.P.O., 1962) pp. 149–150.

ance," is that currently used by the U.S. Department of Commerce. Here the line is drawn under long-term capital on the receipts (plus) side and under short-term capital on the payments (minus) side. Thus, the "over-all balance" may be defined as: [5]

1. Basic balance, *minus*
2. The increase in short-term foreign assets of the United States (U.S. short-term capital outflow)
   which equals
1. The net official reserves balance, *plus*
2. The increase in short-term liabilities to foreigners (foreign short-term capital inflow)

The merit of this concept of the balance is that it treats all increases in short-term liabilities to foreigners as part of the deficit and does not offset any of the domestic short-term capital outflow with foreign capital inflows. Consequently, the picture presented by this concept for a deficit country is as unfavorable as possible. As we have mentioned in Chapter I and shall see below, this may be justified on the ground that all foreign short-term liabilities, because *they may be withdrawn or converted to gold* in the future, are potential drains on official reserves, and thus all increases in them should be counted as part of the deficit.

Finally, we should consider briefly the concept of the balance favored by the International Monetary Fund, the United Nations, and many balance-of-payments analysts. This is known as the "official settlements balance." [6]

Here, we must separate the changes in short-term liabilities (foreign short-term capital inflow) into two categories: those changes which involve liabilities to foreign *official institutions* (mainly foreign central banks and treasuries); and those to foreign *private in-*

---

[5] This balance, as the official definition of the U.S. balance, has been defended in detail by Walter Lederer in *The Balance on Foreign Transactions: Problems of Definition and Measurement* Special Papers in International Economics, No. 5, (Princeton: International Finance Section, 1963). The picture given in the equation is true except for one minor adjustment. A small part of the increase in short-term liabilities to foreigners is included above the line, i.e., is used to offset part of the U.S. short-term capital outflow. This part represents an estimate of "trade credit," i.e., credit granted by foreigners to finance U.S. exports.
[6] This terminology has been used by Hal B. Lary, *Problems of the United States as World Trader and Banker.* (Princeton: Princeton University Press, 1963).

dividuals or institutions. Only the former are included below the line while the latter are placed above the line. Thus, the "official settlements balance" may be defined as:

1. Basic balance, *minus*
2. Increase in short-term foreign assets held by the United States, *plus*
3. Increase in U.S. liabilities to private foreigners
   which equals
1. Net reserves account balance, *plus*
2. Increase in U.S. liabilities to foreign official institutions

This concept, in the case of a deficit country, would show as the deficit only the net loss of official reserves and the *direct* potential drain on reserves, since gold sales are made only to foreign "official institutions."

In recent years, there has been protracted debate over which concept of the balance of payments should be used as the official balance for the United States; the "over-all balance," now used by the Department of Commerce, or the "official settlements balance" defined here. The essential difference is that the latter ignores private individual or institutional short-term claims on the United States while the former includes these as part of the deficit.

A U.S. balance-of-payments committee headed by Dr. E. M. Bernstein—long a leading balance-of-payments analyst—has recommended that the "official settlements balance" be adopted by the Department of Commerce.[7] Table 3 shows that while the "over-all balance" indicates a deficit of $2.8 billion for 1964, use of the "official settlements balance" reduces it to $800 million, a far less frightening figure.

The merit of the latter and lower deficit, apart from its tranquilizing effect on Washington nerves, is that most foreign governments use it. It therefore makes American and other data more easily comparable. Its shortcoming is that the private foreign dollar holdings could be thrown on the foreign exchange market where a foreign central bank would be the buyer. The latter, of course, can convert these dollars to gold. The most prudent view, so it is argued, is to count increases in these short-term claims as part of the deficit.

[7] E. M. Bernstein *et. al.*, *The Balance of Payments Statistics of the United States: Review and Appraisal*, Report of the Review Committee of the Bureau of the Budget (Washington, D.C.: U.S.G.P.O., 1965); see esp. chap. 9.

TABLE 3. U.S. BALANCE OF PAYMENTS: VARIOUS BALANCES, 1950–1964
(billions of dollars)

	1950	1951	1952	1953	1954	1955	1956	1957	1958	1959	1960	1961	1962	1963	1964
Trade balance	1.0	2.9	2.5	1.3	2.4	2.8	4.6	6.1	3.3	1.0	4.7	5.4	4.4	5.1	6.7
Current account balance or balance on goods and services	1.8	3.7	2.2	0.4	1.8	2.0	4.0	5.7	2.2	0.1	4.1	5.6	5.1	5.9	8.6
Basic balance	−3.4	−0.7	−1.6	−2.6	−1.5	−1.5	−1.0	−0.4	−3.7	−4.2	−1.5	−0.6	−1.6	−2.0	−0.1
Over-all balance	−3.6	−0.3	−1.0	−2.2	−1.6	−1.1	−0.9	0.5	−3.5	−3.7	−3.9	−2.4	−2.2	−2.7	−2.8
Official settlements balance [a]	−3.3	0.5	−0.8	−2.1	−1.5	−0.7	−0.3	+1.1	−3.0	−2.3	−3.6	−1.3	−2.0	−1.3	−0.9
Deficits financed by															
(1) Gold sales or purchases (−)	1.7	−0.1	−0.4	−1.2	0.3	0.0	−0.3	−0.8	2.3	0.7	1.7	0.9	0.9	0.5	0.1
(2) Increase or decrease (−) in liquid liabilities to foreign institutions [a]	1.5	−0.5	1.2	0.9	1.2	0.7	0.6	0.3	0.7	1.6	1.9	0.4	1.1	1.6[b]	1.1[b]
(3) Increase (+) in liquid liabilities to private foreigners	0.3	0.8	0.2	0.1	0.1	0.4	0.6	0.6	0.5	1.4	0.3	1.1	0.2	0.6	1.6

SOURCES: Figures for 1950–1959, Hal B. Lary, op. cit., Table 1, pp. 12–13; 1960–1964 figures are revised from U.S. Department of Commerce, Survey of Current Business, June 1965, Table 1, pp. 12–14.
[a] Includes changes in the IMF gold tranche position (see p. 42).
[b] Including net sales of nonmarketable, medium term, convertible securities.

In any event, there is no need to quibble over which concept to use in this study. Any one will do. Table 3 summarizes the actual balance-of-payments figures of the United States under each of these concepts. It is clear that the United States has had sizable deficits by any definition. This book will normally use the Department of Commerce "over-all balance" throughout, although statistics corresponding to the other concepts will be used at specific times as well.

Those items below the line, which in one sense *define* the balance, are often called the "financing" items. Thus, it is seen that a deficit is really a condition when the value of the purchases abroad (of goods, services, or capital instruments) above the line exceeds the value of sales abroad (above the line). The net purchases may then be *financed* by either a decline in official reserves (a sale of gold or official foreign currency holdings), or by a foreign short-term capital inflow (or a negative short-term capital outflow), or both. Similarly, a surplus in the value of foreign sales over foreign purchases may be financed by an increase in official reserves and/or a net short-term capital outflow. At this point it should be evident that short-term capital flows can most easily be considered from the point of view of *changes* in short-term liabilities to foreigners and changes in short-term foreign assets (claims on foreigners).

These changes in short-term foreign assets and liabilities (short-term capital flows) have singular significance in international finance. As we have already seen, they reflect actual payments and receipts for foreign purchases and sales which are initiated in other balance-of-payments categories. They are also the vehicle by which imbalances in foreign purchases and sales are transmitted to the foreign exchange market. To use the United States as an example, if the "basic balance" is in deficit, one effect will be that U.S. banks find their foreign currency (foreign short-term assets) being depleted while foreign banks find their holdings of U.S. dollars rising above the desired level (rising U.S. short-term liabilities). Thus, from both sides of the market, the demand for foreign currency rises and the supply (sale) of dollars increases. If the dollars sold end up in foreign official institutions, which will occur under the present system, they then can be converted to gold.

But other factors affect short-term capital flows besides those which reflect other balance-of-payments categories. These involve transactions which originate in the short-term capital account. Thus, higher interest rates abroad may induce the purchase of foreign short-term debt instruments (a short-term capital outflow), which will increase the supply of domestic currency on the foreign exchange market as buyers sell dollars for the foreign currency. Also, short-term capital movements may reflect speculation on changes in the domestic currency price of foreign currency. If the domestic currency is expected to be devalued (or depreciate) vis-à-vis other currencies, those holding assets denominated in the domestic currency (short-term liabilities to foreigners) will rush to sell them, and domestic institutions that can purchase foreign assets will rush to do so, thus throwing huge volumes of domestic currency on the foreign exchange market in the hope of repurchasing later after a devaluation at a sizable, risk-free profit. This is the essence of currency speculation, of which more will be said later.

However, currency speculation may be much more subtle than the active transfer of funds just described. That is, the speculation may arise in the normal course of payments for exports and imports, by delaying or speeding up payment depending on whether the value of a currency is expected to rise or fall. For example, if the pound sterling is expected to fall in terms of other currencies—either by devaluation or by depreciation within the allowable limits under the present rules—British importers will try to speed up payments to foreigners so as to purchase foreign currency before the external purchasing power of the pound falls. Likewise, foreign importers of British goods will attempt to delay payment as long as possible so as to take advantage of any future fall in the price of the pound. This phenomenon, known as "leads and lags," results in the immediate withdrawal of sources of foreign exchange on the foreign exchange market (by abnormal delay of payment for British exports) and the increase in the supply of pounds on the market (by speed-up of payments for British imports). The sum effect is a massive short-term capital outflow (by increasing short-term assets abroad and reducing short-term liabilities to foreigners) when a currency (the pound) is under speculative attack, even when the expected exchange rate change is small. Of course, when "leads and lags" or other speculation causes sizable short-term capital outflows at the same time that the remainder of the balance of payments is in deficit, the burden of financing the total deficit falls on sales of official reserves. Such has been the case in a number of instances for both the dollar and the pound in the postwar period. The dollar saw such a run in 1960, while the most sizable speculative attack on the pound occurred in early 1965.

Thus, the importance of short-term capital movements, and their reflection of changes in foreign assets and foreign liabilities, cannot be minimized under the present system. However, they are only a part of the total trade and investment position of a country. The investment position deserves more extended discussion before we proceed.

The International Investment Position

The international investment position of a country involves the relationship between the holdings of foreign capital assets of its citizens and government and the value of domestic capital assets owned by foreigners. If the value of total foreign asset holdings of a country exceeds the value of foreign holdings of domestic capital assets—i.e., if total foreign assets exceed total foreign liabilities—the country has a net creditor position. If the reverse is true, the country is a net debtor.

The impact of the capital accounts of the balance of payments on the net investment position is clear. A net capital outflow (positive investment abroad) in any period increases the creditor position (or decreases the debtor position) of the country, while a net capital inflow decreases its creditor position (or increases its debtor position). Of course, the United States and United Kingdom are both sizable international creditors. These net international creditor positions have been built up over an extended period of almost continual net foreign investment and will be considered more explicitly in following chapters. An interesting anomaly is presented, however, in that these two large creditor countries, with foreign assets (in the case of the United States, greatly) exceeding foreign liabilities, have the two currencies for which much concern is currently being voiced.

The anomaly is easily explained away when we break down the

net foreign investment position into long-term and short-term investments. Then we find that the net short-term investment position is important for the continued stability of and confidence in a currency. The short-term investment position is determined by the amount of short-term foreign assets (assets of less than one year to maturity) relative to the short-term foreign liabilities that a country has outstanding at any time. The relationship of this short-term investment (or liquidity) position to the country's balance of payments should be apparent. Taking the concept of the "over-all balance" in the balance of payments, there are essentially two ways to finance a deficit—the sale of reserves, or short-term capital inflow. The latter, which actually consists of an increase in short-term foreign liabilities, obviously impairs the short-term international investment position; that is, short-term liabilities to foreigners increase relative to short-term foreign assets. On the other hand, a surplus in the balance of payments may be financed by a reduction in short-term liabilities or an increase in short-term foreign assets (capital outflow) which obviously improves the short-term investment position. The importance of the short-term investment position lies in the fact that it indicates the potential drain on a country's international reserves of gold or foreign currency; i.e., the loss which could occur if these short-term liabilities to foreigners were suddenly used to buy gold or other currencies.

The net long-term investment position, however, shows the relationship of a country's holdings of direct foreign investment, foreign bonds of over one year to maturity, and foreign corporate stocks to foreign holdings of such domestic assets. These do not have such direct immediate relevance for the position of a country's currency, because they are of a long-run nature and presumably a result of basic economic considerations. Of course, as will be seen below, the United States is a mammoth long-term international creditor, but at the same time it is a sizable short-term international debtor.

Naturally, the purchase of any foreign capital asset (capital outflow) has an immediate adverse impact on the balance of payments. It increases a deficit or reduces a surplus. However, it must be kept in mind that the long-run impact on the balance of payments may indeed be favorable. The incentive to make the foreign investment usually lies in the prospective return of interest or dividends in the future as well as repayment of the principal. Thus, if the investments are truly profitable, they will more than repay themselves in the long run. This repayment will occur through dividend and interest income in the current account and finally a repayment of the principal in the capital account.

With this background, let us proceed to examine how the balance of payments of a country is adjusted so as to eliminate deficits and surpluses.

CHAPTER III

How to Think about Adjustments

THE preceding chapter has demonstrated that any country's payments and receipts must be equal in any period. This is true because the balance-of-payments accounting system, like all double entry systems, is so organized. Nevertheless, it is also true that within this accounting equality there are deficits and surpluses. These arise in certain categories of payments. The rest of the total is considered as a means of financing the deficit or surplus.

This chapter focuses on the responses available to a nation, when it has incurred a deficit or surplus, so that it can return toward equilibrium. It will be apparent throughout that equilibrium is a central concept. Defined most simply, it has been called a state which if attained will be maintained. But this broad definition needs clarification when applied to the balance of payments. Ideally, to be in equilibrium a nation should have a true net zero balance of payments, which is to say that it should have neither a deficit nor a surplus in its balance of payments. The total of its payments, i.e., its outgo, for goods and services, aid, military expenditure, foreign investments, and all other things for which a nation's government and citizens spend money abroad, should equal in amount what foreigners spend in the country in any given time period. If the two figures are equal, equilibrium exists. Since in practice they never are, or only on rare and accidental occasions and hardly ever for very long, the mechanisms of adjustment described herein are actually various steps taken to overcome the inequality and to move back to a position where payments and receipts are equal.

ADJUSTMENT AND LIQUIDITY

To consider the adequacy of the existing international monetary mechanisms which permit a nation to attain equilibrium, two basic conceptions must be kept firmly and separately in mind: (1) the provision of adequate *liquidity*, and (2) the working of an efficient mechanism of *adjustment* to reduce surpluses or overcome deficits, and thereby attain equilibrium.

In order for the citizens of a nation, for example the United States, to buy goods and services from or to invest in, another nation, say France, those private interests in the United States which are doing the buying and investing will also buy French francs in the foreign exchange markets with which to conduct these transactions. Similarly, French buyers and investors in the United States will buy dollars to conduct their business. In addition to private transactions, there also are government transactions. Like the private transactions, they are made for specific purposes, such as aid or military affairs. These transactions also create demand for foreign exchange. It would be an improbable accident if the French demand for dollars and the American demand for francs happened to be exactly equal, as a result of the many daily decisions which create the demand for the respective currencies.

In a very basic sense, it is the inequality between demand and supply for currencies for the purposes noted that creates the balance-of-payments problem. For, to continue the example, if at the end of a year more dollars than francs are supplied to conduct these transactions, the United States will be in deficit vis-à-vis France, which is therefore in surplus vis-à-vis the United States. When the example is expanded to include U.S. transactions with all other countries, then the excess supply of U.S. dollars due to American purchase of other nations' currencies (which is foreign exchange from the U.S. view), over the foreign demand for dollars, constitutes the American deficit.

How is this difference between the supply of and demand for currencies equilibrated? Suppose that instead of dollars, we were talking about another commodity in which people are not so emotionally involved, and can therefore think about clearly, say potatoes. It would then be obvious that the *price* of potatoes would act as the equilibrating mechanism. If, at the existing price of potatoes, the demand exceeds the supply, the price will rise to allocate the potatoes among those willing to pay the new price. If, on the other hand, the supply exceeds the demand, the price will fall, so that potatoes are cheap relative to other goods, and, theoretically, more potatoes will then be consumed, and the market cleared.

Just as there is a price for potatoes, there is a price for foreign exchange—the exchange rates. While, in our example, the price of potatoes could rise or fall freely, reflecting market demand and supply, the fact is that under the existing rules of the monetary game, the price of currencies—of foreign exchange—is set by governments and therefore cannot rise and fall freely. If it could, then the exchange rates—the price of currencies—would continually vary as potato prices do, and the world would have a system known as "flexible exchange rates." In such case there would be no problem of balance-of-payments surpluses and deficits, because the demand for and supply of currencies would be continually equilibrated by variations in the prices. If the system of flexible exchange rates were used by the nations of the world, there would be no balance-of-payments problem. The adjustment mechanism would be automatically provided. One of the major plans for reform of the existing monetary arrangements is indeed the establishment of a flexible exchange rate system.

A moment's thought will reveal that changes in exchange rates would have the same effect internationally as price changes within a country. For example, if there is a surfeit of American dollars in the foreign exchange markets, and there are flexible exchange rates, then the price of American dollars in terms of other currencies will decline by, let us say, 10 per cent. Then a Ford which had cost $3,000 will cost the foreigner $2,700; it becomes a better buy relative to Peugeots or other foreign cars, and the foreigners will buy more of them. Similarly, American shipping, insurance, grains—the whole range of goods and services—will be in greater demand. By the same token, American dollars will buy about 10 per cent less than they used to. The Mercedes that had cost $3,000 now costs Americans $3,300, and many Americans will shift to Buicks instead. The net result of all this is that foreigners will spend more on American goods, and Americans less on foreign goods, and in consequence the foreign demand for dollars increases, the American supply of dollars to foreigners decreases, and at the new price the markets are cleared. If our arbitrary 10 per cent is the wrong figure, there is always *some* price at which the foreign exchange markets will be cleared. If the exchange rates are truly free to vary, the right price will be attained. Thus, exchange rate changes are tantamount to changed prices of goods and services in their relation to the prices of goods and services abroad.

But in actuality, exchange rates are neither free nor flexible. The price of each nation's currency is arbitrarily fixed and administered by its government, or to be more technically correct, by an agreement among governments with respect to the price of currencies. The constellation of exchange rates was initially established in 1944 at the Bretton Woods conference, and, after a basic reshuffling in 1948–1949, has been changed relatively little since. In fact, the "price" of each nation's currency is fixed in terms of the U.S. dollar, which in turn is fixed in terms of gold. Thus, for example, the British pound is fixed at $2.80, the German mark at about 25 cents, and so on for each currency; the dollar is worth 1/35th of an ounce of gold, or conversely a (troy) ounce of gold is worth $35. The current system is known as the "gold-exchange system," or alternatively, when looking at the price of currency aspect, as the "adjustable peg exchange system." The "peg" is the set price for the currency, e.g., the current $2.80 "peg" price for the pound. But these "pegs" can be varied, hence the term "adjustable." They can be and have been changed. The dollar too can be changed in value, by changing the dollar price of gold. Thus, if the dollar were moved down, i.e., devalued, the dollar price of gold would rise by the same amount. But in fact the dollar price of gold has not been changed since 1934.

How do governments, once they pick a peg for the price of their currency, maintain its price at that peg? Natural market forces are in constant flux. The demand for and the supply of each nation's goods and services are always changing with external and domestic circumstances. If governments did not fix the price of their currency, currency prices, too, would change, as we have seen. To keep the currency fixed at its pegged price, governments must create offsetting demand or supply for their currency to counteract the natural forces of change in the market. The method by which governments do this is to use their reserves—their gold or foreign exchange holdings—to buy or sell their *own* currencies, to offset the natural market forces.

For example, the United States has been a deficit country since 1950 (except 1957). This means that the supply of American dollars in foreign exchange markets exceeded the demand for dollars from foreign sources. The United States was obliged to remove the excess of dollars from the markets by selling its reserves—gold (hence the gold outflow) and foreign exchange—for dollars; that is, it bought back its own currency. Any deficit nation must do the same. And, clearly, it must be endowed with a supply of reserves in order to continue to do so. If a deficit nation does not have enough reserves, it must (1) make moves to eliminate the excess supply of its currency—i.e., its deficit—which are the mechanisms of adjustment described below; or (2) it must borrow additional reserves to continue to support its currency, as the United Kingdom did in 1964 and 1965. What about a surplus country? The supply of its currency in the foreign exchange markets is less than the demand for it. Since the price of its currency is not allowed to rise to equilibrate the difference, the surplus country adds to the supply of its own currency in the markets by purchasing gold and other nations' currency with its currency; the gold and exchange purchased are then added to its reserves. Thus, deficit countries decrease their reserves, and surplus countries increase their reserves, as a consequence of the attempt to maintain the pegged exchange rate system.

This defines the *rational* function of reserves. Some people, and indeed some nations, also derive a high, but irrational, satisfaction from the fact that they own a lot of gold. For the moment, let us ignore this irrationality.

While the principle function of reserves is to finance present and future balance-of-payments deficits with fixed exchange rates, owned reserves do not comprise a nation's total ability to finance such deficits. Owned reserves are only one part of a nation's liquidity, which also includes the ability to borrow reserves in addition to those it already owns. Liquidity for a nation may be defined in much the same way as that for an individual. An individual's reserves comprise his assets of money and other assets which can quickly be converted into cash without loss. These are also part of his liquidity. But in addition, should his expenditures exceed his receipts over a given period, he may also be able to borrow money to meet his "deficit," and this ability to borrow must also be considered a part of his liquidity.

Under the present world monetary system, a nation's liquidity consists of its owned reserves and its ability to borrow within the institutional framework. For most nations, owned reserves consist of gold and foreign currencies which are convertible into other currencies, primarily dollars, pounds, and to a lesser extent francs. These owned reserves are, of course, the first line of defense for a deficit country to support its currency in the foreign exchange markets.

A second line of liquidity, which most nations also treat as synonymous with owned reserves, are automatic drawing rights on the International Monetary Fund. These are claims to foreign currencies held by the IMF which may be converted without condition. They consist of the "gold tranche," which corresponds roughly in amount to the one-fourth of the nation's quota which was paid in gold, and the claims on the Fund created when the Group of Ten lend their currencies to the IMF. Since these amounts of foreign exchange are available to the nations automatically, they may be considered as good as technically owned reserves.[1]

A third line of international liquidity resides in the "conditional" drawing rights with the IMF. This consists essentially of the three-fourths of a nation's IMF quota known as the "credit tranche." A nation may borrow foreign currencies from the IMF up to this amount only if the IMF is satisfied that the country is taking measures to cure its deficit. This liquidity, then, consists of conditional credit granted by the IMF.

Finally, there consists other credit facilities which a deficit country may use to borrow reserves temporarily, but subject to the conditions set by the lenders. These may operate through the IMF, such as the Group of Ten lendings to the United Kingdom in

[1] A more thorough discussion of these IMF operations is found in Chapter IV.

1964 and again in 1965, or between individual countries, such as currency swaps and Roosa bonds which the United States has employed. Of course, the scope of such credit facilities depend upon conditions existing at the time and the willingness of surplus countries to lend reserves to deficit countries. Existing arrangements will be discussed in detail in later chapters.

One type of potential liquidity which we shall not consider, but will mention for completeness, is the stock of foreign assets, such as stocks and bonds of foreign corporations which the private citizens of a country hold. In case of extreme balance-of-payments and liquidity strain, such as war, a government could acquire these assets by forced purchase and sell them to acquire foreign exchange. But this would be an extreme measure and could provoke retaliation by foreign countries, and this goes beyond the normal definition of international liquidity. All the same, some British political spokesmen have suggested that these private assets be considered as potential sources of liquidity in Britain's 1964 plight.

Despite all of these borrowing devices, the major and most important component of international liquidity remains owned reserves. These reserves consist of gold and reserve currencies, essentially the dollar and the pound. In a sense, gold and reserve currencies are the core of the existing monetary system. This makes the supply of free world liquidity depend on new supplies of gold and new supplies of reserve currencies, and if these supplies are too low, nations will find it difficult to finance their balance-of-payments deficits.

Why does the need to rely on gold as reserves and as a medium of exchange to settle international imbalances continue? There is an important disadvantage to holding gold rather than reserve currencies. The gold earns no interest, but national currency reserves are literally held in the form of government or other securities, or time deposits, of the reserve currency country, which do earn interest. Again the analogy between a nation and individual may be drawn. The gold a nation holds in its reserves may be likened to the checking account of an individual; neither earns interest. This is idle money and the cost of holding it is the interest lost on alternative assets.

The proclivity to retain gold as the center of the international monetary system may be viewed as a yet unbroken tie with the past.

Historically, within each nation there came a time of transition from the use of gold as money that people carried in their pockets and exchanged for goods, through a period in which *both* gold and paper were used as money, to a period when *only* paper was used. In the United States this transition was not complete until 1934, when the government called in all gold held by its citizens and proclaimed its monopoly right to be the holder and user of monetary gold in the nation. Historically, too, in the United States there existed a bimetallic standard in which silver was used as well as gold; but bimetallism is now of purely historic interest. In the transition gold retained its importance as a domestic currency because people did not trust the paper money issued. Many individual banks had the right to issue currency in the nineteenth century, and the right was often abused, so that some paper money was literally worthless, i.e., it was not convertible to gold. The problem of paper money in the United States ended when the issuance of it became a government monopoly, after the establishment of the Federal Reserve System in 1914.

An analogy between individuals' distrust of paper money and that of governments exists today in the international arena. Governments use gold, and want to acquire gold for both rational and irrational reasons. The rational reason is the fact that many governments distrust all paper units, including the dollar. Indeed, the vast conversion of reserves of dollars and pounds into gold which the surplus countries—notably the Common Market countries—engaged in from about 1958 to the present reflects this mistrust. As the quantity of their holdings of these currencies rose, its quality was questioned. So the use of gold as a reserve to settle balances and to allay this mistrust has been underscored in recent years.

As gold forms the central core of the international monetary system, so, too, many of the proposals for reform revolve around it. The plans for reform include a proposal to return to a pure gold standard; this emanates from Europe and reflects the mistrust of paper. A variant, largely American-inspired, would end the link between gold and currencies altogether.

Biologists have taught us as one of the key concepts in evolution that ontogeny recapitulates phylogeny; that is, the life history of an individual organism goes through the stages of the evolution of its species. Similarly, one of the plans for reform would recapitulate American history on a worldwide scale. It would create a world central bank just as the Americans created the Federal Reserve System. It would substitute for untrustworthy currencies a single universally acceptable international paper currency, called Bancor, to replace gold; or, more precisely, at the outset to live side-by-side with gold and perhaps eventually to replace it. This is the Triffin plan, which will be discussed in detail as one of the plans for reform in Chapter VII.

Just as gold is central to the world's monetary system, so are reserve currencies. A reserve currency is one which is held as a substitute for, or in addition to, gold as a nation's reserve. Just which currency becomes a reserve currency is largely determined by historical factors. There is no conscious choice nor any election among currencies, although one of the major plans for reform is an attempt deliberately to establish a new reserve currency unit, to be called the "multiple reserve unit" or "composite reserve unit." Use of the British pound as a reserve currency arose historically during the nineteenth and first half of the twentieth centuries because pounds were freely convertible into gold, because the holdings of obligations denominated in pounds paid interest whereas gold did not, because the pound was accepted by almost all nations as a means of payment and a unit of account, and because England was a large creditor nation. These characteristics naturally led nations to use the pound as an alternative for gold in their reserves; and these same characteristics which now describe the American dollar have led to the addition of the dollar to the pound as a reserve currency, and indeed in large measure to replacement of the pound by the dollar in very recent times.

When a nation's currency is universally accepted as a reserve currency, the nation benefits because its banking facilities become the world center for settling debts; consequently, its banking system earns large amounts in servicing international trade. But the nation also pays a price. In its internal economic actions it must always keep one eye cocked at the stability of its currency abroad; for the reserve currency becomes one of the backbones of the international payments system, and it is generally thought that "responsible behavior" requires that, in a conflict between internal and external needs, the external shall prevail.

An analogy can be made between the position of a reserve currency nation and a commercial bank. The current gold-exchange standard system is like a fractional-reserve banking system. The reserve currency countries do not own enough gold to convert all of the foreign holdings of their currency into gold. A commercial bank may have total assets in excess of its deposit liabilities, but only some of these assets are sufficiently liquid to be quickly converted to cash to meet deposit withdrawals at any time. Similarly, a reserve currency country may hold foreign assets far in excess of its foreign liabilities, as the United States does in the form of stocks, bonds, plant, and other investments abroad owned by its citizens. But only gold can be used to meet the demands of the "depositors," that is, those surplus nations who have "invested" in dollars or dollar obligations. The commercial bank avoids runs on the bank by keeping the confidence of its depositors. In the nineteenth and early twentieth centuries in the United States, there were periodic runs on banks which forced banks in turn to call in loans prematurely, forcing further liquidations and bankruptcies. To end these "liquidity crises" the Federal Reserve System was established to stand behind individual member banks to lend them cash so that runs could never go far. In the minds of those plans for reform designed to convert the IMF into a supercredit agency to guarantee national liquidity (Triffin, Roosa, and others) lies a historic analogy with this American development. But at present, the world has no true lender of last resort.

In the recent past, great attention has been paid to liquidity problems, defined either with reference to a single nation, or sometimes as the aggregate supply of reserves available to the free world. One purpose of international trade is thought by many to be the earning of reserves, which can be converted to gold and hoarded. Few nations are exempt from this prejudice. Much of the American concern about the balance of payments focuses on the U.S. loss of gold.

Most plans for reform of the world's monetary system are also plans to improve the system's liquidity. While they focus on the aggregate world supply of liquidity, there is implicit the idea that each nation will share in this increased supply; thus the bridge from total to any nation's liquidity.

Insufficient attention has been paid to balance-of-payments adjustment. With more efficient adjustment mechanisms, less liquidity is needed. If this section deals with adjustment at greater length than many treatises on this subject, it is in part to compensate for past inattention, in part to point out that improved adjustment will do much to solve the liquidity problem.

The bridge between liquidity and adjustment is *time:* The one rational function served by hoarding of reserves by nations is their use of reserves to support their currency and thus buy time when they are in deficit—time to adjust easily rather than abruptly. Given the vicissitudes of world trade, it is natural to expect that nations will periodically encounter abnormal years. In these they may incur deficits and reserves will give them time to make some type of adjustment to return to equilibrium. So again, a nation, like an individual, might rationally want to earn some surplus as a reserve against difficult times—a reserve which can be used to tide over the period of adjustment.

Adjustment Mechanisms

The persistent loss or gain of reserves is symptomatic, and should serve as a signal, of a maladjustment in the economic position of a nation vis-à-vis the rest of the world. The deeper element that is maladjusted—or to use the usual term, in disequilibrium—is the structure of *prices* and *costs* of the nation in comparison with those of the rest of the world. Thus, if American Fords at $3000, and other goods and services correspondingly priced because they cost roughly as much to produce, are so expensive that the world is unwilling to buy enough of them—to spend enough of its currencies for them to equal what the United States spends abroad—then the United States must have a deficit. This does not imply that only the current account (exports and imports of goods and services) must balance with the rest of the world, but that the current account balance must be able to compensate for U.S. expenditures in the other sectors, including capital investment, tourism, and aid and military budgets, which are not so sensitive to changes in relative prices.

So, basically, the root of the deficit lies in a disequilibrium in relative prices, which reflect costs of production. In consequence, it will hardly be surprising that three of the four mechanisms of adjustment available to a nation in disequilibrium rely heavily on changes in the nation's prices relative to those of other nations. These three are, first, changes in the exchange rate; second, the "classical medicine," i.e., inflationary or deflationary steps designed to change a nation's internal price structure and level of income compared to others; and a third, called an "incomes policy" in Europe and "wage-price guidelines" in the United States, which could theoretically be a substitute for inflation or deflation. The fourth mechanism of adjustment is direct control, of some variety, over various elements in the balance. For example, quotas and tariffs can restrict imports, or exchange controls can restrict capital outflow, or serve other similar purposes. Unlike the first three mechanisms, direct controls deal with the symptoms and do not attempt to alter the price relationships—which have been termed the root of the disequilibrium.

Exchange Rate Adjustment

Changes in the exchange rate are discussed first in the sequence of price altering mechanisms because, logically, one would expect this device to be the first one used by a nation. In practice, it has become the last technique to be used, after all others have failed. It has already been noted that freely flexible exchange rates would automatically adjust international price relationships as the supply of and demand for a nation's currency vary, thereby keeping deficits and surpluses from arising. With pegged exchange rates, the same kind of price adjustments will be achieved only when the nation's money managers move the peg upward by "revaluing," or downward by "devaluing," its currency; this automatically moves the nation to a new price level in comparison to other nations. Before the money managers and politicians can make such a move, disequilibrium must have been in effect, evidenced by the fact that the nation has been consistently losing or gaining reserves—i.e., been in deficit or surplus.

If the nation has been gaining reserves, further surpluses can be stopped by making the nation's currency more expensive to the rest of the world by revaluation. Actually, this has been done only once in the postwar period when in 1961 Germany and Holland revalued their currencies by 5 per cent. If, on the other hand, the nation has been losing reserves, a reduction in the price of its currency by devaluation would tend to eliminate its deficit.

How much revaluation or devaluation should occur in a given situation? Given the present state of economic knowledge, this is a guess. And a shot in the dark always is likely to miss. But some light is thrown by two considerations. The first is the *elasticity* of demand and supply for a nation's exports and imports. Simply stated, elasticity measures how much more of a nation's exports will be taken abroad with a given fall in its prices—or in the price of its currency, which comes to the same thing; and also how much less it will import as a result of the rise in price to its people of foreign goods and services. Most nations conduct studies of their relative elasticities; the numerous estimates available should inform the money managers, to some extent, of the needed size of the devaluation or revaluation. The second consideration is how severe the disequilibrium has been, that is, how big a deficit or surplus is to be removed. The movement of the peg is a step adjustment, unlike the small and constant adjustments that would have taken place with flexible exchange rates. Given the elasticities, the larger the disequilibrium, the bigger the necessary step movement to a new peg.

When should a nation move the peg? There is no certain or even widely accepted criterion. But two points may be made with reference to the question of timing.

First, deficit countries are limited, in the time they have to adjust, by their reserves (liquidity) and their willingness to use them up in defense of their currency. Surplus countries, on the other hand, are under virtually no pressure to adjust. Nothing in the IMF rules, or in economic logic, really militates strongly against the cumulative piling up of gold or other reserves. Indeed, the mercantilist bias of most Europeans has favored it. In this respect the present system is asymmetrical, placing pressure on the deficit countries alone. Since in practice devaluation has been rarely used as a method of adjustment, this asymmetry forces the use of other adjustments by the deficit nations. As will be seen, the other adjustments are largely deflationary in nature. Therefore, the pegged exchange system, coupled with a strong antipathy to devaluation, has inherent in it a deflationary (or at least anti-inflationary) bias much as the old gold-standard system had in the 1930s.

Second, the articles of the IMF and writings of many economists offer as a criterion for exchange rate adjustment that of "fundamental disequilibrium." This concept is rather nebulous. In retrospect one knows when a nation is in "fundamental disequilibrium," but one never knows exactly when it got or gets there. The usual symptoms are a prolonged deficit or surplus, of such a magnitude that it cannot be eliminated without special steps to restore equilibrium. It is not of the temporary or superficial nature that is apt to right itself, given the vicissitudes of changing world trade patterns. Ragnar Nurkse has added by way of definition that if a chronic deficit does not right itself when a nation is in recession, then fundamental disequilibrium exists. Whatever the fuzziness of definition, when these conditions exist, the present rules of the IMF legally permit a change in the exchange rate as a method of adjustment. In the last analysis, just when to make this adjustment is a matter of judgment of a nation's leaders.

In the postwar period, the two major deficit nations have been the United States and the United Kingdom. Neither has chosen to devalue its currency (in Britain's case, since 1949), because, as the world's bankers and as reserve currency countries, they have felt it would be irresponsible to do so. Other countries which are not reserve currencies have assumed different postures. In 1948–1949, virtually all European nations were in deep deficit and devalued. Subsequently, when in deficit, France did not hesitate to devalue as late as 1958. Italy, on the other hand, refused to do so in its 1963–1964 deficit period. In lieu of devaluation there are other methods of adjustment available.

Domestic Deflation and Inflation

It has been noted above that the ultimate purpose of the first three mechanisms of adjustment is to change a country's prices relative to those abroad. Without changes in the exchange rate, how may this be accomplished? The most obvious method is for a government, through the use of its monetary and fiscal powers, to increase or decrease the level of aggregate demand relative to output inside its own country.

A decrease in the level of aggregate demand will result in those consequences commonly known as "austerity," or deflation; that is, there will be less purchasing power in the nation, and if there were free competition the price of goods and services would fall. In addition, or perhaps in substitution for falling prices (because in the modern world some prices—particularly labor—are not flexible downward), real income and employment will fall. These phenomena are the symptoms of economic depression. If a little depression is insufficient to do the job, then a larger degree of depression is necessary.

The mirror image sequence is true of inflation. If any country chose to inflate its prices deliberately—there is in practice great resistance to this idea—it could do so by increasing its aggregate demand relative to output by reducing taxes, pumping more money into its income stream through the banking system, or similar devices.

This technique for adjusting imbalances in international accounts by changes within a single country is known as the "classical medicine." It is, in short, the traditional method by which balance-of-payments disequilibriums are to be adjusted when the exchange rate stays fixed. Under the old gold standard which the world abandoned in the 1930s, prior to the "gold-exchange standard" under the Bretton Woods agreement which still exists, the "classical medicine" was the major prescription to adjust the balance of payments.

How does the "classical medicine" work to equilibrate the balance of payments? A deficit country, for example, by increasing taxes or by other deflationary methods, can reduce the level of aggregate demand, which sets up forces to improve the balance of payments. This may not *reduce* its costs and prices absolutely, under modern conditions, but it will slow down the rate of increase, so that other countries can increase—inflate—at a more rapid rate. Eventually this will result in a relatively lower structure of costs and prices for the deflating country, thereby stimulating exports and inhibiting imports, and increasing its earnings in the balance of payments. This sequence of events may be called the price effect. Similarly, a surplus country could stimulate its aggregate demand so that its prices rose more rapidly than those of deficit nations, resulting in a mirror image sequence of the deflationary procedure described above. In fact, however, no surplus country has chosen deliberately to inflate to help its deficit neighbor. This underscores the observation that the existing system places its major pressure against deficit countries.

But this mechanism does not rely solely on price effects. The income stream of a nation is also increased or decreased by inflationary or deflationary monetary and fiscal policies. In the case of a deficit country deflating, the reduction of the income stream will act to reduce the quantity of imports its people buy from abroad, and thus assist the balance of payments. Indeed, this is one of the objectives, along with price effects, of deflationary policies of deficit countries. That this is not simply a theoretical formulation is evidenced by the British experience. The aggravating factor in the recent balance-of-payments crises in the United Kingdom has been an excessively rapid increase in imports, as aggregate income was allowed to rise in each inflationary, or "go"—following each deflationary or "stop"—period. Surplus countries, by inflating, would increase their domestic income streams and hence their imports more rapidly.

To the extent that inflationary and deflationary policies are carried out by interest rate changes, international capital movements will be affected. For example, a deficit country in pursuing its deflationary policy may increase interest rates. In consequence, short-term capital, seeking a higher return, will flow into the country; the country's own capital outflow will be inhibited, since domestic capital can now earn more at home. These flows should improve a nation's balance-of-payments position. Conversely, a surplus country with an inflationary lower interest rate policy would find its balance on capital account declining.

The interest rate effect may be overwhelmed by speculative capital movements in some cases. When a deficit nation raises its interest rate after having "fundamental deficit" for some time, investors may fear this to be a signal that its currency will be devalued. Thus, they may not lend to the deficit nation, even at a premium interest rate, for in devaluation they would sustain a capital loss. That this possibility is not purely theoretical is again evidenced by the British case; even a 7 per cent bank rate in 1964 failed to prevent investors and governments from switching out of pounds. Domestic austerity may not only be costly and unpopular by suppressing economic growth, but may also reduce the nation's capacity to produce and export in the long run and thus be harmful to its balance of payments. Some analysts favor high interest rates to hold capital and an easy budgetary or fiscal policy to stimulate growth, achieving both goals with the traditional tools of policy. But it is likely that there are limits to the possibility of such a divorce between monetary and fiscal policies.[2]

In summary, the mechanism herein described relies on a price effect, an income effect, and an interest rate effect. With reference to a deficit country, the price and income effects improve its current account balance; the interest rate effect improves its capital account balance. The reverse is true of a surplus country which follows an inflationary policy. The use of this theoretical mechanism is limited by certain practical considerations. With respect to a deficit country, the effects of deflation are costly and unpopular. They reduce the level of employment and cause hardship to workers and business. They inhibit the level of growth and consequently reduce the potential level of living. In short, they place difficult burdens of a depressing nature on the deficit nation. With reference to the surplus countries, the theoretical mechanism is blurred by the fact that virtually none of them has followed these policies. Instead of inflating or reducing interest rates each has fought inflation, sterilized its additions to reserves, and continued to earn surpluses much of which were converted to gold. From the point of view of the French and the Germans who are earning surpluses, none of these theoretical steps makes any sense. Price stability is as much a goal for them as for other nations. The shortcomings of inflation as a technique lie, therefore, not in the fact that the French and the Germans are unwilling to do things which they deem harmful to themselves, but rather in the system itself. The proposal to return to the gold standard is in fact a proposal to widen and deepen reliance on this "classical medicine." However, this mechanism is also the major weapon available to nations under the existing gold-exchange system, if existing exchange rates are to be maintained. The fundamental similarity of the current gold-exchange system to the old gold-standard system

[2] See James E. Meade, "The International Monetary Mechanism," *Three Banks Review*, September 1964, p. 10.

still requires deflation for deficit countries, in an age when no population will accept unemployment—indeed, when full employment and economic growth have become the major goals of economic activity in all nations.

Incomes Policy

The objective of an "incomes policy" as it is called in Europe, or of its American first cousin, "wage-price guidelines," is to change internal prices to obtain the price effect while avoiding the income effect and the interest rate effect. To do so requires that money wages and profits be moved up or down—be increased or decreased—in response to the needs of the international balance-of-payments position. Theoretically, with a successful incomes policy, prices and costs can be lowered without affecting economic growth or real output. If an incomes policy functioned well, the money managers could inflate or deflate domestic demand through their monetary and budgetary policies so as to achieve the desired level of domestic employment and the best attainable rate of economic growth. At the same time the level of costs and prices could be adjusted relative to those of foreign competitors by directly lowering wages and profits through an incomes policy. For example, a deficit country with a successful incomes policy could simply reduce, or at least inhibit increase in money wages and profits thereby lowering costs and prices, while other countries were not doing so, and gain a relative advantage in its international current account balance. An incomes policy, therefore, attempts to introduce, through wage and profit manipulation, a flexibility which the nation might have if its markets were entirely competitive, without really having a competitive economy in which to function. For a deficit country, the objective is to hold money wages and profits to a level of increase lower than the increase of *productivity*, so that the level of costs and prices will fall, or at least not rise as much as costs and prices in the surplus countries. Ideally, a surplus country, if one ever tried to use this mechanism to reduce its balance-of-payments surplus, should allow money wages and profits to increase *more* rapidly than productivity. Needless to add, no nation has ever followed this prescription.

While this mechanism is theoretically ideal, deficit countries that have attempted to use it have encountered two stubborn institutional barriers. The first is that trade unions have been wholly unwilling to surrender their wage-determining prerogatives to incomes policy planners. The second is the oligopolistic nature of modern corporations, which do not want to see their profit levels fall and have many ways to get around an incomes policy. An incomes policy has had some success in certain countries for limited periods of time, notably in Holland—until the pressure of inflation made it impracticable there—and in Sweden. The longest and most agonizing experience with this device has been in England.

The United States has used its "wage-price guidelines" with moderation. About 1962 the government began to intervene in wage negotiations to assure that wage increases remained within the bounds of productivity increases so that prices did not rise relative to those abroad and, thus, further increase the American international deficit. President Kennedy's intervention in the steel controversy in 1962 was based on this doctrine. The doctrine has continued to be espoused by the Johnson Administration; but since American prices were relatively stable from 1958 to 1964, wage-price guidelines have not been pursued as vigorously as incomes policies in Europe. Should inflation become the American problem, perhaps in consequence of the current drive to increase the level of employment, greater use may be expected.

As a device to solve balance-of-payments problems the effective use of incomes policy still seems a long way off, and will require fundamental changes in the political and social institutions, as well as the economic structure, of the Western democracies.

Direct Controls

Basically, there are three types of direct controls for balance-of-payments purposes. It is only with these that we are concerned. First, there are those which inhibit imports, including quotas, tariffs, and similar devices. Second, those which stimulate exports include tax rebates, favored credit conditions, and a range of devices designed to assist exporters and, therefore, the balance-of-payments position. Some of these stimulants are outlawed under the GATT agreement, others are not. Some are honored in the breach, others in the observance, by virtually all countries. A third genre primarily affects the freedom of international capital movements. Restrictions on investment and bank lending abroad as well as discriminatory taxes on investment abroad are among the chief weapons of the American anti-deficit arsenal. The United Kingdom uses these, as well as other devices. On the other hand, Germany and some other surplus nations discriminate against foreign investments coming into their nation to reduce their surplus.

The underdeveloped nations use so many direct control methods to conserve and allocate foreign exchange that this may be said to be their main means of adjustment. The concern of this analysis, however, is with the major trading nations only.

Direct controls may be compared to price controls. Both deal with the symptoms of a maladjustment and not with its causes. If the root of the balance-of-payments disequilibriums is relative price differences among countries, the use of direct controls cannot cure the trouble at its origin. Direct controls, like price controls, must therefore be considered holding operations—temporary expedients—until more profound measures may be applied. Unfortunately, like so many temporary expedients, they tend to become permanent. Once institutionalized, direct controls introduce further distortions into a situation already distorted by more basic causes.

The objection to direct controls is that they are illiberal. They are movements away from free trade and investment. This antipathy to controls is more than a matter of sentiment favoring freedom. The maximum efficiency of the world's economy is thought to be correlated with, and dependent on, free mobility of goods and the factors of production in response to prices. To the extent that this is blocked, the optimum allocation of resources is not achieved. To the extent that controls spread, the world is in danger of moving back to the autarchy and anarchy of the 1930s, which it is the express purpose of the Bretton Woods agreements, the GATT, and most nations' expressed policy to avoid. Like all controls, moreover, these create a need for economic managers whose judgment is superior to the market's, a difficult task at this stage of economic knowledge. Further, these controls give rise to the problem of enforcement and to black markets.

Direct controls are always put into operation as short-term expedi-

ents, although once instituted some have a perverse way of linger-
ing on. It is significant that no plan for reform put forward to date—
and there have been many—has suggested direct controls as a method
of solving balance-of-payment difficulties, because this type of thinking is universally reprehensible to the economic spirit of our times
among free nations. Nevertheless, the deficit countries, the United
States and United Kingdom, are now using these devices—temporarily, of course—and their use is described, without much sympathy,
in Chapters V and VI.

While none has done so, it is theoretically possible for surplus
nations to consciously use a type of direct control to rid themselves
of surpluses by increasing payments to foreigners. For example, in
the capital category, European surpluses could be reduced by certain
types of government-directed expenditures. Increased aid to developing nations is an obvious example. It is true that France's aid
per capita to her former colonies is sizable, but it has not increased
with her surpluses, and other European nations are, by most criteria,
not major aid givers. Also, the private investment of European capital abroad could be stimulated by a variety of devices. Simply reducing the impediments to borrowing in European, and, notably, French,
capital markets would go far to this end.

In the current account category, the surplus countries could increase their share of joint military expenditures, although this question has major political ramifications. Probably more current, in
view of the Kennedy round discussions, is the possibility of tariff reductions by surplus countries. The Common Market, whose countries
are the major surplus countries, could take a liberal position in the
current GATT negotiations. By reducing tariffs, surplus countries
would enable their people to import more, thereby reducing their
surpluses. Instead, the EEC has adhered to an illiberal position.

If the surplus countries increased their expenditures by some of
these means, a good part of the payments would go to deficit countries and assist the equilibration of the world payment system. But
since the surplus countries have no major incentive to adjust, the
use of new direct controls has, and will probably continue, to be a
device used by deficit countries.

CHAPTER IV

The Rise of the Bretton Woods System

THE basic outline of the existing international payments system was set by the world monetary conference that met at Bretton Woods, New Hampshire, in 1944. The negotiations and discussions which preceded the conference, beginning as early as 1942, produced a number of different plans, and the end result represents an essential compromise among these plans. The institutions established as a result of this conference are the International Monetary Fund (IMF) and the International Bank for Reconstruction and Development (IBRD, or World Bank). Our concern is primarily with the IMF. The World Bank is an institution designed to make convertible currency loans to the reconstructing European countries, and later to the developing nations, which is outside the scope of our discussion.

THE FIRST WORLD MONETARY SYSTEM: THE GOLD STANDARD

International monetary *systems* are a recent development in man's history. For most purposes, the nineteenth century "gold standard" may be deemed the first organized international monetary and financial system. Prior to this, international trade was limited and there were only rudimentary foreign exchange markets. More important, most countries relied predominantly on coins of precious metals as the *domestic* money supply. When traders wanted to convert one national currency to another, the rate of exchange was set by the ratio of the amount of the precious metal (primarily gold) in one type of money to the amount in the other. Thus international exchange rates were fixed between national currencies because the various currencies consisted of coins containing the same precious metal.

It was out of these characteristics of the domestic money supplies of the Western countries that the international gold standard system grew in the middle 1800s. Essentially, the international gold standard requires two features: first, that the domestic monetary unit be defined in terms of gold and that any domestic money other than gold —silver, paper, or demand deposits—be convertible into gold; and second, that the monetary authorities of a country buy and sell gold at a fixed price in terms of its own currency. These two requirements, if sustained, accomplish the essence of the gold-standard system; the domestic currency is as good as gold *and* any of the domestic currency held by foreigners is also as good as gold, that is, gold can be demanded for it at a fixed price.

The British were the central factor in implementing the international gold standard as a world monetary system. Britain, as the site of the world's major banking establishment, production facilities, and commodity markets (especially the major gold market), as well as the center of the most successful colonial empire, became the center of world trade and finance in the late eighteenth and early nineteenth centuries. The British pound sterling, in fact, was used as the domestic money supply by some of the colonies; and because of the advanced banking facilities in London, the pound was used to finance international trade not only between the United Kingdom and its trading partners but also between third countries. Thus when Britain made the gold sovereign legal tender in 1816, she went on the gold standard while many other countries continued on bimetallic standards, including gold and silver. By making gold fully convertible with paper currency, both externally and domestically, and with her central position in the London gold market and international finance, Britain became the center of the international payments system. Her early success (after 1816) with the gold standard, which enhanced her position, led other countries to adopt the procedures necessary to become gold standard countries. Most of the European countries had "gone on gold" by 1875, and the United States achieved internal (and external) convertibility of domestic currency to gold in 1879.

The "world," at that point, was on a gold standard which prevailed until World War I.

Aside from the domestic circulation of gold coin and the ready convertibility of noncoin money to gold coin, how did the gold standard operate internationally? First, the gold standard *fixed* exchange rates among the various national currencies within narrow limits. For example, if the United States defined its dollar as X amount of gold and the United Kingdom defined its pound as Y amount of gold, the par rate of exchange of the dollar for the pound was X/Y. The actual exchange rate could not diverge much from X/Y because a holder of either pounds or dollars could acquire gold from the monetary authorities at the fixed price. But the rate of exchange of dollars for pounds could fluctuate within the narrow limits set by the cost of transporting gold between the two countries. The Englishman who held dollars which he desired to convert into pounds would not pay above a certain dollar price for the pounds. Otherwise, he would be better off converting his dollars to gold in the United States, shipping the gold to Britain, and converting the gold to pounds. Thus the maximum he would pay for pounds would be $X+T$, where X is the dollar price of a pound and T is the cost of transporting a dollar's worth of gold to Britain.

The same principle applied to the exchange rate between any two of the currencies that adhered to the gold standard, as well as to the cross-rates between currencies. The gold standard was a fixed exchange rate system with minimal actual fluctuations in exchange rates in the foreign exchange markets. This condition persists today, under the Bretton Woods agreement. The 1 per cent maximum fluctuation of a currency on each side of parity is a carry-over from the gold export and import points of the old gold standard.

More important was the adjustment mechanism to eliminate balance-of-payments disequilibriums under the gold standard. With the fixed exchange rates implied, balance-of-payments deficits and surpluses were settled by transfer of gold from the deficit to the surplus country.[1] The primary feature of this transfer, which appeals to gold-standard advocates today, was that it set up an automatic

[1] It should be noted that early in the gold-standard game, the pound as well as gold became a component of other countries' reserves, especially the British colonies. These countries transferred pound balances in London as well as gold in settlement of balance-of-payments deficits.

chain of events that corrected external imbalances. Theoretically, the pre-1914 gold-standard system automatically eliminated surpluses and deficits by causing the respective countries to inflate and deflate their domestic economies when gold was transferred. Thus the surplus country acquired gold with foreign exchange which increased its money supply, since gold was part of the money supply and the basis for issue of the rest. This, of course, caused the appropriate movements in prices, income, and interest rates needed to eliminate the surplus. The reverse was true for the deficit country which lost gold.

The smooth operation of this adjustment mechanism required that the rules of the game be followed, which essentially meant that each nation allow the impact of gold movements to be felt on its money supply. In addition, it was thought that private capital flows in response to interest rate changes would cushion the adjustments to balance-of-payments disequilibriums. Changes in interest rates as a result of gold movements would induce rapid and sizable capital flows to the deficit country, thus reducing the gold loss and reversing the deficit.

Moreover, the relative inflation and deflation in prices and money wages needed to balance the external accounts could be achieved relatively painlessly in accordance with the "quantity theory" of money. The "quantity theory" predicted that the price level would move in direct proportion to the money supply. Thus, if a deficit country lost 5 per cent of its gold stock and allowed this to reduce its money supply by 5 per cent, then its average price level would soon fall by the same percentage. Any reduction in real output or employment that happened to result would be only a temporary transition phase, and the economy would automatically return to full employment at the lower price level in a short time.

Thus the textbook version of the gold standard system is a beautifully self-equilibrating system. But, in fact, hindsight indicates that the pre-1914 gold standard hardly followed the picture presented by the theoretical version outlined above. First, the central banks did not follow very closely the rules of the game, and often offset (neutralized) the effects of gold movements on domestic money supplies.[2]

---

[2] See Arthur I. Bloomfield, *Monetary Policy under the International Gold Standard* (New York: Federal Reserve Bank of N.Y., 1959), pp. 48–52.

To the extent that this was done, the theoretical balancing mechanism was not allowed to operate and countries insulated their domestic economies from the classical medicine. Second, short-term capital movements appear to have been generally stabilizing in nature, thus reducing the strain placed on price adjustments.[3] Third, both the volume of exports and imports, and price levels, indicate remarkable parallelism in movements among countries, rather than the divergent movements predicted by classical theory. Thus when prices rose the rise was spread among all countries, not just the surplus countries. Furthermore, there was never any sizable downward movement in money wages, as the theory would predict for a deficit country.[4]

If then the gold-standard system prior to World War I did not conform to the theoretical model, why did it apparently work so well, and why does the nostalgic longing for the good old days persist among many of our contemporaries?

A number of reasons suggest themselves. First, the countries involved in the system were of roughly comparable size and exhibited the same general economic tendencies. Trade was more or less balanced before countries attached themselves to the system, and was thereafter maintained with minimum adjustments. Second, there was general world prosperity during the heyday of the gold standard, from, say, 1880 to 1914, making classical adjustment to the external balance relatively painless as prices and production moved in the same direction in each country. Also, the world was much closer to the economist's concept of perfect competition than was the case by the 1930s. Firms were relatively smaller, entry to industries was easier, and the iron laws of supply and demand operated more freely, making price adjustments possible without creating severe unemployment. In short, economic conditions were favorable for the operation of the gold standard, even though it did not operate very close to its theoretical model. It is improbable that the gold standard caused the favorable economic condition; rather, the environment permitted relatively painless adjustment of the balance of payments.

[3] Bloomfield, *Short-Term Capital Movements under the Pre-1914 Gold Standard*, Studies in International Finance, No. 11 (Princeton: International Finance Section, 1963), esp. pp. 91–93.
[4] Robert Triffin, *The Evolution of the International Monetary System: Historical Reappraisal and Future Perspectives*, Studies in International Finance, No. 12 (Princeton: International Finance Section, 1964) pp. 6–9.

The gold standard was abandoned first in World War I in 1914. Free convertibility of national currencies to gold was universally abandoned during and after the war—a necessity in war. Foreign accounts, especially those of the enemy countries, are blocked and not allowed to be used. In addition, imports of needed war goods must have first priority, and exports must be controlled to keep goods from being sold to the enemy. Virtually the entire balance of payments comes under direct government control, and exchange controls— the control of conversion of domestic currency for foreign currency— are the means by which this is accomplished. The adjustment mechanism in the foreign balance is almost totally by direct control. The same sequence, of course, occurred in World War II.

At the end of World War I, exchange controls, inconvertibility of currency for gold, and therefore, flexible exchange rates with central bank interference prevailed. There was, however, overwhelming sentiment in most countries for a return to the gold standard. But the war had seen a rapid and sizable rise in world prices, while monetary gold had increased by only a fraction. For most countries, so much paper money had been issued during the war that domestic convertibility was out of the question. Furthermore, various countries had experienced widely divergent rates of inflation, so that the configuration of exchange rates which would balance trade before the war was not at all similar to that which would balance trade after the war. And those countries which had suffered from inflation the most—the belligerents—had the least gold at the war's end.

The Gold-Exchange Standard

Even with these difficulties, the movement back toward gold began, but it was not the same gold standard that had existed before 1914. Rather, a "gold-exchange" standard was adopted in which most countries held both gold and foreign currencies as reserves. Exchange rates—between currencies, and between gold and foreign official holdings of a nation's currency—were fixed within the narrow limits of the gold export and import points.

By the time Britain returned to convertibility between foreign-held pounds and gold in 1925, the gold-exchange standard was the monetary system of the major countries. But Britain's return to gold may well have contributed to the eventual downfall of the system. Winston Churchill, then Chancellor of the Exchequer, insisted that the United Kingdom re-establish the prewar parity of the pound to gold. Since British prices had risen greatly during the war, and gold holdings had declined, this necessitated a policy of deflation between the war's end and 1925 when convertibility was re-established. The deflationary monetary policy not only kept Britain's prices from rising, but created considerable unemployment. Thus, although convertibility was achieved, it had severe attendant costs, from which the economy did not recover by the time of the depression of the 1930s.

The gold-exchange system of the 1920s differed considerably from the old gold coin standard.[5] The rapid rise in prices and paper money and the scarcity of gold resulting from the war made it necessary to conserve gold in the payments mechanism. Most countries, with the United States as the notable exception, therefore, did not re-establish convertibility for domestic citizens between gold and currency, and most did not mint gold coins. Hence, governments had a monopoly on monetary gold holdings (now primarily gold bullion rather than coin) which were used primarily for settling international balances.

Also, the new system relied much more heavily on the holdings of foreign exchange as international reserves in addition to gold. While governments had held some foreign currency before the war, foreign exchange—which was convertible to gold—was now a major element in the system, allowing gold to be conserved by providing a source of reserves which did not rely directly on gold.

Under the gold-exchange system, which lasted until its collapse in 1931, the primacy of the pound as the world's major currency was somewhat displaced by the U.S. dollar. The United States had suffered least among the major countries from the war, and had extended considerable credit, during and after the war, to its allies. Also, the United States maintained convertibility of the dollar to gold and gained considerable gold during the war. For these and other reasons, the dollar, as well as gold and the pound, were held in the reserves of foreign countries.

[5] For an excellent discussion, see Shigeo Horie, *The International Monetary Fund* (New York: St. Martin's Press, 1964), chap. III.

But the use of national currencies as reserves created a problem which has persisted and been compounded in the post-World War II period. That is the problem of speculative attacks on currencies when doubts arise as to their continued convertibility to gold at the existing price. Such attacks occurred on the pound after 1925, and it was such an attack that forced the United Kingdom to abandon convertibility in 1931.

There was another change in climate in the 1920s from that which had prevailed under the earlier gold standard. It was no longer assured that a country's price level was highly responsive to changes in the money supply without major changes in employment and output. In Europe, Germany was a prime case in point—a feeling that the domestic economic welfare was a primary consideration which might well be at odds with the discipline imposed by a gold standard was becoming widespread. Thus the focus of attention shifted toward domestic employment and output, and neutralization of gold flows to insulate the domestic economy from the balance of payments became widespread. Another manifestation of this economic nationalism was the movement away from the free trade atmosphere of the prewar period. With the gold-exchange standard, maintenance of the fixed exchange rates without domestic inflation and deflation left tariffs, import quotas, and other restrictions as the only means of achieving external balance, and their use increased in the 1920s.

The Collapse of the Gold Standard and World War II

The world monetary system collapsed in the general depression of the 1930s. It is difficult to accept either of the positions that the depression caused the collapse, or that the world monetary system caused the depression. In many aspects, the two were mutually reinforcing. It can hardly be denied, however, that the gold-exchange system accentuated the spread and severity of the depression.

First, the assumption of price flexibility, necessary to make the gold standard operate, was rapidly proved invalid by the depth and duration of the depression. The very elements of Keynesian economic theory that make income and employment dependent on aggregate demand for output had been largely ignored prior to the depression by both academic economists and policy makers. The existence of the depression made it a fact of life, and prices did not fall enough to restore full employment. Under such conditions, it is certainly to be expected that the international monetary system becomes a matter of relative unconcern. Indeed, the fixed exchange rates of the gold-exchange standard were thought to deepen and spread the depression. When one country enters depression, its imports decline, which reduces the demand for output in its exporting partners, which in turn suffer from unemployment and falling output. In such instances, the external accounts and the exchange rate are looked upon as a burden too costly to bother with.

The international economic conditions prior to the depression were also contributory to the collapse of the system. The United States was running a current account surplus in its balance of payments and was lending to the European countries, although it still had an over-all surplus and gained some gold. In the late 1920s, the United States and the United Kingdom reduced lending (both governmental and private), which placed considerable balance-of-payments pressure on European countries; they needed capital imports to cover their current account deficits. When a major source of this credit disappeared, it became impossible for Germany to meet reparations payments and for other countries to meet war debt repayments. As a result, tendencies toward European deflation and protectionism were stimulated to balance their current accounts.

The immediate cause of the collapse rests in the mobility of capital internationally, which was accentuated by the holdings of foreign exchange as national reserves and the use of foreign deposits by commercial banks in a number of countries as reserves for monetary creation. In 1931, the largest bank in Austria, which was a large depository of foreign-owned funds, collapsed and could not meet demands for withdrawals. This shook public confidence in the safety of deposits in Austria, and then in Germany, precipitating a panic as foreign holders attempted to withdraw their funds and convert them to domestic currency. Since the United Kingdom had considerable foreign deposits in Austria and Germany which were now blocked, a speculative run on sterling occurred which forced the United Kingdom to suspend gold sales, and the first step to total abandonment of the gold-exchange standard had occurred. Britain, in suspending gold payments, was in effect letting the pound fluctuate in price with respect to gold and other currencies. However, a sizable group of her colonies and other countries kept their currencies tied to the pound rather than remaining on gold.

Two years later, in 1933, the United States for different reasons cut the tie of the dollar to gold. Until then, gold coin still circulated in the United States, and domestic currency was convertible to gold. The United States, perhaps mistakenly, attempted to reflate the domestic price level by removing the obligation of the government to sell gold at the old price of $20.67 per ounce, after which the gold price was allowed to fluctuate for roughly a year. In 1934, gold was nationalized and removed from private circulation. Domestic convertibility was abandoned, but international convertibility was restored at a new dollar price of gold at $35 per ounce, a devaluation of the dollar of over 41 per cent from the earlier level.

In the years following, most countries gave up convertibility, either by allowing their exchange rate to float or by devaluing with respect to gold and other currencies. During this period international trade declined drastically, protectionism was rampant, and competitive depreciation and devaluation of currencies was the order of the day.

During the interim from 1931 to 1936, the pound was allowed to fluctuate in value on the foreign exchange markets, but the British attempted to manipulate the rate through the Exchange Equalization Account. Without attempting to establish a fixed rate, this account would buy and sell pounds for foreign exchange, in order to exercise some control over the level of the rate. After the abandonment of convertibility in 1931, the pound fell significantly, and the fact is that the Exchange Equalization Account was used primarily to sell pounds to keep the rate from rising when short-term capital inflows occurred.

Similar stabilization funds were established in other countries. Even though most of them were not on the gold standard, they used gold as the means of carrying out the fund operations. This then was not a system of flexible exchange rates with official intervention, but a means by which the price of a country's currency with respect to gold was managed.

Within this uncertain framework, speculative short-term capital movements, seeking capital gains through exchange rate changes, exerted highly destabilizing influences on exchange rates. Day-to-day fluctuations in exchange rates were sizable, and the stabilization funds were unable to offset them because of limited resources. This experience with destabilizing short-term capital movements under flexible exchange rates has been used as an argument against flexible rates, although the period in question could hardly be considered normal.

Flexible exchange rates have been condemned because they were associated with the events of the 1930s. However, this was a period of rampant nationalism ending too often in fascism, of "beggar-thy-neighbor" policies with respect to tariffs and exchange rate manipulation, and of economic autarky in the face of world depression. There was a will to use devices to interfere with free trade; flexible exchange rate manipulation was one manifestation of such interference. Had fixed rates prevailed throughout, the various countries probably would have engaged in competitive devaluation of currencies rather than depreciation. Nurkse's [6] strong condemnation of flexible rates, especially as being prone to violent fluctuations due to speculative capital movements, has been adopted almost universally as sufficient proof that flexible exchange rates will not work. But the evidence of the 1930's is no basis for such a wholesale rejection. Speculative capital flows would have been destabilizing even with fixed rates, as in fact was the case in the speculative attack on the pound in 1931 which forced the United Kingdom to abandon the peg. Thus, citing the chaotic conditions of the 1930s as an argument against flexible rates is not a valid basis for rejection, but is a form of guilt by association.

By 1936, considerable alteration had occurred in the structure of exchange rates, and the United Kingdom, United States, and France entered into a tripartite agreement pledging to attempt to stabilize exchange rates and avoid currency depreciation. A number of other countries adhered to the agreement, and by 1940 exchange rates had been more or less stabilized at new levels. But the means by which the stability was achieved remained gold and foreign exchange reserve holdings, essentially the same system that had collapsed in 1931.

The outbreak of World War II brought exchange controls over

[6] *International Currency Experience:* Lessons of the Interwar Period (Geneva: League of Nations, 1944).

all uses of foreign exchange. Governments again found it necessary to control all external transactions. The wartime controls provided the hiatus during which plans for a new monetary order could be discussed, in hope they could be agreed upon and implemented when peace was achieved.

THE APPROACHES TO MONETARY REFORM

The prelude to the Bretton Woods conference took place in an environment of international monetary chaos; first, the collapse and competitive devaluations of the 1930s, and then the exchange controls and bilateral trade of the war years. But the framers of the plan for reform had a number of specific fears in mind which, it was hoped, any new monetary order would avoid.

First, the gold standard had proved unworkable. The new environment, in which nations were primarily concerned with domestic full employment policies and growth, made it impossible to return to a system that tied domestic monetary policies closely to movements in the external balance. Deflation for balance-of-payments purposes was too costly, as the depression had proved, and a new set of rules was needed. A world with inflexible prices was not one in which the gold standard was feasible.

Second, the exchange controls and economic nationalism that were the aftermath of the depression should be removed in the new system. In a sense, exchange controls represented an intermediate stage between the gold standard and something else that was to come, the IMF system. Not only did exchange controls allow a country to balance its external accounts; this balance was, to a relatively large extent, achieved while a country's money supply was being managed for domestic ends. For example, the United States had nationalized gold in 1934, and since then domestic monetary policy had, at most, been only indirectly determined by the balance of payments. The exchange controls of the late 1930s and World War II provided the means for this separation. The more extreme examples of Germany and Italy could be cited, wherein the state assumed a much greater role in managing the economy; and exchange controls over external transactions allowed greater direct monetary control over domestic industry and expenditures.

The corollary to exchange controls was greater emphasis on bilateral balancing in international trade. This inevitably led to a proliferation of restrictive practices which tended to suppress international trade. The negotiators for a new international monetary system not only rejected the old gold standard, then, with its automatic balancing and automatic control over domestic policies, but also were fearful of the controls that had replaced it. These bred a dependence on bilateral international transactions which distorted trade and gave the national governments a high degree of control over the major part of international transactions.

Finally, there was the fear that capital movements would continue to be disruptive, as they had been during the exchange market chaos of the depression years. This led to the widely held belief that flexible exchange rates would be unworkable because speculative international money flows would bounce exchange rates up and down at random, also distorting trade.

In essence the world was afraid of the gold standard, of flexible exchange rates, and of exchange controls. What was needed was a new monetary order to avoid the difficulties of each.

In the years immediately preceding the Bretton Woods conference, a number of ideas for reform gained currency. Two of them emerged as the basis for bargaining at the conference, representing the views of the two principal powers, the United States and the United Kingdom. By the close of the second world war, the United States had become *the* major economic power and the world's principal creditor nation. Britain remained the center of the Commonwealth and the sterling area, and the country with the most experience in international monetary matters. It was not accidental then that the White Plan, as the statement of the U.S. position on reform, and the Keynes Plan, representing the U.K. view, became the plans upon which attention was focused and formed the bases for the compromise eventually adopted. As these plans have been discussed in detail by others, we will present only a brief outline of each.[7]

[7] For more thorough discussions of the two plans, see R. F. Harrod, *The Life of John Maynard Keynes* (London: Macmillan, 1951); R. N. Gardner, *Sterling-Dollar Diplomacy* (London: Oxford University Press, 1956); W. R. Scammell, *International Monetary Policy* (London: Macmillan, 1957); Shigeo Horie, *op. cit.*; and F. Lutz, *The Keynes and White Proposals*, Essays in International Finance, No. 1 (Princeton: International Finance Section, 1943).

The White Plan

The White Plan was primarily oriented to eliminating the bases
for a number of problems which it was feared would develop at the
end of World War II. After the first world war the United States
had crawled into its isolationist shell. It had become more protec-
tionist in the 1920s and had tended generally to neglect international
monetary matters. In addition, the victors of World War I had imposed virtually impossible economic conditions on the losers which
hindered their reconstruction and economic growth. It was only
reasonable that a connection was drawn between the unfavorable
economic conditions in Germany and the rise of Adolf Hitler, and
the United States was determined not to make the same mistakes
after World War II.

Thus, the United States was considerably more internationally
minded and desired not to return to passive isolationism but, indeed,
to exert a primary role in shaping the world environment—including
the economic environment; and it was thought that multilateral
trade, in which a country accomplished external balance with all
other nations rather than with each of its trading partners as had
been the trend under the bilateralism of the late 1930s, was the only
way economic nationalism could be avoided.

Furthermore, the United States was fearful of being discriminated
against in international trade, which was one manifestation of bilateralism. Such had been the case after World War I when the
dollar was a relatively scarce currency because the United States was
the only major country that retained its full capacity to export
throughout. Likewise, early in the war it looked as if the same
situation would evolve after World War II; and while the United
States understood the necessity of discrimination against dollar goods,
it was not willing that the discrimination should eventually lead to
collapse of the system. Rather, under U.S. guidance, it would be
eliminated as the war-ravaged nations attained economic viability.

The U.S. position, as stated in the plan authored by Harry Dexter
White, Under Secretary of the Treasury, therefore, was directed toward achieving multilateral trade within a system which would allow the United States to exert its economic influence throughout.
The first version of the White Plan was considerably more inter-

national in nature than the later versions. The basic arrangements of the first version can be summarized briefly:

1. Exchange rates would be fixed, within narrow limits, and subject to change only upon the agreement of three-fourths of the members of the new monetary agreement. There were exceptions for the first three years of the agreement, when unilateral exchange rate adjustment was possible under explicit conditions. But after the transition phase, exchange rates were to remain fixed except when it was *generally agreed* that a country's balance of payments was in "fundamental disequilibrium." This provision had two primary purposes: It was intended to avoid repetition of the competitive devaluations of the 1930s; and it was thought that the United States could exert its vast economic power only under a system of fixed exchange rates. With flexible rates, the United States or the system could not exert influence on countries that were chronically inflationary or deflationary.

2. Each member should abandon all restrictive controls on foreign exchange transactions (except some pertaining to capital transfers) as conditions permitted, and no new bilateral clearing or trading arrangements should be entered into. This provision gave implementation to the U.S. desire for multilateral rather than bilateral international relationships.

3. An international *stabilization fund* would be created which would hold $5 billion in gold and national currencies, received from the member nations on a quota basis. The quota would be based on a number of factors such as foreign exchange holdings of the country, the past balance of payments, and national income. Each country must pay 30 per cent of its total quota in gold to the Fund, the remainder being paid in its own currency, or up to 50 per cent in government securities. These quotas would represent the assets of the Fund.

The Fund would create its own unit of account, the "Unitas," which would be fixed in terms of gold value (equal to $10 worth of gold at the existing dollar price of gold). The gold value of the Unitas could not be changed without an 85 per cent majority vote of the members. In addition, each nation's currency would be defined in terms of the Unitas, and the actual market fluctuations of currencies against each other would be within a narrow range set by the Fund. But the Unitas was only a value reference point—a unit of account equal to $10—and not a medium of exchange; so that nations would not receive Unitas deposits, but all Fund dealings would be in national currencies.

The objective of the Fund would be, of course, to extend short-term credits to the national members. This would be accomplished by selling foreign exchange to deficit members for their currencies, upon condition of implementing appropriate balance-of-payments policies decided upon by the Fund. This provision was directed primarily toward alleviating foreign exchange difficulties due to current account fluctuations and speculative capital flows; that is, the Fund's resources would be made available to members to give them time to adjust to balance-of-payments changes without altering the existing exchange rate.

Finally, the Fund would have the power to buy and sell gold and currencies, and also could issue its own bonds to sell in a member country's capital market to acquire the currency of that country. This, of course, would allow the Fund to sell bonds in a surplus country to acquire the country's currency which it, in turn, could resell (lend) to a deficit country in order to finance its deficit. In this sense, the Fund would act as an international financial intermediary through which surplus countries would lend reserves to deficit countries.

The first version of the White Plan also included a provision for establishing an *international bank* to be capitalized at $10 billion by the member countries. This bank would not only lend to countries for reconstruction and development after the war—as the World Bank which was finally established at Bretton Woods was to do— but also make investments in and extend credit to countries in time of depression, to keep world reserves from falling and to provide a means for financing members' deficits. These provisions were dropped from the later versions however.

It is evident in retrospect that the United States has not been well served by the Bretton Woods plan, even though it was the product of American ingenuity. Indeed, the United States would have been better served by the Keynes Plan, as it turns out, and even better served by a plan that made life easier for deficit countries than either

the White Plan or the Keynes Plan did. The ironic fact is that successive versions of the White (American) Plan became more conservative, by which it is meant that they bore down harder on deficit
countries and tied the system closer to the old gold standard because White and other government officials compromised their plan
with conservatives in Congress. It was to satisfy these conservative
forces that the White Plan was trimmed in successive versions so
that the Congress—increasingly restless and increasingly Republican
—would in the end ratify it. It must be remembered that in this
period Congressional conservatism was associated with such terms as
"globaloney" and "giveaway" plans. Basically, the conservatives saw
the Europeans as impecunious beggars and the United States as the
only strong power in the world. Their vision could not extend to a
time when this imbalance would be corrected. Nor were they willing
to see introduced into the plans that type of generosity which the
United States could now well use, and which would in fact make for
greater world trade rather than the preservation of the gold asset.

Thus the White Plan, which became the Bretton Woods plan,
was actually less a compromise between the United States and other
more liberal countries than a compromise between the original liberal
intent of the Treasury and the conservative Congress. It is note-
worthy that by the 1960s, in contrast to the 1940s, the composition
and functioning of Congress had changed to such an extent that the
most sophisticated analyses of the balance of payments have been
those encouraged by and submitted to the Joint Economic Committee of the Congress.

The final version of the White Plan had three primary provisions:
(1) fixed exchange rates and a fixed price for gold; (2) rejection of
direct controls and bilateralism to achieve balance-of-payments equilibrium; and (3) a fund of currencies which could be lent to deficit
countries to carry them over temporary balance-of-payments difficulties while maintaining convertibility of their currencies. The forward-
looking provisions allowing the Fund to sell its own bonds or the
"Bank" to make its own investments were dropped.

Furthermore, the adjustment mechanism implied by this proposal
remained remarkably close to the gold standard. There was no presumption that a country would tie its domestic currency to gold, but
it was implied that a country would achieve and maintain gold

convertibility of its currency held by foreigners. Adjustment to balance-of-payments difficulties must therefore be effected by domestic relative deflation and inflation. Since it would be the deficit countries that would use the Fund's liquidity resources, the sanctions imposed by the Fund would always hit the deficit countries, forcing them to do the adjusting and placing little pressure on the surplus countries.

The Keynes Plan

The Keynes Plan, which basically represented the British bargaining position at Bretton Woods, had some basic differences from the White proposals. In large measure, the Keynes Plan was the embodiment of a final stage in the long evolution of Lord Keynes' ideas on international (and national) monetary matters. The ideas were tempered with some consideration for the facts of life in the war years when the plan was developed. First, it was obvious that the United Kingdom, and other European countries, would need U.S. aid for postwar reconstruction. Second, while the professional economists in the British government were sympathetic with the American view on nondiscriminatory, multilateral international settlements, there was a considerable body of British opinion in favor of discrimination, especially in so far as the Commonwealth tariff preference system was concerned and with respect to controls over capital movements. It seems clear that Keynes considered these two factors in his proposal.

The premises upon which Keynes based his plan had been set out in his earlier writings. A country should not tie its domestic money supply to gold; instead, domestic policies should be dictated by the needs of full employment and domestic price stability. The randomness of gold production made a domestic monetary standard based on gold incapable of achieving these goals. But the simple nationalization of gold, so that only central banks held it and its only use was in international settlements, was also not enough to divorce domestic economic policy from the external balance. Thus, exchange rate adjustments were necessary in the longer run, while gold movements, together with proper central bank manipulation of short-term interest rates and the forward exchange rate to induce balancing international capital movements, would allow adjustment with fixed exchange rates in the short run.[8] In short, Keynes very early viewed fixed exchange rates for the short run, and variable par values in the long run, as the proper international monetary arrangement.

In his later *Treatise on Money*,[9] Keynes suggested a "supranational bank" with the power to create reserves in addition to gold, since an international system based solely on gold was overly rigid and did not allow a sufficient degree of discretion in the management of international reserves. These ideas represented the broad framework of the Keynes Plan which was presented for consideration in 1943.[10]

As with the White Plan, the Keynes Plan proposed that exchange rates have fixed parities, but be alterable under certain circumstances, and that nations need not have recourse to controls, restrictions, and bilateral balancing techniques. With this as a reference point, Keynes proposed the establishment of an international clearing union, with some of the characteristics of a central bank. The clearing union proposal provided for the following:

1. A new international currency (called Bancor) would be created by the clearing union. This currency would be in the form of deposit balances with, and the liabilities of, the clearing union and the assets of the member countries for which it would serve as part of their international reserves. The Bancor unit would have a fixed value in gold, and each national currency would be fixed (but alterable) in price relative to Bancor. The member nations would agree to accept Bancor deposits, transferred from other countries, in settlement of international imbalances. The clearing union would operate much as a check clearing house operates between banks, except that Bancor would be transferred rather than dollars or pounds. A surplus country would accumulate Bancor balances with the clearing union, while deficit countries would find their balances declining, or eventually would have a negative balance (be in debt to the clearing union). In this manner, the clearing union could finance deficits by *creating* reserves of Bancor.

[8] John Maynard Keynes, A *Tract on Monetary Reform* (New York: Harcourt, Brace, 1924), pp. 190–205.
[9] (New York: Harcourt, Brace, 1930), pp. 388–411.
[10] *Proposals for an International Clearing Union*, Cmd. 6437 (London: H.M.S.O., 1943).

2. Member countries would receive a quota of Bancor in the beginning to be revised annually, based on past exports and imports. Changes in the actual Bancor balance (positive or negative) would require the payment of a penalty to the clearing union. Thus a surplus country would gain Bancor, and a charge of 1 per cent per year would be levied on the excess over 25 per cent of its quota, and another 1 per cent on the excess over 50 per cent of the quota. A deficit country with a negative balance would have similar penalties applied to it. This would provide an incentive for both surplus and deficit countries to adjust external imbalances. Furthermore, deficit countries with negative balances in excess of 50 per cent of their quotas would be required to pledge assets of gold, foreign exchange, or bonds as collateral for the loans.

3. Chronic deficit countries which accumulated negative balances could be required by the clearing union's governing body to alter their exchange rates, impose restrictions on capital movements, or pay gold or foreign exchange to the Union. If the negative balance exceeded a limit, further credit (negative balances) could be cut off. Similar sanctions would be applied to chronic surplus countries with excess positive Bancor balances. The Union would have considerable power over member countries in adjusting exchange rates, imposing internal inflation or deflation, or permitting restrictive practices on payments; but this power would extend to the surplus countries as well as the deficit countries.

4. Total world liquidity could be adjusted upward or downward, as needs dictated, by changing the quotas of the members proportionately. Quotas could be reduced if world inflation appeared imminent, or increased if deflationary conditions prevailed.

5. Gold still would play an important role. First, countries could agree to settle imbalances in gold (although no country could require gold rather than a Bancor balance). Second, the Union would buy gold with Bancor at the agreed price but would not be obligated to sell gold for Bancor. One-way convertibility between Bancor and gold would have been an important step toward eliminating the metal as a cornerstone of the international payments system.

The Keynes Plan, then, foresaw short-run exchange rate fixity with long-run flexibility. It would have partially replaced gold with a new monetary asset, Bancor; whereas the White Plan was content with a new unit of account, Unitas, which in the last analysis was really the U.S. dollar. The lending (negative balance) provisions in the Keynes scheme were explicit and an integral part, which would have automatically increased world liquidity, up to a point. The requirements imposed for adjustment applied to both deficit and surplus countries, and any deflationary bias in forcing a deficit country to carry the sole responsibility of adjusting would have been eliminated.

The Keynes Plan was a highly advanced and sophisticated plan which foresaw a considerable amount of conscious world monetary management—although within strict rules. It represented a major departure from the gold standard, and this may well be a reason for its not being accepted. What did evolve from the Bretton Woods conference was a compromise between the Keynes and White plans; but the compromise contained less of the Keynes and more of the White plans—and certain vital provisions of each were dropped. In a U.S.–U.K. meeting in 1943, the Keynes Plan was replaced in favor of the White Plan as the basis for negotiation. The resulting "Joint Statement" became virtually the common bargaining basis of the United States and United Kingdom at Bretton Woods, as well as the broad outline of the final IMF agreement.

The Bretton Woods System

We are here concerned primarily with the International Monetary Fund, not its sister institutions. The International Bank for Reconstruction and Development (World Bank) and the International Finance Corporation are for more limited and specific objectives, and affect the world monetary system to a far less extent.

The International Monetary Fund is a fund, or pool, of *national* currencies which are available to the member countries through "drawings," that is, the purchase of foreign currencies from the Fund with the national currency of the drawing country. These drawings are for the purpose of financing balance-of-payments deficits under a fixed exchange rate (at least in the short run) system.

The IMF's resources, its stocks of gold and national currencies, were acquired by payment of quotas levied on the members. These quotas are based on an imprecise formula involving reserves, volume of trade, national income, and other factors. The quota of a country is important because it (1) provides the basis for determining the country's right to use the Fund's resources, i.e., its drawing rights; and (2) determines the voting weight for each country. Twenty-five per cent of a country's quota, or 10 per cent of its official reserves of gold and dollars—whichever is smaller—must be paid to the IMF in gold, the remainder being paid in the country's own currency. Any Fund holding of a national currency must have a guaranteed value in gold to protect it from loss from devaluation.

The payment of the quotas to the IMF, then, establishes a pool of currencies upon which deficit countries can draw. Naturally, a deficit country will want to draw the currencies of the surplus countries which it can sell on the foreign exchange market and thereby keep its own currency from falling in price. Thus the Fund provides an immediately mobilizable source of foreign exchange for deficit countries. It is the financial intermediary which provides the surplus countries' currencies to the deficit countries in the form of drawings—the essence of the White Plan. In supplying foreign exchange to deficit (drawing) countries, the IMF makes the "credit" only to an official institution (central bank or Treasury) of the drawing country in the form of a sale for the domestic currency of the drawer.

There are a number of restrictions upon the drawing rights imposed by the IMF Articles. As to the amount a country may draw, the provisions are complicated but explicit. A country may not draw foreign exchange in excess of the amount which would make the Fund's holdings of its own currency (with which it "buys" the foreign exchange) equal to 200 per cent of the drawer's quota. Since in the beginning each country paid 75 per cent of its quota in its own currency, it could normally draw 125 per cent of its quota in foreign exchange. Of course, should its own original currency deposit have been drawn by another currency, its drawing potential may be more. In addition to this ultimate limit, there are other restrictions. For example, a country cannot normally draw more than 25 per cent of its quota in one year. The first 25 per cent drawing is automatic, but the Fund may then review the policies of a drawing country to satisfy itself that satisfactory measures are being taken to correct its balance-of-payments deficit.

Restrictions also apply to the use to which foreign currency drawings may be put. These are normally used to cover deficits in the current account in the balance of payments, or for certain types of normal capital transactions. These restrictions on use are designed to avoid the use of the Fund's drawing rights for reconstruction, reparations, or simply to acquire and hold foreign exchange reserves. In essence, the foreign exchange must be needed to support the value of a country's currency in the course of normal international transactions.

Resorting to IMF's resources for prolonged financing of international imbalances is to some extent precluded because of limits on the amount and duration of drawing. Moreover, each drawing has a service charge of ½ of 1 per cent levied, and drawings which place the Fund's holdings of the drawer's currency above its quota are subject to a cumulative additional service charge. The procedure for limiting the duration of drawings involves a complicated formula requiring repurchase of the country's currency held by the Fund in excess of 75 per cent of its quota at a rate dictated by its reserve holdings; but in no event will the Fund allow a drawing to persist beyond three to five years, depending upon the problem for which the foreign exchange was used.

In essence, the IMF provides a progressively conditional source of liquidity for its members, the limit of which is a *fixed* quota. It does not supplant other sources of international reserves, nor does it allow any discretion on the part of its managers to adjust liquidity availability—except within the very narrow limits which allow flexibility in granting drawing rights. The inadequacy of the size of the Fund can easily be seen when one compares the original American quota of $2.75 billion, giving the United States a maximum drawing amount in the beginning of 125 per cent of that amount, with its over $3 billion deficit in 1958. Certainly, the liquidity available from this Fund is not overwhelming, even with the increase in quotas by 50 per cent in 1959 and the 25 per cent increase in 1965. More basic, however, is that the Fund provides no automatic source of new liquidity—each must be negotiated. Likewise, there is no automatic source of new reserves outside the Fund.

While the IMF provides only temporary "credit" to deficit countries, the IMF Articles set the framework within which the members must operate. Most important is the exchange rate provision. The IMF exchange rate system is one of fixed rates. The IMF Articles require its members to fix the par value of their currencies in relation to gold or the U.S. dollar. The dollar is fixed in value only in relation to gold, i.e., at $35 per ounce. Each nation's currency is therefore directly or indirectly tied to gold. A country may allow its currency to fluctuate on the foreign exchange market by no more than 1 per cent on each side of the par rate, the limits at which a central bank must support its respective currency by buying or selling reserves for it.

The par value of any nation's currency can be changed only in the event of a "fundamental disequilibrium" in the balance of payments. The Articles do not define "fundamental disequilibrium," and its determination appears to be a matter of judgment. In any event, before a change in an exchange rate can occur the country must present a formal proposal justifying its view that a fundamental disequilibrium exists. If the proposed change from the initial par value (when the IMF Articles went into effect) is 10 per cent or less, the Fund will raise no objection, but if the reevaluation is greater than that amount, the Fund has the right to concur or object. Exchange rate adjustments are not at the discretion of members, except for an initial change of 10 per cent from the 1945 rate, but require the Fund's acquiescence.

There are no rules which either (1) give the Fund the right to change par rates as with the White Plan, or (2) set up conditions under which the Fund could require exchange rate adjustment, as in the Keynes Plan. The IMF statements relating to changes in par values are so nebulous as to be of little help either to a country contemplating such a change or to the Fund as a precedent of a proposal for change. As a result, the postwar period has seen a solidifying of the exchange rate structure.

The Bretton Woods conference took a solid position on the desire to eliminate restrictive practices, especially exchange controls, in order to restore a multilateral, nondiscriminatory system of world payments. The Articles of Agreement make it an obligation for each member to avoid restrictions on current account pay-

ments, to avoid discrimination in foreign exchange dealings, and
to establish and maintain convertibility of foreign-held balances
into gold or other convertible currencies. Under certain extreme
circumstances—which prevailed in the immediate postwar period
due to wartime exchange controls, and still prevail in underdeveloped countries wherein foreign exchange is very scarce—provision
is made for the avoidance of these basic objectives. The major
provision permitting selective exchange controls is the so-called
"scarce currency clause." Under conditions where the supply of a
country's currency is severely limited for foreign transactions, as the
dollar was in the immediate postwar years, the other members may
institute exchange controls on that scarce currency. This provision
passed out of the limelight when the dollar shortage disappeared
with the sizable U.S. deficits of the late 1950s.

THE OPERATION OF THE IMF SYSTEM
IN THE POSTWAR PERIOD

Three essential characteristics of the IMF system emerge. First,
it is a fixed exchange rate system with inexplicit provisions for
altering exchange rates. Second, the system was designed to avoid
the use of restrictions for balancing international payments and
receipts. Third, it supplements world reserves of gold and foreign
exchange with a pool of liquidity, fixed in size, thereby giving
more time for balance-of-payments adjustments. In the postwar
period the IMF underwent shaky beginnings and did not emerge
into a viable force until the late 1950's under the leadership of
Per Jacobson.

While exchange rates have become more rigid in the postwar
period, this is not a direct result of the IMF Agreement. A majority of the original IMF members have devalued their currencies
since 1945, but most of the devaluations took place in the aftermath
of the war, in 1948–1949. These devaluations reflected primarily
the inappropriate rates with respect to the dollar originally established, rather than the use of exchange rate adjustments as a continuing means of adjusting the balance of payments. Since the
middle 1950s, only France has resorted to devaluation among the
major countries.

The emergence of the American and British deficits as significant problems in the late fifties and early sixties required, by most criteria, an alteration in exchange rates; but none occurred, and the reasons normally given strike at the very foundation of the Bretton Woods system.

The argument usually employed is that a reserve currency (the dollar and the pound) should not devalue because that would cause capital losses in countries which hold these currencies as reserves and catastrophic disruptions of trade and of international transactions. The Bretton Woods system virtually presupposes a reserve currency system. Its lending facilities (drawing rights) are too small to finance a major deficit for any reasonable period. It has no provision for removing gold from its central position as the ultimate reserve; and since gold cannot increase fast enough, countries will substitute currencies which are convertible into gold as reserves. The pound was, by the 1920s, a reserve currency. The dollar came into its own in the postwar period as a major reserve currency, since it was the only currency freely convertible to gold.

As a result of these factors—a continued reliance on gold, and limited IMF resources—the major source of expansion of world reserves in the postwar period has been the dollar holdings of foreign countries gained through the persistent U.S. deficit; and it has been these very dollar holdings that have ostensibly kept the United States and United Kingdom from devaluing when the possibility arose that they might be massively converted to gold. Thus a rigidity has been imposed on the exchange rate system which, even if the IMF were willing, makes deficit reserve currency countries reluctant to devalue their currencies. This problem was compounded when the major currencies removed their major exchange controls in 1958, thereby allowing capital to flow relatively freely among countries. The basis was then set for massive speculation against reserve currencies.

If we can assume that exchange rate adjustments have been limited—and the IMF can supply reserves only in limited amounts for relatively brief spans of time—and that restrictive practices for balance-of-payments purposes are to be avoided, how can a deficit country and a surplus country adjust to eliminate the imbalance? The only method left is by relative inflation and deflation, the very process required by the gold standard, although possibly less severe and over a longer period. The deficit country *must* lower prices, restrain imports, and raise interest rates because (1) it can use IMF drawings only to a limited extent, and (2) it loses gold and foreign exchange, of which it has a limited amount. The surplus country, however, does not have to inflate since it can pile up reserves in unlimited amounts. In neither case can the IMF require an exchange rate adjustment, regardless of how fundamental the disequilibrium appears.

A second major problem, aside from the absence of any adjustment mechanism which does not place the burden on the deficit country, is the prospective failure of world reserves to grow fast enough. The IMF is a fixed quota system, thus drawing rights are relatively fixed. Reserves can grow only through new gold or new deficits by reserve currency countries; and the latter lead to currency crisis when confidence in a currency becomes impaired. Thus, the IMF system has a basic contradiction, if exchange rates are to remain rigid.

EVOLUTION OF THE IMF

Although we have thus far pictured the IMF as a relatively narrow institution, far from the clearing union proposal of Keynes, it has not remained static, and has seen the Western countries through 20 years of rapid economic growth. It has extended drawings to a host of member countries, and has a dedicated and competent staff who have provided incalculable technical assistance on monetary matters. The fact remains, however, that the evolution which has occurred has been primarily within its role as a financial intermediary between surplus and deficit countries. Whatever improvements in the adjustment mechanism have occurred, it is because of the IMF's facilitating better understanding of economic theory and economic policy and not because of the system itself.

The most obvious evolutionary steps have been the increases in IMF quotas in 1959 (50 per cent) and in 1965 (25 per cent). In both cases, other adjustments were made in individual countries' quotas to bring them into line with their changed international economic status. The quota increases, of course, raise the potential drawing power of the members—i.e., the pool of currencies is larger —and thereby increase world liquidity. Such increases do not improve the condition of a deficit reserve currency country such as the United States or United Kingdom, nor improve the adjustment mechanism.

The IMF also instituted the so-called stand-by credits in 1952. These are merely an advance guarantee that a certain maximum amount of foreign currencies can be drawn by a country over some period. Thus, the country may deem these as automatic drawing rights as comparable to owned reserves. They are of considerable benefit for some countries, especially the underdeveloped, when balance-of-payments problems are foreseen. Such stand-by credits have been between $1 and $2 billion since 1961.

The major improvement in the liquidity aspects of the Fund is the "General Arrangements to Borrow," adopted in 1962. This agreement, which is allowed under Article VII of the IMF Agreement, is between the IMF and ten of its major members. Under the agreement, these countries are committed to lend up to $6 billion to the IMF, which may in turn lend to a deficit country in balance-of-payments difficulties that require resources in excess of those available through normal IMF channels. It was through this agreement that the massive "rescue of the pound" was accomplished in 1964. The Group of Ten arrangements are another means of the surplus countries extending credit to deficit countries with the IMF acting as a financial intermediary.

Another development, further outside normal IMF channels, is the Group of Ten's London gold pool, which makes available a pool of currencies for stabilizing the price of gold in the London gold market. Through this pool, gold losses from speculative gold purchases are shared among the group of countries, rather than falling primarily on the United Kingdom. Gold purchases are shared among the group on a quota basis.

While other devices have been developed to stabilize foreign exchange markets and increase the credit granted by surplus countries, they have occurred largely outside the IMF, although with its blessing in most cases.

While the Fund has matured as a source of liquidity, these developments are *ad hoc* additions to the relatively restrictive IMF

Articles. The adjustment mechanism has not been improved, and it is still doubtful that the IMF can solve the liquidity problem when the United States eliminates its deficit. Plans for reform are therefore relevant and needed. The essential problem is how best to reform the system, a problem upon which the following chapters focus.

The receptiveness of the IMF itself to new reform proposals appears to be mixed. In the 1965 *Annual Report* written by the Fund's staff, and approved by its executive directors, it is implied that there is no urgent need for supplementing the volume of reserves, and that existing methods of creating liquidity may suffice to meet the world's needs for a time. But it was also noted in the report that further progress should be made toward an international consensus about the way in which the international monetary system should develop.

CHAPTER V

The United Kingdom: Plight and Prospects

AMERICAN concern with many British problems is qualitatively different from its concern with those of other nations. The visible, and even the subtle, ties are obviously closer. With respect to the balance of payments, the dollar and the pound are the two reserve currencies. Moreover, both nations have been deficit nations since 1950. But while the United States, within an over-all deficit, has huge surpluses on current account, the British do not. Britain has undergone a series of balance-of-payments "crises," each calling forth restrictive economic action of the "classical medicine." In October 1964, a supercrisis emerged which produced a speculative run against the pound and threatened an involuntary devaluation of the pound and perhaps other currencies. Indeed, the balance of payments remains the major British economic problem to whose needs other activities must be tailored.

To the solution of the balance-of-payments problem itself the entire National Plan,[1] with its targets for growth of output and productivity, is oriented. The Plan is thus a vast attempt to alter the structure of British industry so that in the long-run the balance of payments will, hopefully, be removed as an underlying weakness of the British economy, permitting a sustained growth of the British

---

[1] *The National Plan*, Cmnd. 2764 (London: H.M.S.O., 1965), pp. 69–83.

economy, uninterrupted by periodic crisis, and with it rising living standards and renewed political strength.

If the 1964 sterling crisis had resulted in a forced devaluation of the pound at that time, the dollar may not have withstood the ensuing speculative pressure against it. Fear that forced devaluation of these two key currencies would topple the whole system of international monetary arrangements inspired the extension of approximately $3 billion to Britain by the Group of Ten, and an additional $1 billion of credit from the IMF to "rescue" the pound. Another such credit, smaller in amount, was again extended in September 1965. Such action is indicative of the fact that the British problem is closely intertwined with the whole complex of international financial arrangements as well as the U.S. balance-of-payments problem.

The analysis of adjustments to a balance-of-payments deficit (Chap. III) emphasized that in some way a nation incurring deficits must reduce its costs and prices compared to those of its competitors. Devaluation is, of course, one method of doing so. But the favorable longer-term effects of devaluation will be achieved only if the competitive advantage which the deficit nation thus gains is not eaten up, either by internal inflation or by the competitive devaluation of others; and there are other methods to reduce cost-price relationships as well. The United Kingdom has placed reliance on these other techniques. It is convenient to examine them and their alternatives from the point of view of the time periods over which they operate: the short, the intermediate, or the long run, and it is along these time axes that this chapter is organized.

In the short run, the alternatives are devaluation or deflation (coupled with some direct controls over capital movements). In the intermediate term the problem is to keep inflation under control so that whatever benefits are gleaned by a successful short-run policy may be sustained. The alternatives available here seem to be an "incomes policy," or an economic policy designed to keep output below capacity. In the longer term, the problem is one of restructuring the economy in order to increase output per worker—another cost-price reducing technique—and to shift industrial output to fit contemporary competitive conditions.

It is evident that the Labour government has chosen deflation and controls in the short run, an "incomes policy" in the intermediate range, and the National Plan in the long range as its *modus operandi*. This chapter analyzes the chosen, as well as the alternative path in each case.

Whatever techniques are employed, it is implicitly an American desire that the British should succeed in the re-establishment of a strong economy and with it rising living standards and a strong voice in the international politics of our day.

THE PROBLEM

Traditionally, Britain, with few natural resources and a population in excess of 50 million has exported finished manufactured goods and services in exchange for imports of goods and raw materials. This remains the British position. But the great transformations of world power that have occurred since 1918 have forced Britain to shift from her role as center of a worldwide quasi-imperial network of markets and sources of supply to an industrial nation among many nations, independent and competitive rather than center of a complimentary trading pattern.

Britain has not increased her exports fast enough to pay for the imports needed to allow rapidly rising living levels. More important, her product mix has not sufficiently shifted toward more sophisticated engineering and technological output, which is required to compete with new trading partners in Europe. The failure of British exports to expand sufficiently in the post-World War II period has resulted in a decline in her reserves of gold and foreign exchange. Thin at the end of World War II when the gross total was about $3.4 billion, they have grown thinner, to $2.3 billion in mid-1965. Thus a small change in Britain's payments or receipts has a major impact on reserves. Fear that deficits would further deplete thin reserves has led to policies which "stop" economic activity in Britain, to the further detriment of her economic growth. This would be bad for any major trading nation. Temporarily rescued from the vicious cycle of balance-of-payments deficits to reserve crisis to "stop" policies by the 1964 and 1965 Group of Ten and IMF credits, the basic British problem remains to be solved, and now in such a way that sufficient balance-of-payments surpluses are earned to repay the credits as well. The task is thus temporarily eased, but in the long run is enlarged. Politically, failure to grow has led to a shrinkage for Britain. Under the National Plan, military and aid commitments will be cut or restrained. Only economic growth can restore a strong political voice to the United Kingdom.

Innumerable statistical series have been deduced to show Britain's relatively lagging international industrial status. The following table shows the relative growth rates of Britain compared to other countries. Its rate of growth in output and productivity is the lowest of all of the countries shown over the past decade, and it is also the lowest, except for the United States, in output per capita growth.

TABLE 1. SOME GROWTH COMPARISONS, 1954–1964
(annual averages)

	U.K.	U.S.	Germany	France	Italy
National income (constant prices)	2.6%	3.4%	3.4%	4.9%	5.3%
Output (physical)	2.6	3.2	7.6	4.4	5.9
Productivity (output per labor unit)	1.9	2.1	5.3	4.0	4.1
Wages	4.4	3.6	8.6	8.8	5.9
Per capita production	2.2	1.6	6.5	4.4	5.9

SOURCE: J. Polk, "British Crisis and Response," National Industrial Conference Board Record, March 1965, p. 31.

With respect to exports, while the value of Britain's exports have risen from about £2.1 billion in 1950 to £3.9 billion in 1962, its share of the world export market has fallen; the United Kingdom's share of the total of 12 industrial countries had amounted to over 25 per cent in 1950, but only 15 per cent by 1962.[2] Yet the burden on export receipts to achieve external balance today is greater than it was in the past. As late as 1938 Britain needed to export goods of only about two-thirds the value of its imports. The balance came from income on overseas investment and other invisible earnings (banking, insurance, shipping, etc.) Thus in 1938 Britain imported some £846 million while its visible exports totaled £562 million and "invisible" exports, £243 million. By 1962 visible exports were needed to pay for over 96 per cent of imports (£3,991 vs. £4,059 million); invisibles totaled £509 million, a figure larger in amount than the pre-

[2] Key Statistics of the British Economy (London: H.M.S.O., 1964).

war days, but far smaller as a per cent of imports. The enormous liquidation of British assets to pay for World War II has forced far greater reliance on the exports to maintain balance-of-payments equilibrium. If the level of living is to increase, exports must rise faster.

Moreover, the trading partners have changed over the years. Even in the postwar years from 1950–1955, nearly half of all British exports had gone to the sterling area countries, which imported an average of about £1,300 million per year, and were by far the single most important market for British exports. Yet while exports to the sterling area stayed at nearly the same level in subsequent years, Western European nations increased their imports of British goods rapidly, but obviously not rapidly enough. By 1962 these nations were the major importers of British exports; Western Europe and the sterling area each took about one-third of British exports (£1,360 and £1,342 million, respectively); North America took roughly one-sixth (£518 million); and the rest of the world, a sixth (£572 million).

The task of shifting Britain's output toward more sophisticated manufacturing and engineering industries raises qualitative as well as quantitative problems. The task calls for more efficient production and greater investment; it probably requires new magnitudes of educational endeavor, and perhaps a rearrangement of social values, all of which are aspects of the "structural change" problem, which are discussed later in this chapter.

The new National Plan acknowledged that such a shift is necessary and has indicated the type of shift desired. The 3.8 per cent per year average industrial growth (25 per cent in the period 1964–1970) projected by the Plan is to result from reductions or slower growth in the older industries—coal, textiles, and older consumer goods—and by much higher rates of growth in new industries. The most rapid expansion is to be in mechanical and electrical engineering, at a rate of some 6 per cent per year. This expansion is vital to secure the needed increase in exports and investments. Further, chemicals, oil refining, man-made fibers, and communications are expected to grow at 8 per cent to 10 per cent per year.

The Plan itself is avowedly open to periodic review. In nature, it resembles the French model of "indicative planning" rather

than Socialist-type plans. However, while the key French control
is the supply of credit to industries, the advanced British capital
market denies the government access to this key. Save exhortation
and cooperation, there is yet no way to force conformity to the Plan,
although some type of power to do so could be in the offing.

The Plan has received a mixed reception. While it unquestion-
ably gives all parties concerned a tangible goal and enlists the economic development councils as "adrenalin carriers," it has been
assailed by the *Economist* [3] as the "National Platitudes"; by others
it is said to be unrealistic and to fail to allow for new "spurt"
growth.

But even with these optimistic projections, the balance of payments remains the principal immediate problem. It is difficult to see
how the United Kingdom will earn sufficient balance-of-payments
surpluses to repay the Group of Ten and IMF credits by 1970,
let alone build reserves.

ANATOMY OF A CRISIS

The anatomy of the most recent (1964) balance-of-payments
crisis will illustrate the nature of that problem. Table 2 shows exports, imports, and the deficit on the visible trade account since
1958. In the last crisis (1960), imports had risen by over $1.6 bil-
lion in the year, while exports had increased by less than half that
amount. This resulted in a run on the reserves to which the government's response was another of the periodic "stop" policies in
Britain, in which the economy was restricted. Credit, via the bank
rate increase, was tightened, and other steps were taken to slow
both consumption and the growth rate. As the trade deficit fell
toward its normal $1.5 billion level, and as the restriction drove un-
employment up toward 500,000 persons, a "go" period appeared
warranted and credit and other restrictions were eased.

As growth accelerated, the conditions were generated for another
balance-of-payments crisis. One of the conditions, which the table
does not show, is the persistence of internal inflation in Britain. A
"go" period creates added demand for labor, which in turn results
in higher wages, incomes, and profits. This added income has three

[3] September 18–24, 1965, p. 1,071.

TABLE 2. VISIBLE TRADE BALANCE
(*millions of dollars*)

	Exports	Imports	Trade Deficit
1958	$ 9,290	$10,494	$1,204
1959	9,691	11,152	1,461
1960	10,349	12,715	2,366
1961	10,752	12,309	1,557
1962	11,054	12,564	1,510
1963	11,855	13,496	1,641
1964	12,275	15,552	3,277

SOURCE: Polk, *op. cit.*, p. 30.

effects: (1) It is spent for goods, many of which are imported, hence imports rise; (2) it pulls goods into the internal consumption stream which would have been exported; (3) it raises prices, including those in the export sector. An increase in imports, accompanied by a *slower rate* of increase of exports, lays the ground for a new balance-of-payments crisis. In the 1964 crisis, imports jumped by over $2 billion, while exports, restrained by the rising prices of the "go" phase, increased by only $400 million. As the trade balance worsened, confidence in the pound declined. A force devaluation was feared. Thus, the external trade crisis was compounded by a massive speculative outflow of short-term deposits held in London. In addition, foreign trade financing worked against Britain. Through the "leads and lags" phenomenon, payments from foreign currencies into pounds were postponed, in fear of devaluation. Some experts estimate the lag to be $1.5 billion. This combination reduced British gold and dollar reserves drastically. The result was the previously mentioned rescue operation, and an even more extreme "stop" of the British economy than had been resorted to in earlier crises.

Not only did the 1964 crisis result in a rise in the bank rate to the crisis level of 7 per cent, but also Britain resorted to an import surcharge (tariff) of 15 per cent, which was antithetical to the general free trade movement and certainly to the espoused objectives of the European Free Trade Association. Moreover, steps were taken in the Labour government's first budget to curtail the export of capital from Britain; in general, the budget taxed more heavily and was designed as a restrictive, as well as a further equalitarian, device.

A brief comparison of the United Kingdom's export totals and prices with those of other countries is revealing. While the United Kingdom's exports rose by 48 per cent in the decade 1953–1963, the increase was a sad performance compared to Germany, France, or Italy, which rose 233, 136, and 303 per cent, respectively. On the other hand, British export prices rose faster, despite all the periodic "stop" policies.

TABLE 3. CHANGES IN EXPORTS AND PRICES, 1953–1964 [a]

	Prices of Manufactured Exports	Volume of Manufactured Exports
	(%)	(%)
United Kingdom	+19	+ 48
United States	+18	+ 16 [b]
West Germany	+ 7	+233
France	+ 3	+136
Italy	−18	+303 [c]

SOURCE: S. Brittan, *The Treasury under the Tories, 1951–1964* (London: Penguin, 1964), p. 280.

[a] First quarter 1964 only.
[b] Base is average 1952–1954.
[c] All exports.

The table covers a long span and conceals the improvement in the American position and the deterioration of the Italian near the end of it; but it gives a fair picture of the United Kingdom over the whole of the eleven-year period. Even if Britain's competitive position should begin to improve very soon, the eleven-year deterioration will have exacted a heavy toll in lost economic growth.

Naturally, the position of the U.K.'s reserves will be a logical consequence of the export story. Adequate exports would have permitted adequate imports and also could have added to Britain's thin reserves. More adequate reserves would not only cushion the shock of external changes on internal policies, but permit increased overseas investment, aid, and other British goals.

In May 1965, Britain's gold and hard currency reserve totaled £840 million, or $2,352 million. A year earlier, the reserves were

£969 million ($2,713 million). As Chart I below indicates, Britain's liabilities (debts) to foreigners in 1964 were some $11 billion. The ratio of reserve to liabilities has been very thin, and is growing thinner. Hence, British domestic policy has been excessively sensitive to even the slightest change in the balance of payments. Every time reserves fell significantly, pressure mounted for a "stop" period—a deflationary crackdown on employment and growth in the home market accomplished by increased bank rate, higher taxes, an increase in unused capacity—policies detrimental to economic growth.

CHART 1. PERSPECTIVE ON STERLING LIABILITIES TO FOREIGNERS

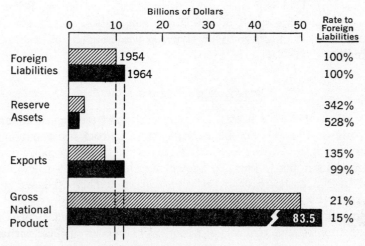

SOURCE: IMF, International Financial Statistics.

Since 1958 British *domestic* prices rose *less* rapidly than those on the Continent excepting Germany (see Table 2, p. 170); however, Table 3 above shows the U.K.'s *export* prices rose more rapidly. Thus, the deflationary impact of "stop" periods was not reaching the export industries, probably because they had failed to invest over the years sufficiently to increase productivity.

By September 1965, after the "rescue operations," the British reserve position was again strengthened, but on a loan basis. The initial $1 billion IMF loan, contracted in December 1964, was for three years; an additional $2.4 billion credit advanced in May 1965 is due in five years. The $3 billion multinational loan of "rescue operation" days had been repaid with these borrowings. The September 1965 credit is also due in the future. Thus additional liquidity, in the form of IMF loans, was used as a substitute for an adjustment process. The proceeds are to be used to support the pound at the pegged $2.80 rate, a rate which some argue is largely responsible for the balance-of-payments deficit, and hence responsible for the need for a loan.

But borrowed reserves, unlike earned reserves, must be repaid, plus interest. Whether this borrowed additional liquidity will buy time to effect structural changes to enable Britain to earn surpluses as it is hoped, or will simply constitute a huge burden on Britain depends upon the speed of structural change. It is clearly a vast gamble on the effectiveness of future policy, and not a basic adjustment.

DEFLATION OR DEVALUATION

It was noted in Chapter III that a deficit resulting from an overvalued currency can be reduced by a cutback in a nation's costs, prices, and income, which serve to increase its exports and decrease its imports. This can be accomplished either by a devaluation of the currency or by relative deflation. These policies are alternatives to achieve the same end.

Both the Conservative and Labour parties have in fact eschewed devaluation for different sets of reasons. The policies of these parties may be considered in turn.

From 1951 to 1964 the Tories never faced a balance-of-payments crisis of the magnitude of that of 1964. They relied on periodic applications of deflation and reflation—the "stop-and-go" policy that many severely criticized. Aware of the policy's shortcomings, the Tories apparently hoped that longer-term devices would eventually eliminate the need for "stop and go," including a successful incomes policy and profound structural change to be precipitated by entry into the Common Market. But historical circumstances were such that neither was possible to institute.

In more detail, the "stops" were instituted when the balance-of-payments deficit was rising. Restrictions were placed on the economy in the form of increased interest rates, credit restrictions—particularly on hire-purchase (installment credit)—to dampen the demand for consumer durable goods, and alterations in tax rates. The "go's" were set off by rising levels of unemployment—when the 500,000 level was approached—and by improvement in the balace of payments.

This policy was criticized for several reasons. The techniques used were crude. Consummate timing is required to manage such an economy, but it was alleged at the time, and subsequently in J. C. R. Dow's study that both the timing and techniques could have been much better. Most important, the policy discouraged investment in labor-saving equipment by creating uncertainty with respect to the level of future demand and sales.

Thus Lord Robbins wrote:

We have been attempting to drive our car through this difficult post-war country with steering gear out of action, the wheels lashed rigidly in one direction, our only means of equilibration an occasional stop, every few months, for the wheels to be unlashed and turned at another angle—while Ministers stand on the roof and deliver salutory exhortations.[4]

Chart 2 shows the relation between the "stop-and-go" policy and industrial production in the decade 1954–1964. The policy was said to be mistimed because the "stops" were introduced after production was already on a plateau, although the balance-of-payments deficit, which lags economic developments, was still rising. The "go's," particularly the tax relief budgets of 1955, 1959, and 1963, were implemented after the turnaround when output was already rising but when the balance of payments was still improving. Thus, the added stimulus of demand tended to set the stage for the next balance-of-payments crisis.

The Tory hope that "stop and go" could be replaced or supplemented by an incomes policy and structural reform was frustrated. The former, toward which the Tories moved in the early 1960s, was blocked by the refusal of the Trades Union to cooperate, and for other reasons. The "pay-pause" of 1961, a form of limited incomes policy aimed mainly at government employees, proved sterile,

4 Polk, *op. cit.*, p. 29.

CHART 2. STOP AND GO

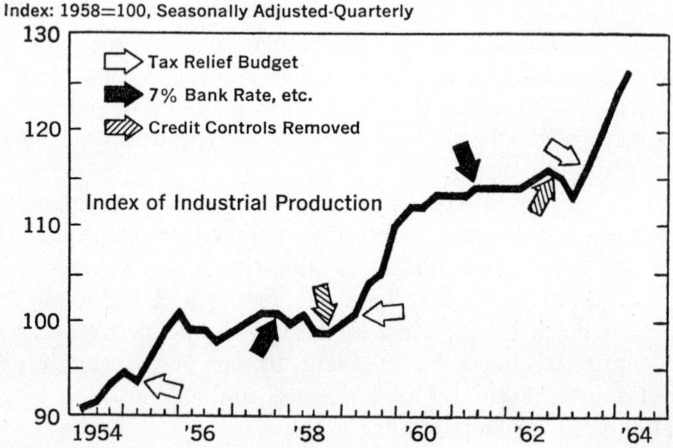

Index: 1958=100, Seasonally Adjusted-Quarterly

SOURCE: S. Brittan, *The Treasury under the Tories* (London: Penguin Books, Inc., 1964), p. 24.

as teachers' strikes, civil servants' complaints, and other difficulties forced its abandonment. President de Gaulle's veto prevented the move to structural reform, which the Tories hoped would be forced onto the British economy by membership in the Common Market through the competitive influences of Europe.

Labour gained power in October 1964 in the midst of the worst sterling crisis since 1950. Devaluation was then advocated by economists of various political persuasions,[5] including many within the Labour party. The party's leaders, however, despite advice to the contrary, decided against it in any form. The choice seems to have been dictated by political considerations. The sole economic argument against devaluation—that the pound is in fact not overvalued, but that exports are low because of inefficient selling and delivery—is belied by the vast effort that has and does go to reduce domestic prices and costs by a variety of techniques. Moreover, the volume of imports to Britain, which precipitated the crisis, is further evidence of overvaluation. To combat it, a surcharge on imports, initially 15 per cent and later reduced to 10 per cent, was imposed.

[5] See as an example, F. Hirsch, *The Pound Sterling: A Polemic* (London: Gollancz, 1965).

This serves to increase import prices, or, put differently, is somewhat similar to a devaluation of the pound for this purpose.

While the political considerations which led Labour to reject devaluation have not been made explicit officially, they seem to have been both domestic and international origins. At home, Tory propaganda had, over the years, effectively labeled Labour as "the party of devaluation." If Labour could nevertheless have blamed a 1964 devaluation on past Tory ineptitude, they did not so choose. Further, the 1949 devaluation had not had the desired effect, because subsequent inflation as well as more sizable Continental devaluations had offset its advantages. Internationally, concern lest devaluation should harm England in its role as banker for the sterling area and others, its relations with the international monetary establishment, and perhaps, above all, should precipitate a speculative run on the dollar—possibly culminating in forced U.S. devaluation and a collapse of the international monetary system—militated against British devaluation.

In lieu of devaluation, the Labour party has instituted a series of policies with different time dimensions, designed to eliminate balance-of-payments crises in the short run, and to lower British costs and prices vis-à-vis the rest of the world in the longer run. The provision of vast international credits in the 1964 "rescue operation" and again in the fall of 1965 has permitted Britain to forego devaluation in 1964, and has allowed time to attempt this series of policies. Most immediately, Labour embarked on a familiar "stop" policy, restricting credit to inhibit the economy and raising the bank rate (to 7 and, later, 6 per cent) to attract or hold foreign capital. This "stop" was supplemented by certain direct controls; foreign investment was severely restricted and the import surcharge was imposed. In the intermediate term, an incomes policy was undertaken to control inflation. In the longer run, the National Plan is designed to restructure the economy, and to raise productivity.

The die having been so cast, devaluation or a floating exchange rate has become an academic question. Because the question may rise again, however, if government policies change or the present plans do not succeed, the question is still worthy of some analysis. Remember that while foreign credits have provided additional liquidity and time to the United Kingdom, these borrowings must be repaid. To do so, Britain needs a balance-of-payments surplus of approximately £300 million per year if the debt is to be repaid by 1970 as presently scheduled. The maturity of the debt may be lengthened, but it has not yet been, and given the present Plan, it is difficult to see how repayment will be possible.

Devaluation for the United Kingdom raises four key questions: Will it not raise import costs and thus cause inflation which will vitiate its value for the trade balance? What about relations with the sterling area and others who hold reserves in sterling? Is it effective, i.e., will it not be offset by countervaling devaluation elsewhere? Finally, how will it affect relations with the international monetary system?

On the first question—inflation—antidevaluers usually argue that Britain depends heavily on imports both for domestic use and to process and re-export. Devaluation would raise the price of imports from those nations which had not devalued. Therefore, as a direct effect, higher import prices would result in some higher export prices, offsetting in part the price advantage on exports, which Britain had initially gained by the devaluation. Indirectly, higher import prices would increase the cost of living inside the United Kingdom. Some will demand higher wages to offset this; others would automatically get them where cost-of-living wage clauses exist. Pensioners and others with fixed incomes would suffer.

Those who favor devaluation point out, however, that the foregoing arguments are only effective if Britain were operating at peak capacity and had no unused resources of either labor or plant. If there *is* spare capacity, both output and productivity can rise in response to increased demand for exports. The increase in productivity, of course, means that higher import costs, as well as higher labor costs, can be absorbed without raising prices. Moreover, when unused capacity exists, the pressure for wage increases is less and can be resisted by employers. Since prices need not rise under the condition of devaluation with unused capacity, pensioners and others with fixed incomes should not suffer. The net effect would be greater exports without price rises and a higher level foreign exchange receipts. Clearly, the degree to which this analysis holds depends on the extent of unused capacity and the ability to control demand when devaluation is introduced.

The major point implicit here is that a *planned* devaluation, accompanied by the control of demand or preceded by the creation of some unused capacity is needed if inflation is not to eat up the benefits of devaluation. Unfortunately, the tendency of most governments to wait too long to devalue, to undertake it as a last gasp antidote to a balance-of-payments crisis, and to fail to plan for it is evident historically. This observation however does not negate the inherent value of the devaluer's argument.

If flexible rates (the floating pound) were used rather than a devaluation to a new fixed rate, the inflation argument takes another twist. Some think that without the discipline of limited reserves an economy's managers will not resist inflation so forcefully. But this argument seems weak. The managers should attempt to achieve price stability with or without the fear of losing reserves. Moreover, in Britain, where far more people are directly effected by higher import prices than by reserves of gold and dollars one would expect more political pressure for a "strong pound" with a flexible exchange rate rather than without one.

The second question is concerned with the sterling area and other "depositors" who would incur a capital loss on their sterling holdings if the pound were devalued. The question would seem to involve a priority of values, as much political as economic in nature. Those who favor devaluation are known as "little Englanders" on this score; they argue that the cost of "responsibility" to the sterling area is too great for the United Kingdom to bear. It inhibits needed economic change, slowing Britain's move toward a fully competitive economy. They would rather save England than save the $2.80 pound. They point to the decreasing level of trade with the area, as both the United Kingdom and the Commonwealth have increasingly turned to Europe and the United States as trading partners. At the same time, a growing and viable United Kingdom could provide more aid, capital, and export markets for the area, so that it would be of mutual benefit that Britain succeed even if this required devaluation. It also remains a question whether members would in fact quit the sterling area if there were a devaluation. Most did not in 1949; probably some would and others would not, particularly if access to London's long-term capital markets continued to be open to them. Certain non-sterling "depositors" also hold reserves in London and are encouraged to do so. Those favoring devaluation can demonstrate that these balances have been among the most volatile among Britain's short-term liabilities. With a stronger pound, even a devalued one, and an improved balance-of-payments position, these deposits would probably grow in size, and certainly be less volatile. This question may now be largely academic, because few official balances are held in sterling (apart from members of the area).

It has been suggested that other countries with stronger currencies "fund" the British liabilities to foreigners. Funding would provide for planned and orderly withdrawals of balances from London in exchange for guarantees against capital loss if there were devaluation of the pound. It should be noted that those who would guarantee are in effect making a long-term loan to the United Kingdom which would probably, in the end, absorb the capital loss. Under a funding arrangement, those nations which make guarantees would not only help Britain but also benefit themselves, since their trade and exports to the sterling area members could then continue unabated.

Third is the question of countervailing devaluations. Clearly, a devaluation is worthless if powerful trading competitors also devalue. As France has demonstrated, unilateral devaluation(s) can be very effective; the present French strength is due in large measure to the franc devaluations of the 1950s, while other significant currencies stayed at par. Many informed analysts believe that a 1964 British devaluation would have caused countervailing devaluations only in some of the Scandinavian nations, outside of the sterling area. They also believe that a two or three billion dollar "currency swap" between the U.S. and Continental currencies would have enabled the United States to defend the dollar successfully against speculation. In short, a 1964 or 1965 devaluation would have been successful for the United Kingdom without international disaster ensuing. Future actions will, of course, depend on future circumstances, and on the general level of cooperation within the international monetary establishment.

Finally, there arises the questions of relations with the international monetary system and the "establishment" which essentially controls it—the IMF, the Group of Ten, and the Bank for International Settlements. In retrospect, the Labour party leaders were clearly sensitive to the desires of this group, particularly so because of the allegedly delicate position of the dollar in 1964 and the British desire for continued close relations with the United States. In accepting vast credits, rather than devalue, the British have further submitted to "multilateral surveillance." It is implicit that a nation heavily in debt should justify the loan by appropriate internal policies, which to date has meant internal "discipline," i.e., relative deflation. Some economists object to an enlarged role for the central bankers to influence domestic policies. The central bankers are relatively independent of their governments and not subject to direct popular control; they have been called an "international House of Lords." But it would seem that with pegged exchange rates and the subsequent need for some form of international harmonization, the influence of the "establishment" is not apt to diminish, but to grow. With respect to the future, Britain is apt to be even more sensitive to the desires of the "establishment," particularly since she is so deeply indebted to it. Thus the question of future devaluation, indeed, of any future action, depends on the circumstances of future relations between Britain and the international monetary system as a whole.

INTERMEDIATE-TERM SOLUTIONS: THE CONTROL OF INFLATION

It has been noted that the Tories tried to institute some form of "incomes policy" in the early 1960s, and Labour has picked up the effort. So an attempt at incomes policy is the order of the day. How does it fit into the grand design? What is it? Can it work, or more precisely, what are its difficulties? Are there alternatives?

We need another stone . . . namely, a policy for directly raising or lowering money prices, wages and costs without relying on the indirect slow process of inflation or deflation of demand for this purpose—which has come to be called an "incomes policy."[6]

A functioning incomes policy, J. Meade calls:

Undoubtedly the ideal means of adjustment. The authorities could then inflate or deflate domestic demand through their monetary or budgetary policies so as to achieve the desired economic growth. If there were a

[6] Meade, op. cit., pp. 10–11.

simultaneous deficit on the balance of payments this could be corrected through incomes policy by a reduction in the rate of rise of money wage rates so that, with increasing productivity, the country's prices and costs were reduced relative to those of other competing countries.[7]

Thus the essence of an incomes policy is the ability of the managers of the economy to push wages and therefore costs up or down at will; they would put wages and costs down when British costs were too high, as evidenced by relatively low exports, high imports, and a threatening balance of payments.

Surely this is a proposal full of promise. But two obvious questions must quickly come to mind. First, the trade unions have something to say about wages. Thereby hangs the first difficulty of an incomes policy. The unions have been reluctant to surrender their wage-bargaining function to "incomes policy" planners. To surrender this function requires a change of heart by trade unionists which has not yet come.

The second question is more subtle: Do wages (or even "incomes") alone determine costs? Do we live in a cost-push economy? Or are wage increases not in fact validated by a level of aggregate demand which, in fact, reflects a government's monetary and fiscal policy—how much money it puts into or fails to take out of the incomes stream? There is among advocates of incomes policy a remarkable bias toward the belief that cost-push and not demand-pull economics determine costs. And this consideration leads to what has often been posed as the alternative to a "wages" or "incomes" policy. It is known variously as the "Paish" theory or the "unused resources" theory.

As early as 1947, the first postwar Labour government saw the need for a wages policy to (1) use as a lever to regulate wages in the fashion described by Meade, or, failing that much power at least, (2) restrain inflation by keeping wage increases below productivity increases, and (3) reallocate labor among industries as the "plans" required, chiefly to the export industries. After some lively debate, the government realized it could not persuade the trade unions to relinquish wage-bargaining power even to Labourites, which a wages policy implies. It opted instead for direction of labor—a policy

[7] Ibid.

which proved too unpopular to be usable.[8] Unable to plan, the Labour party redesignated plans as targets by 1950.

The Tories' troubles with an incomes policy have been outlined. Labour has hardly had fewer. From past experience, Labour had learned to approach an incomes policy gingerly. First, since it was evident that the trade unions were going to surrender few if any of their bargaining prerogatives, the purpose of the current incomes policy is to try—by methods of persuasion mainly—to keep over-all wage increases at a level equal to or below the level of increasing productivity. While this, if successful, would inhibit inflation from the cost side, it is hardly the flexible level that Meade discusses. This is probably one sense in which Meade terms the policy "impracticable." A second relates to the "equity" problem. The terms "wage policy" and "incomes policy" have been used interchangeably. The fact is, however, that it is wages which must be controlled under the theory. But one of the major objections the unions had to a wages policy was its injustice since other incomes—rents, profits, salaries—are not similarly controlled.

In practice, the current incomes policy is broad and permissive, and dependent almost entirely on persuasion, that is, on the voluntary cooperation of all concerned. The Machinery White Paper [9] calls for a review by the NEDC (or its successor, the Department of Economic Affairs) of the "general movement of prices and money incomes of all kinds. . . . the Government, Management and Unions will be expected to take any action that may be required." To investigate "particular cases of price and income behavior" there is established a National Board for Prices and Incomes, working in two separate divisions—one for price review, the other for incomes.

What is the general policy? It is, briefly, that wage increases should be kept below the annual growth of output per head, which

[8] See S. E. Rolfe, "Trade Unions and Central Planning," reprinted, W. A. Leeman, ed., *Capitalism, Market Socialism and Central Planning* (Boston: Houghton Mifflin Co., 1963), and B. C. Roberts, *Trade Unions in the New Era* (London: International Publishers, 1948) p. 17. Also see B. C. Roberts, *National Wages Policy* (London: Allen & Unwin, 1959), and J. Hennessey's contribution to *Policy for Incomes?* (London: Institute of Economic Affairs, 1965).

[9] *Machinery of Prices and Incomes,* Cmnd. 2577 (London: H.M.S.O., February 1965).

is estimated at 3 per cent now (compared to about 2 per cent in the 1950s); this is expected to rise to 3½ or 4 per cent per capita from 1964–1970, yielding a 25 per cent growth in that period.[10] The National Plan of September 1965 confirms this growth target. It also reaffirms that the chief mechanism to keep price rises within productivity bounds will remain the incomes policy toward whose effective utilization the Plan claims "an encouraging start has been made."

The incomes policy—its timings, its content, its logical and administrative shortfalls—have been mercilessly criticized. To cite a few examples:

John Vaizey has written, ". . . by the timing and manner of the present policy it is fairly sure that the dice are loaded against any such policy." [11] Nicholas Davenport has written that the overdue tax reforms were to "persuade the employees and non-owners of capital to cooperate in the national incomes policy. . . . But so far it has failed to do so." [12] At the outset, the incomes policy has in fact failed to restrain increased earnings. Indeed, the following chart shows that (average weekly) earnings increased by mid-1965 at the greatest rate since 1955, and casts real doubt on the effectiveness of that policy, at least as late as mid-1965.

Christopher Hollis' poetic summary is scorching:

THE WORKERS SPEAK TO MR. BROWN
The naked pound was hot in spring,
    By wage restraint and credit squeeze
Saved barely from devaluing
    And marked as yet with grave disease.

The Engineers will breach the dyke,
    The Doctors ballot for their fees,
And he gets left who does not strike
    And who goes striking gains increase.

The wages rising day by day,
    The prices rising every night,

[10] *Prices and Incomes Policy*, Cmnd. 2639 (London: H.M.S.O., April 1965).
[11] John Vaizey, "As the Crisis Approaches," *Spectator*, June 18, 1965, p. 749.
[12] Nicholas Davenport, "Financial Policy Reviewed," *Spectator*, June 11, 1965, p. 764.

Bid them be swift for higher pay,
So blue the funk, so green the light.

The Blackleg sings to him, "Brother, brother,
If this be the last song you shall sing,
Sing low, for you may not sing another,
Brother, sing." [13]

CHART 3. WAGES AND EARNINGS, 1955–1965

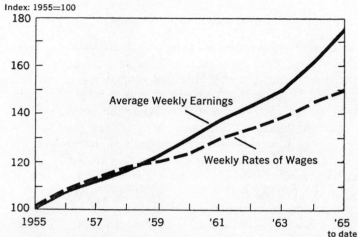

SOURCE: *Financial Times*, July 13, 1965, p. 12.

Other criticisms abound. How can a "pay creep" be controlled? Even if stated wage rates move within the productivity confines, piecework rate increases, upgrading of labor, and fringe benefits can be used and add to weekly income. If wages drift up and a company cannot raise prices, or fears to be pilloried for trying, a profits squeeze ensues. By standard American theory (and experience), this leads to more managerial efficiency, investment in machinery to substitute capital for labor and other desirable actions. But if British experience is a guide, it might lead instead, to quality dilution, a lower propensity to invest with profits expectations declining, and the rest of the vicious downward spiral, unless appropriate longer-term structural changes are made effective.

[13] *Spectator*, June 18, 1965, p. 781.

In summary, even if a wages or incomes policy is not based on dubious assumptions—that is, on the "cost-push" side while trying to ignore the "demand-pull" side which only appropriate monetary and fiscal policy can control—it nevertheless encounters some severe difficulties.

Under present institutional arrangement, it is likely that an effective incomes policy will still encounter trade-union resistance. A policy honored in the breach will not be effective.

CONTROLLED DEFLATION

To those who believe an incomes policy ineffective in controlling price increases, the other means must be restricting the rate of increase in aggregate demand. Here, the ultimate control of inflation is achieved by generating a margin of unused labor and capital resources by holding demand slightly below the output potential of the economy through the judicious use of monetary and fiscal policy. By so doing, upward pressure on wages, and, hence, prices, is reduced, a stable price level can be achieved with steady market expectations conducive to capital investment. This has been offered as an alternative to the British practice of "stop and go."

Any policy which restricts aggregate demand is of course a variation of the "classical medicine," a form of deflation. But there is a significant difference between deflationary pressure which is suddenly and crushingly applied as in the "stop" periods and one which is applied in a more sophisticated fashion, particularly when it can be tied to a longer-term policy of investment and growth.

If the approach to deflation is quantitative, it will serve to answer at least three critical questions which must occupy the minds of the managers of the economy, and which until very recently have not been answerable.

The first is, just what level of deflation is necessary? Is one talking about unemployment and depression of the magnitude of the thirties or something far more tolerable? Second, when and on what levers are the instruments of policy to be used to secure the desired degree of deflation? Third, how does the policy of deflation fit into a longer-term pattern ultimately aimed at strengthening the economy?

With the recent appearance of J. C. R. Dow's book, *The Manage-*

ment of the British Economy, 1945–60,[14] widely hailed as a classic in its field, one is inclined to concur with the judgment of F. W. Paish in his review of it that the publication of Mr. Dow's book "should serve to remove much, if not all of the confusion, at any rate, of the excuse for it."[15]

The policy prescriptions of the Dow-Paish school of thought derive from the refinement of the well-documented statistical relationship between rates of money wage increases and the level of unemployment first examined by A. W. Phillips.[16]

In brief outline, the "Phillips curve" analysis shows that lower unemployment rates are associated with the faster increases in wages as increasing competition for scarce labor pushes up wage rates. Extending the argument an additional step, when the rise in money wages exceeds the rise in labor productivity, it is evident that prices will also rise in rough parallel, either because business can pass on higher labor costs to consumers or because the tight labor market reflects tight goods markets where prices are already rising.

Thus inflation has its counterpart in low unemployment rates, and policy makers are faced with a play-off between less inflation (and perhaps slower output growth) and more unemployment, or, alternatively, less unemployment and faster price rises. The essence of the case rests in the fact that the structure of the economy will not let full employment exist side by side with price stability.

These disturbing relationships are not confined to the United Kingdom but exist in most highly developed countries.[17] The im-

---

[14] Cambridge: Cambridge University Press, 1964.

[15] "The Management of the British Economy," *Lloyd's Bank Review,* April 1965, pp. 1–17.

[16] Some of the major contributions, in chronological sequence include: A. W. Phillips, "The Relation Between Unemployment and the Rate of Change in Money Wage Rates in the U.K., 1862–1957," *Economica,* November 1958; L. A. Dick-Mireaux and J. C. R. Dow, "The Determinants of Wage Inflation in the United Kingdom, 1946–1956," *Journal of the Royal Statistical Society,* Series A. Vol. 122, Pt. 2, 1959, republished as National Institute of Economic and Social Research Reprint Series No. 23; F. W. Paish, *Studies in an Inflationary Economy* (New York: The Macmillan Co., 1962), esp. Ch. 17; W. A. H. Godley and J. R. Shepard, "Long-Term Growth and Short-Term Policy," National Institute *Economic Review,* August 1964; and J. C. R. Dow, *The Management of the British Economy, 1945–60, op. cit.*

[17] P. A. Samuelson and R. M. Solow, "Analytical Aspects of Anti-Inflationary Policy," *American Economic Review,* May 1960, pp. 177–194, have examined the relationship for the United States. For a general survey of the theory, see

plications for Britain, with its high degree of dependence on external trade, make the relationship much more critical than for a country with a relatively small foreign sector, such as the United States. Rising prices at low unemployment levels are not only bad per se for the United Kingdom but will quickly cause a deterioration in the current account balance in the balance of payments as so often has been the case in the postwar period.

In adopting the "Phillips curve" analysis as a basis for policy recommendations—which may, for convenience, be called the Dow-Paish recommendations—a number of sophisticated estimates have been derived. During the period from 1947 to 1959, the British unemployment rate averaged 1½ per cent,[18] and the price index for total output rose by 57 per cent. But Dow estimates that had the British unemployment rate been 2¼ per cent, prices would have risen only 17 per cent or by 40 per cent less than they actually did, certainly an uninflationary figure, and one which would have prevented most, if not all, of Britain's balance-of-payments crises.

As a basis for indicating appropriate monetary or fiscal policy to control inflation, the unemployment rate leaves much to be desired. The most important consideration is the fact that changes in the unemployment rate *lag* behind changes in the utilization of capital capacity and changes in output. Thus, the Dow-Paish analysis would not base policy on the unemployment rate alone but rather on the broader gauge of "unused productive potential." This is a measure of idle capital capacity (unused plant and equipment) and is expressed as the per cent of total output capacity unused.[19]

One of Dow's objectives is to arrive at a figure of unused productive potential which will achieve price stability. In accomplishing this objective he notes that, first, unused productive potential shows

Martin Bronfenbrenner and F. D. Holzman, "Survey of Inflation Theory," *American Economic Review*, September 1963, pp. 630–639.

[18] The U.K. and U.S. unemployment rates are not comparable because of definitional differences. A rule of thumb is that 1 per cent should be added to the U.K. figure to make it *reasonably* comparable to the U.S. figure.

[19] The physical measurement of the margin of potential was made public by the Treasury in their *Economic Reports* for 1961–63. The National Institute of Economic and Social Research has created an "index of productive potential" from 1951, which has by now become a sufficiently fine tool to use. For a discussion of the problems of measurement, see Paish, *Policy for Incomes?* (London: Institute For Economic Affairs, 1964), pp. 31–38.

greater variation than changes in the unemployment rate; and, second, the growth of money income moves in roughly equal percentage changes, but in opposite directions, with unused productive potential. As a result there exists some per cent of idle capital capacity which if maintained will permit the growth of national income to be approximately equal to the growth in output and thereby achieve price stability. This critical percentage of unused productive potential appears to be between 5 and 6 per cent. Given the relationship between unused productive potential and unemployment, this is the approximate equivalent of an unemployment rate of 2¼ per cent. With the historical trend in the increase in capital capacity, the resulting growth in real output would be somewhat less than 3½ per cent per year; but since the rise of income would also be held down to a level of less than 3 per cent per year or about equal to growth, the consequences would be noninflationary for the economy. The rate of increase of wages per year would be within the bounds of increased productivity—which is, of course, the objective of the incomes policy, if it were effective.

From these data the economic managers are able to answer two of the major questions posed at the outset. The first provides the magnitude of unemployment or capacity of unused resources which must remain idle in order to combat inflation. The objective is 2¼ per cent unemployment, or 5 to 6 per cent unused capital capacity. Second, managers know more about the timing. Changes in unused capacity lead changes in the unemployment figure by six months or more. This is the prime indicator on which the managers of the economy should focus.

With reference to the best policy tools to be used, Dow also makes some interesting observations. Basically, there are four: (1) physical controls (import quotas, rationing, capital-export quotas, etc.); (2) control of public-sector fixed investment (housing, transport, etc.)—the instrument widely advocated before and during World War II as the chief weapon in the contra-cyclical armory; (3) fiscal policy (changes in taxes, budget subsidies, or other transfer payments); and (4) monetary policy (interest rate changes, quantity of money control, and other financial control).

Among the policy tools, Dow prefers fiscal policy—changes in taxes. He observes that contra-cyclical policy has been affected only by those taxes which change the rate of personal consumption in the months immediately ahead. Tax changes designed to effect the level of investment operate only after a considerable time lag, and thus do not touch the shorter cycles. These changes may, in this context, be considered part of a longer-term structural reform policy. The Dow-Paish analysis suggests that a broad-based tax on consumer goods (and perhaps services) is in order. This could take the form of a "turnover" tax with variable rates, similar to that used in many European countries both for revenue and inflation control. It can be argued that such taxes are regressive. But the fact remains that "regressive" is a term that needs to be reconsidered in an affluent society whose crying need is for more investment relative to consumption rather than vice versa.

To be consistent, the economic managers should not rely on increasing interest rates to restrain demand. This accounts for the poor results of past policy. It acts as a further disincentive to long-term investment, particularly in the private sector, and in housing, too.

Finally, the difficult question of growth. The case against any deflationary policy, including the maintenance of a reserve of unused capacity, is that while it will admittedly slow or prevent inflation, such a policy will also slow the rate of economic growth. To create a noninflationary economy, without growth, would be a policy of stagnation. Therefore, it has been argued by some, let there be the inconvenience of inflation to stimulate growth. With this view the Dow-Paish view disagrees, but only in part. First, Dow argues from his data that "if the pressure of demand had been somewhat lower, and the margin of unused capacity . . . larger than in most of the post-war years, there could have been steady expansion of expenditure, output, and output per head as rapid as that which in fact occurred." [20] Thus he holds that had his anti-inflation prescriptions been used, growth would have been at the same rate as it was in fact, but without (or with less) inflation. But even if this argument is accepted, there are yet many who want *more* rapid growth than that which occurred. Dow notes that "the pursuit of faster growth requires action aimed directly at accelerating the growth of capacity. A faster expansion of demand without such action seems likely to

[20] *Op. cit.*, p. 361.

lead to an insupportable degree of excess demand." [21] Paish goes further in his argument: "Without effective competition it is impossible to ensure the elimination of inefficient managements; and the surest way of slowing down the rate of growth is to conserve inefficiency." [22] While Paish is not arguing that the restrictions of demand will stimulate growth by the euthenasia of the inefficient he does contend that this is a desirable precondition to growth, which, as Dow argues, still requires special stimuli.

Of course there must be economic growth to keep the productive potential of the economy rising, as well as to increase living levels, create surplus monetary reserves, and for all the other "good" reasons. Without sufficient growth, it is possible (via an incomes policy or a Dow-Paish demand control) to hold the rise of money incomes down to the 3 per cent or so per year, and yet have inflation. For if money incomes, though rising no faster than output, are rising at a rate faster than can be permanently maintained, there will still be inflation. This, in essence, is the concept of a "sustainable level" of rising output and income. It points once again to the inescapable need to focus on the longer-term reform goal, which is structural change designed to encourage and allow economic growth.

Before turning to that subject, however, it might be well to attempt to summarize, at the risk of missing the finer points, the way the Dow-Paish analysis finds the U.K. system works, and how it should be managed.

The major weapon of economic management is monetary and fiscal policy. The objectives of policy are three:

1. To create a steady growth of demand in line with the growth of capacity. In contrast, "stop-go" policies upset the policy of growth; moreover, "stop-go" produces periods of excess demands, which inspire inflation.

2. To hold demand at a level which leaves a greater margin of spare capacity on the average (probably 5 to 6 per cent) than was true in the past. An incomes policy would probably be ineffective to do this, at least at the outset, and indeed until some institutional changes in unions and management take place. Greater price stability is desirable, and also as a means of getting the growth of ex-

21 *Ibid.*, p. 403.
22 "The Management of the British Economy," *op. cit.*, p. 9.

ports to pay for the imports needed for current needs and faster growth.

3. Growth policy requires different action, aimed directly to that end.

There are, of course, objections to this policy. First, while Dow-Paish may be right in presuming that the same *rate* of growth may be achieved with 2¼ per cent unemployment (or 5 to 6 per cent unused capacity) as at 1½ per cent unemployment (or the related amount of unused capacity) it is nevertheless true that the unused resources do represent lost output. The fact is that at 1½ per cent unemployment more goods and services would be produced. Applying the same 3½ per cent growth rate at the lower unemployment figure, output in each future period will be higher than with the Dow-Paish 2¼ per cent unemployment. But the cost involved is added inflation, a cost which England is ill-prepared to bear because of the international position.

There is a political corollary of this economic observation. Primarily, a 5 to 6 per cent level of unused capacity, or 2¼ per cent unemployment, seems too high to those whose first priority is full employment. But the extent to which employment should be "full" is yet a point of issue; supporters of Dow-Paish reply that full employment which assures inflation and crises, in fact robs the nation, including those workers who are supposed to benefit by full employment.

Another anti-Dow-Paish position holds that even if a 2¼ per cent unemployment figure sounds innocent enough, it requires much higher (and unconscionable) levels in some geographic areas. The level of unemployment is not uniform throughout the United Kingdom. It is relatively high in Northern Ireland, less in Scotland, Wales, and the North of England, and very low in the midlands and the South, where the bulk of British labor is employed. Paish, however, replies that the 2¼ per cent unemployment figure sought allows for these regional variations, and takes into account the very low level of labor mobility among regions, estimated at only some 36,000 per year average from 1959–1962. If unemployment levels were uniform it has been estimated that the noninflationary level of unemployment could be reduced to some 1.7 per cent.[23] To attain

[23] *Policy for Incomes?, op. cit.;* see also *Studies in an Inflationary Economy, op. cit.*

uniform unemployment levels it would be necessary to increase the movement of workers to jobs—which is said to be difficult because of regional preferences, housing shortages (which in turn are maintained by rent controls and subsidies)—or to move plants, hence jobs, to areas of labor surplus. The latter task is part of the longer-run structural change problem, specifically of distributing growth among regions.

Another objection holds that if uneconomic railways, mines, shops, etc., were closed, or featherbed rules reduced, additional labor could be found for the system, and more unemployment would be unnecessary. Since the limiting factor to growth is the labor supply, this would allow for growth with less inflation. In part Paish has answered this objection when he says that demand restriction would eliminate the inefficient units of the economy, at least in the private sector, freeing this labor for more economic uses. Dow-Paish supporters would further ask just who and by what means are these things to be accomplished? The managers of the economy have yet to show the kind of proficiency required to do so.

LONGER-TERM GOALS: STRUCTURAL CHANGE AND ECONOMIC GROWTH

Structural change in Britain has been urgently advised for a long time. The following timely statement describes pre-World War I conditions:

The British economy vis-à-vis the world economy was deteriorating . . . exports and productivity . . . compared unfavorably with growth-rates abroad, especially with . . . Germany and the U.S. . . . Britain's relatively poor economic performance can be attributed largely to the failure of the British entrepreneur to respond to the challenge of changed conditions.[24]

The question of structural change cuts deeply into the psychological and sociological fabric of the nation—its attitudes toward class, education, and trade as a way of life, the alienation of its working classes, the backwardness of its unions and management.

All parties agree that structural reform is necessary. A difference of approach becomes manifest with the appearance of the Labour party's National Plan; for it is based on certain assumptions with

[24] D. H. Aldcroft, "The Entrepreneur and the British Economy 1870–1914," *Economic History Review*, March 1964.

respect to the operation of the economy. These include the view that incentives per se are not sufficient to restructure the economy. The Plan states explicitly that while it believes in a mixed economy, "the forces of competition often operate too slowly." The Plan must therefore provide more specific targets or indicators to which industry can move. Moreover, the economic development councils acting as channels of stimuli and information can continue to check progress. Implicit is the view that without the prodding of government the private sector would not restructure the economy properly or rapidly enough. Another view—and it is not necessarily a Conservative party view, for that party may well adopt indicative planning as well—is that with adequate incentives industry will rise to the task. Indeed, this argument runs that the disincentives of high interest rates, "stop-and-go" policies, restrictive labor practices, and the like have slowed the economy despite industry's wishes to the contrary. This view would also hold that it is impossible to outline the future statistically. Some industries should advance, in response to market conditions, even more than the Plan can now foresee; others less. This view would also hold that a Plan operating within the confines of the Labour party policy based on an incomes policy and perhaps on the retention of an excessively valued pound actually make restructuring more difficult than it would otherwise be.

There has been so much talk of the long-run economic problem within Britain that, if nothing else, the British are probably the best educated nation in the world on their own domestic difficulties. From some time in the mid-fifties a torrent of ink and a gale of words have descended on British heads, all containing, roughly speaking, one common plea: that Britain would never break out of its vicious circle of export weakness, sterling crisis, economic cutback, and then more export weakness unless attention was turned to the redesign and reconstruction of the whole economic machine. If this was heresy at the outset, it has now become dogma. And the danger of overstatement is so great that many in Britain have come to believe their crisis is of a greater magnitude than it is in fact, and perhaps insoluble. Yet if these ideas are reduced to a simple chart (below) the relative strengths and weaknesses of Britain can be seen fairly quickly.

Output per man hour in manufacturing is probably the key variable to watch. It can be raised by appropriate investment. It is the major target of remedial direct economic action. In Britain it has

CHART 4. GROWTH IN OUTPUT PER MAN-HOUR IN MANUFACTURING, 1962–1965

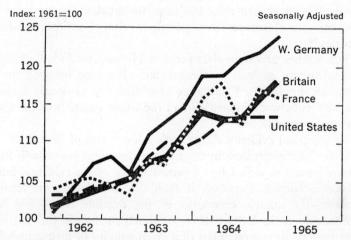

SOURCE: *The Economist*, August 7, 1965, p. 540.

increased roughly 4½ per cent a year between 1961 and 1964—higher than America's 4 per cent and nearly as high as France's 4¾ per cent, but still well below Germany's. The point being made is that the improvement of this datum has neither been wholly lacking nor is its further improvement to compete with the best by any means impossible, given appropriate action to make the economy more dynamic.

There are a number of important economic areas in which longer-term reform can be focused—all with the aim of bringing Britain from its imperial past into the contemporary competitive world of efficient mass production and distribution. Three areas, investments; the quality of management—both in its producing and selling functions—and competition are examined here. Whether a plan or market incentives or some combination is used, these three require attention.

INVESTMENT POLICY

No analysis of the British position would be complete without some analysis of the question of the rate of investment in industry. New investment is commonly thought to be the fuel behind growth of the economy. But some qualitative refinements need to be added. The simpliste faith that raising the percent of GNP in investment will allow high growth rates has been undercut in recent years by some analysis of comparative growth-investment ratios in various countries.[25]

These studies, and some data presented below, conclude that qualitative elements, as well as the amount of money invested in industry, are important. Qualitative considerations obviously include selectivity as between industries, and the whole question of the quality of management.

The statistical evidence shows both a lower rate of investment in the United Kingdom than in any major nation, and less growth from that investment as well. Chart 5 presents some of the evidence. Since it covers a fairly long period, it should be noted that the leading countries—the miracle economies of the wartime Axis—have had more trouble in the latter half of the timespan than in the first half in getting the same growth out of a given amount of investment. To some extent this reflects a phenomenon well advanced in the United States; as an economy grows additions to output come less in manufacturing than in the services, where automation, technology, and growth are harder to institute, and where one sees less growth from investment than in more "basic" production. But this refinement aside, the lag in Britain's performance in *both* investment and growth is clear. If a given rate of investment (measured as a per cent of GNP) yielded the same growth (again a percent of GNP) in all countries, all countries would fall on the diagonal line. In fact, however, Japan, with an investment rate of 30.3 per cent, showed a growth of 9 per cent above the norm. Germany, investing 23 per cent of GNP, grew some 5.6 per cent. Britain, investing 17.2 per cent, grew by only 2.7 per cent. The same figures for the years 1950–1956 would show a faster growth rate from investment than prevailed in the 1957–1963 period, plotted in Chart 4. For example, in 1950–1956 in Japan, investment of 19.8 per cent had brought growth of 8.7 per cent; Germany, 20.3 per cent and 9 per cent; Britain, 14.2 per cent and 2.6 per cent.

[25] See for example, S. Kuznets, "Quantitative Aspects of the Economic Growth of Nations," *Economic Development and Cultural Change*. July 1961.

CHART 5.   GROWTH AND INVESTMENT, 1957–1963

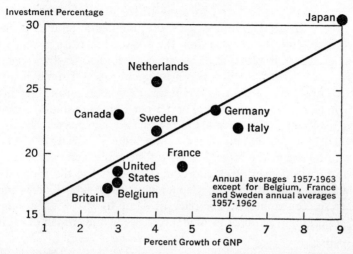

SOURCE: *The Economist*, January 15, 1965, pp. 233–234. Investment is Gross Fixed Investment of all kinds, divided by GNP, both at factor cost to obtain above percentage.

In any event, it is probably not in the cards for the United Kingdom to grow as rapidly as the miracle economies even when it steps up its investment level from about 14 per cent average to over 17 per cent. Why not? Because in the United Kingdom (as in France and Sweden) the labor force is expanding very slowly. There are no pools of refugee, farm, or even foreign workers to pull into industry to be rigged out, so to speak, with a standard set of tools. (As the pools of underutilized labor are absorbed in the miracle economies, this fact and the following analysis will come to apply to them as well.)

The National Plan devotes great attention to the question of manpower shortages, and to the related question of improving technical skills, that is, of shifting workers from low to high productivity areas. While great emphasis is placed (in Chap. 3 of the Plan) on policies the government has adopted to retrain workers, to present and intended improvements in the unemployment benefits system, and similar devices, the Plan nevertheless concludes that in the end the amount of labor available to attain the goal will be in short supply. In part this is to be rectified by a more even spread of industry throughout the country, to areas where unemployment is now high. Nevertheless, the anticipated need for an extra 800,000 workers of which 400,000 are to come from the expected increase in the labor force, possibly supplemented by another 200,000 if the regional policies are successful, still leaves a manpower gap of some 200,000.

It is hoped in the Plan to attain an increase in output per head of 21 per cent from 1964–1970, or 3.2 per cent per annum, a figure larger than that which prevailed in the past decade. Nevertheless, it is expected that distribution of manpower among industries will continue to be one of the more difficult tasks the planners face.

The focus of investment effort must be on what the economists call a substitution of factors. Capital investment—machinery—must replace scarce manpower. The relevant figure to watch is not simply the proportion of national income invested, but the growth of capital per man.

How does the United Kingdom compare to other nations in this respect? Table 4 shows the growth of GNP per employee (Col. 1). The growth of capital stock per employee is shown in Column 2. The contrast between Columns 1 and 2 is shown in Column 3.

From the table there appears a marked disparity between the British performance and those of the fast movers, particularly Holland, Germany, and France. The disparity is much less marked in Column 2 than in Column 1. Thus the British rate of investment per employee has been $6/7$ that of Holland, but the rate of growth of output per employee in Holland has been $1\frac{1}{2}$ times as high. With respect to France, the growth of capital per employee has been about the same, but the French output per employee has grown nearly twice as fast.

Were is not for the fact that there is such a diverse mixture in the output of the various countries considered, Column 3 might be considered indicative of the relative effectiveness of capital formation in the different countries. To the extent that difference in product can be ignored, the ratios in Column 3 again indicate the disparity between the fast-growing nations—Germany, France, and Holland—whose capital formation has then been relatively effective. Some may argue that the foregoing figures are too aggregated; that if they were

TABLE 4. GROWTH AND INVESTMENT PER EMPLOYEE,
1950–1960 (in percentage) [a]
Annual average rate of *real* growth of:

	(1) GNP per employee	(2) Capital stock per employee	(3) (1) ÷ (2)
West Germany	5.0%	4.6%	1.09%
France	3.9	3.0	1.30
Netherlands	3.6	3.5	1.03
Sweden	3.3	1.7	1.93
Norway	3.1	4.9	0.63
Belgium	2.4	2.6	0.92
United Kingdom	2.1	2.9	0.72
United States	1.9	2.8	0.60
Canada	1.9	4.2	0.45

SOURCE: T. R. Sargent, *Out of Stagnation*, The Fabian Society Tract 343,
London, 1963, p. 3. Part of the logic on which certain reforms for investment
proposed are based is to be found in this provocative work.

[a] The countries are listed in decreasing order of growth of GNP per employee.

NOTES: GNP and capital stock are in *real* terms, i.e., corrected for price changes;
capital stock includes in principle all durable goods in public and private enterprise except military installations, forest, land and livestock, stocks in consumers'
hands.

broken into component industrial or similar parts, a different picture
would emerge. There seems to exist no comprehensive set of data
which would throw light on this hypothesis. But students who have
analyzed the British position tend to believe that the data above are
accurate to the extent that they do indicate the fundamental problem of Britain in comparison with other nations.

The question then is why should British investment, which has
risen in gross amount, be so ineffective? The answer would seem to
reflect the lack of harmony between the relative rates of growth of
capital and labor. Since the labor supply was so short and there was,
as we have seen, a consistent pressure on wages which in turn stimulated and thus put a constant pressure on sterling, the connecting
link between the relative lack of growth of a labor force compared to
capital lies in the fact that those in control of economic policy chose
to tackle the scarcity of labor and wage inflation by "stop-and-go"
methods designed periodically to restrain the demand for goods and
services.

Consequently, output, being held back through fear of wage inflation, and through the fear of constantly shifting demand targets, was prevented from growing at a rate commensurate with the growth of capital which was being achieved.

If this actually is correct, one would also expect to see the share of wages and salaries in the national income tending to rise. In fact, that share of the GNP rose from 64.3 per cent in 1954 to 67.7 per cent in 1960.

The "stop-and-go" policy, coupled with a policy of overfull employment had several other consequences which were harmful to labor-saving investment. The major one, of course, was that interest rates were high and have kept going higher, not only to restrain the general level of demand but also to attract foreign capital or at least to prevent its flight. The second was that firms were afraid to invest in labor-saving machinery, which of course involved high overhead costs even in the face of fluctuating demand. They preferred to rely on labor rather than fixed cost capital on the theory that it could always be laid off. The fact that they subsequently tended to hoard labor, particularly skilled labor, even in periods of falling demand does not contradict the fact that they could live in the belief that they were always more flexible with labor than with fixed capital.

It is interesting that analyses of other economies which have also grown slowly, for example, the Belgian, have reached much the same conclusion. In A. Lamfalussy's suggestive studies of Belgium,[26] there are a number of insights which appear to be appropriate for Britain as well. One is that capital intensive investments, intended to substitute factors, i.e., capital for labor, will generally be of a lumpy, or indivisible, kind. Thus variable costs (wages) are transformed into fixed or overhead costs (depreciation, obsolescence, and interest charges) which cannot vary as sales vary. Conditions in which the future fluctuations in demand induced by "stop-and-go" policies are expected will, of course, retard investments of this kind.

The National Plan tackles this problem rather obliquely. While pointing out "there will have to be a large investment in manufacturing industry," the Plan simply states "it is also important that in

---

[26] A. Lamfalussy, *Investment and Growth in Mature Economies: The Case of Belgium* (London: Macmillan, 1961). See also his *The United Kingdom and the Six* (Homewood, Ill.: Richard D. Irwin, 1963), esp. Chaps. 6 and 7.

making investment decisions businesses should not be unduly influenced by temporary fluctuations and uncertainties." It is thought that "little NEDDIES," the National Economic Development committees can assist here by focusing the attention of industries on demand two years and more ahead and on the growing shortage of manpower over the decade which will necessitate more labor-saving investment. The Plan, however, is silent on methods by which regularity of demand must be substituted for "stop-and-go" methods as indeed it must be. In this context the Plan only makes sense because it assumes that the incomes policy will be so successful that "stop and go" will prove unnecessary. This yet remains to be seen.

Let us resolve an apparent paradox. Is is possible to argue that conditions that have not inhibited capital investment in general have nevertheless inhibited labor-saving capital investment? Capital projects have various objectives. The expansion of capacity must be performed unless a company or an industry is to run the risk of having to turn customers away unsupplied. But the substitution of capital for labor depends on a comparison of their costs over what their costs are likely to be in the future. If there is little to choose between the factors of production as regard to their costs and, indeed, if the capital cost may be a burden in periods of "stop," the motive for emphasizing labor-saving investments is weak. If, however, capital funds had been cheaper and more plentiful, and if the prospect for demand had been less fluctuating it is likely that even if the total amount of investment had been no greater, more of it would have been devoted to labor-saving machinery.

If this analysis is correct, the methods by which British investment may be made more effective are almost self-suggesting—at any rate, they have been suggested often by analysts of both the relative "left" and "right." Let us review them briefly. They fall into two categories. The first category comprises steps to be taken whose impact falls *within* the confines of industry; and the second, those external conditions which apply to the economy in general.

Within the confines of industry three major proposals have been made. The first is a payroll tax, which is to increase the cost of labor to the firm and to make the hoarding of labor disadvantageous. Actually, under Selwyn Lloyd's tenure as Chancellor of the Exchequer such a system was proposed, but it was originally intended that the tax should be in the area of 4 shillings per week per employee, which critics thought too little. There is some level at which management is forced to consider the additional cost of labor and to look for substitutes. In addition, it has also been proposed that a greater share of national insurance payments fall directly on employers. It has also been proposed that the payroll tax should not be uniform in all industries as investment in labor-saving machinery is not equally possible in all fields, and indeed in certain services it is nonexistent. In addition, it has been proposed that a reduction or abatement of the payroll tax for industries moving into areas of labor surplus would be an inducement to do so. Those who oppose this tax argue it simply increases British costs, including exports, without an assured offset in greater productivity.

Perhaps as important as the financial stick which the payroll tax would provide is the fact that it would forcefully bring to the attention of managers the *need* for a substitution of capital for labor; it thus acts additionally as a mechanism of persuasion. And persuasion is the second method which can be used within industry. The National Plan relies heavily on the various industry economic development councils to act as instruments of persuasion, and this they will probably do effectively. Realists will ask who will persuade the unions to allow change, even if managements were willing to institute it. There is clearly no simple answer, but there are several partial ones. The first is that some unions are Luddites and some are not. Labour would argue that the unions' cooperation with the National Plan will bring changes in union behavior. A conservative approach would place greater emphasis on tangible carrots and sticks to change union practice. As the areas of union intransigence become clear, special steps, including persuasion, wage-differential inducements, and even antimonopoly legislation which restricts bargaining to a plantwide level and excludes it from certain elements of cost control may constitute further answers.

The third device within industry relates to better depreciation allowances on new equipment, designed to induce replacement of old machinery, and to encourage the use of new. Innumerable studies exist that underscore the penchant for using obsolescent equipment in British industry. But government stimulus can and should be provided to make it desirable and even profitable to replace that machinery. Thus a study conducted by the American Treasury,[27] found that average life of industrial equipment is five years in Sweden; eight years in Belgium; ten years in Canada, France, and Germany and the Netherlands; sixteen in Japan; and twenty-seven in Britain. Moreover, the annual rate of write-off worked against Britain. The proportion of initial cost of equipment which can be written off during the first year of life is relatively high in Britain, second only to Japan. But with regard to the first two years, Britain drops down to fifth, and with regard to the first five years to the bottom again. The National Plan offers no specific remedies on this score. It simply states that the government is currently examining the whole question of fiscal incentives for investment to see if the present method can be improved or whether there should be other methods.

So much for the proposals that would have an affect within industry. There are several general economic conditions widely thought conducive to increase the effectiveness of capital investment. But two are especially important, and ramify widely. The first is the provision of a steady level of demand rather than periodic "stop" and "go's." Even if the level of demand is such that it maintains a $2\frac{1}{4}$ per cent unemployment level as Dow has suggested, management would not be beset by the uncertainties of the past. Dow and others have argued this position so capably there is hardly need to repeat it.

The second is the availability of cheap credit for investment purposes. Had there been a devaluation of the pound, and with a shifting of Britain's external obligations to the IMF or to some other stronger asset base than Britain can muster, a high interest policy would not need be maintained in order to attract or keep speculative money on deposit balances in London. Nor need a higher interest rate be maintained to restrict demand and to control inflation, if Dow's suggestion of a broadly-based consumption tax, discussed earlier, is followed. It has been suggested that if a cheap money policy is not possible without devaluation, it is yet possible to provide special low interest rate loans to industries specifically for the purpose of the type of capital investment which replaces labor. Part of the effectiveness of the French plan lies in its judicious use

[27] Published in the London *Times*, February 15, 1962.

of credit instruments to stimulate movements of industry in the direction it indicated. There is as yet no similar device within the British National Plan, and the Plan itself is silent on the question of low interest rates, general or specific, as incentives to investment.

In the critically important area of labor-saving investment incentives, many of the ideas developed in the 1960s assumed tax reform as a precondition to success. The Labour victory in late 1964 has meant a marked shift in thinking in this respect. For example, the initial tax reforms proposed by Labour tended to move away from incentives for business toward greater equalitarianism, a move thought to be the price paid to the noncapital owning classes in return for their cooperation in the incomes policy. There was a sharp disappointment with respect to some elements discussed above. Thus the *Economist* wrote:

. . . investment allowances, designed to encourage British firms to modernize . . . will fall sharply in value under Mr. Callaghan's present proposals.[28]

Within one year after the Labour victory, it is too early to attempt judgments. This is so because modern Labourites seem far more flexible than those of the 1940s, and,

. . . by about the time of the General Election of 1964 . . . the intellectual and administrative preconditions for modern capitalist planning had been created. . . . There were, however, still some critical questions left unsettled . . . not primarily by the adoption of the right legislative programme. It is rather a matter of how to employ the *incidental* power of the state from day to day. . . .[29]

As the relationship between the state and industry unfolds in contemporary Britain, the effective use of incentive devices should be one of the keys to successful structural reform.

THE QUALITY OF MANAGEMENT

One of the important long-run growth considerations for the United Kingdom is the improvement of the quality of its man-

28 *The Economist*, May 1–7, 1965, p. 500. See also N. Lawson, "Disquieting Budget for 1966," *Financial Times*, April 8, 1965, p. 15.
29 A. Shonfield, *Modern Capitalism* (London: Oxford University Press, 1965) p. 109.

agement, and on this subject certain major points may be made. The first is that there is obviously great difficulty attendant in an effort to move the best brains and focus of attention of the British elite to commercial enterprise—in both its producing and selling aspects—from its long-term focus on other affairs, in which it has developed an expertise nowhere else matched. Obviously, this implies vast shifts in social orientation which at best can take a long time. On the other side of the ledger there is the fact that certain tangible economic steps may be taken which will assist in the improvement of the quality of management. Perhaps most important, there is clearly a strongly expressed will, not only among government planners but among industrialists, that this change should come about. This contrasts with past sentiments in Britain. It has been alleged that insufficient incentives have existed for management to seek self-improvement. Paish has argued that the economy, operating at near-capacity levels, has failed to punish the inefficient. Others have held that, while sales efforts by British firms have left much to be desired, British production management has been as good as any. While the National Plan is still geared to full utilization of capacity, the attempts by the economic development councils to stimulate more efficient production processes reflect a severe questioning of the ability of managements to produce well.

Michael Shanks has collected a number of examples of relative British inefficiency.[30] In 1956, the British machine tool industry recruited two university graduates while 500 were hired by its German counterpart. The industry's technological lag is such that the value of a ton of machine tool imports is double the value of a ton of such exports. British shipyards in 1960 required an average of nineteen months to build a ship while Japanese yards required eight months.

With reference to sales, which is as integral a part of the commercial system as production, for every one salesman employed in the British export trades, Germany employs 2.9, the United States 2.8, and Japan 3.4. Undoubtedly, British selling has suffered from the market condition of most of the postwar period. Home markets, supported by a constantly rising high level of demand, have too eas-

[30] M. Shanks, *The Stagnant Society* (London: Penguin Books, 1961).

ily absorbed goods which should have gone into export markets. Moreover, the past relationship with the sterling area has not helped. In the early postwar years Britain had a virtual monopoly in many important export markets, particularly in the sterling area. At one time this area took over 60 per cent of the British exports, and still takes over a third. These were not only soft protected markets, but were also English-speaking markets which did nothing to raise the competitive achievement of the British sales force.

To raise the quality of British management and also industrial efficiency requires increased investment in human resources, specifically through education and training.

It is not our purpose to analyze the British educational system, with its traditional bias toward the classics and the humanities, its preference for the amateur and distrust of the specialist, and its strong preference for the "whole man" in an age of specialists. The various British reports—of Lord Robbins, Sir Geoffrey Crowther, and others—have covered this ground thoroughly. Yet the root of the difficulty would seem to lie in the educational system. The very number of persons in all kinds of higher education is almost the beginning of the problem. While there were approximately 135,000 full- and part-time students—British and/or foreign—in the British universities in 1962–1963 there were some 4,250,000 students in American universities. Indeed, with 286,000 nonwhites, the American universities have more Negroes than there are all types of British university students combined. With reference to educational programs, the National Plan has tabulated anticipated increases of considerable magnitude; [31] It is expected that by the autumn of 1969 the number of entrants each year to universities will rise to make a full-time student total of about 199,000 compared to 117,000 in 1960.

One result of this lack of general higher training is a broad lack of well-trained people for industry. While 36 per cent of the managers of British industry have been to a university (and they are highly concentrated in the big companies), the comparable figure in Japan is about 80 per cent, with a 100 per cent goal.

Within the general problem of education there is specifically the problem of technical education. Britain trains far fewer technologists

[31] See The National Plan, op. cit., pp. 192–199.

per head of population that the United States, Russia, or Germany. The gap in technical education is even more marked than the gap in general education. Only now is Britain undertaking a technical university, which most of her Continental counterparts have already done. Developments comparable to MIT or Cal Tech, or the large number of technological training adjuncts to the American state universities are still a far goal. Among the technologists who are trained to fulfill jobs in industry, the "brain drain" to the United States and to other countries reflects, at its root, the relatively low pay of British management, and also the unwillingness of too many firms to use technological graduates to their full capabilities. Far fewer engineering or scientific graduates reach the board of directors or high positions in British industry than in Germany and the United States. This again reflects the educational bias against the specialist. One of the basic tenets of British society is that no expert or specialist should be trusted to take an executive decision. Quite naturally, industry's distrust of the intellectual is reciprocated. As industrialists prefer their experts to be on tap and not on top, the intellectuals have rarely chosen willingly to go into industry, particularly when it means working in the provinces. Therefore, teaching, the civil service, or the professions are the most usual preferences. In the case of scientists and engineers either pure research, or, in too many cases, immigration to the United States or other countries where the attitudes are quite different, is the solution. This again contrasts strongly with the United States where it is quite usual for a bright student to want to go into industry.

One of the methods by which quality of management could be improved is money. Direct salary payments for executives have risen less in Britain than in most Western European nations. Consequently, in nearly every department, British executives are at the bottom in relative advance, or near it. A recent survey conducted by the Associated Industrial Consultants [32] makes for some interesting comparisons. The 1965 Budget came down hard on expense account living for the British, thought to be a form of tax evasion. Yet even prior to this budget the survey revealed that only the French executives, who are allowed 2.1 per cent unaccountable expenses, were worse off than the British. In other countries the amount

[32] Reported in the *Daily Telegraph and Morning Post*, May 21, 1965, p. 26.

rose from Belgium with 3 per cent to Germany with 12 per cent and Austria with 26 per cent. In terms of executive salaries, the absolute level is highest in France, followed by Belgium, Germany, and Britain, among the surveyed nations. A comparison of the changes in salary since 1960 is revealing. Persons designated "head of design and research" in Britain had incomes rise 29 per cent; those in Germany had risen 38.2 per cent and those in Belgium 89.5 per cent. "Works managers" in Britain had had a median rise of 32 per cent compared to 64.9 per cent in France and 54 per cent in Belgium. Accountants' median salaries had risen 28.5 per cent in Britain to 41.7 per cent in France.

On the premise that salaries measure the importance societies and individual companies attach to jobs, and in view of the great need for exports in Britain, it is surprising that the median export manager's salary in Britain had gone up by 17.5 per cent since 1960 while the home sales manager's had risen about 25 per cent. In Germany, in contrast, the exporter's salary was up 44 per cent, while the home sales manager's had risen 39 per cent.

One of the surprising lags in British industry is the absence of bonus plans or stock option plans. Stock options, which are widely used in the United States and elsewhere, are one of the cheapest carrots yet invented. They convert the manager from a bureaucrat to a profit seeker very quickly. They are virtually absent in England. In comparison to other countries, while about one-third of British executives receive bonuses, 43 per cent do so in France, 64 per cent in Germany, and 85 per cent in Holland.

The role of the business school in education at one time was hotly contested in the United States. There is no question that business schools have contributed to the improved quality of American management. In addition to expertise, their major contribution has been to impart some professionalism, self-assurance, and social *élan* to the middle and upper reaches of business bureaucracies. They have also provided a mechanism for capturing relatively bright youths and bringing them early into the series of attitudes and techniques which work for business success. Yet it is only within the past year that business schools have been introduced into England. That the need for them is clearly recognized is evidenced by the fact that the initial subscription of about £3 million was oversubscribed immediately by British business.

It was the original intention of the planners of the two business schools, in Manchester and London, that these schools should focus their efforts among the middle reaches of the existing managements, where they believed they could obtain the quickest results. However, it was subsequently decided, to some audible regrets, that younger students straight from their university course would be admitted. It will be several years, therefore, before the 400 immediate post-graduate students on a 40-week course and the 400 post-experience students on a 20-week course are loosed on industry. Yet the very establishment of these schools is clearly a step in the right direction. The extension of the business school system into the universities has not yet been accomplished. A number of observers [33] have argued that industry would be better served if the minimum age of entry to these top-level business schools were made 25 or 26, thus restricting entry to those who have had a few years of business career experience. Not only would the education be more meaningful to more mature students, but, in addition, it is likely that the young graduates will, in the main, be employed by the progressive firms where they will be preaching to the converted.

One of the major problems, however, that will continue to stand in the way is the very attitudes of the community toward trade—i.e., toward producing and selling—as an important aspect of life. The belief that "getting and spending" is an American-type lunacy which Britain should not import recurs constantly. The following quotes from two recent pamphlets, one by David Howell, a leading young Conservative, and the other by Thomas Balogh, now a Labour government adviser, spell out the problem. Howell writes:

A number of British firms absorbed these lessons and as a result achieved remarkable productivity increases. The majority have not. And the reason? Almost certainly in most cases—and this perhaps sounds trite—because they have had no desire to do so. It is not just that the effort of it all—notably, the frustration of trying to soothe the fears and suspicions of labour leaders—has seemed too much of a deterrent. Beneath that lies a nagging doubt whether higher productivity and greater efficiency are the kind of goals after which decent people should be chasing anyway. Scratch an Englishman and you find underneath, not an anti-American perhaps, but certainly a man who feels that the

---

[33] See, for example, Gareth Jones, "Opportunity for Skill," *The Conservative Opportunity* (London: B. T. Batsfords, 1965).

American life is a materialist, ulcer-ridden hell. There is more, he will tell you, to life than that.

This view of America, and of the dangers of pursuing the goal of economic efficiency too exclusively, persists as strongly as ever in Britain today. In no quarter has it been advanced, developed and accepted more enthusiastically than in and around the British Labour Party. The pursuit of material wealth has become a national goal which no one dares support without hurried reservations. We must not, it is explained again and again, become like America.[34]

In unconscious corroboration, Professor Balogh writes:

It is when it comes to ultimate human values, the final ends of economic activity, that the fissure is complete. The Tory ideal seems to reproduce as much as possible the present-day U.S. way of life as the result of 25 years of intense endeavour. . . . For the Labour Party, and, I am sure, the majority of the British people . . . to approximate America . . . with its spiritual insecurity, its lack of fulfillment, its neuroses and fears, its increasingly strident mass-conditioning, while social endeavour remains relatively backward, is surely an unattractive prospect.[35]

COMPETITION

The purpose of a policy designed to encourage competition is in one sense negative. It would be naïve to assume that the alternative states of economic organization are on the one hand monopoly and on the other competition. Quite clearly, between lie some forms of "imperfect competition" which are neither and yet which serve effectively to restrict price competition, but also to give industries some degree of security which they desire, and without which a high and sustained level of investment in new machinery might be difficult. But the evidence, particularly from American experience with antitrust, suggests that in the more traditional role, legislation to ensure competition functions not because it "busts trusts" or destroys oligopoly, but because it keeps the door open to new competition. In addition to the classical use of legislation to enforce competition,

[34] David Howell, *Efficiency and Beyond*, C. P. C. No. 308, London, March 1965.
[35] Thomas Balogh, *Planning For Progress*, The Fabian Society Tract 346, London, July 1963.

the effects of increased competition on both management and labor are also examined to some extent in this section.

With reference to the traditional legislation, given the continual changes in the conditions of supply and demand, the constant changes of technology and tastes, and the possibility that established companies degenerate into cautious bureaucracies, losing that verve for success which characterized their youth, there are always existent in society forces tending naturally to break down monopolistic arrangements, and to reward effective competitors. Therefore, while it may not be possible to devise a legal framework which would curb all restrictive practices, the purpose of legislation should be, first, to avoid aiding those who wish to use restrictive practices and, second, to maintain an open door to the utilization of new techniques, to the satisfaction of new tastes, to the incorporation of new managerial ideas—in short, to the competitive forces which are in the last analysis the real destroyers of the restrictive power of "imperfect competition."

In the United States with its enormous emphasis on its internal economy, the shape of the solution has been largely in the form of antitrust policies aimed to minimize restrictive policies and price agreements. In an open economy like Britain's the problem is further complicated. In effect, inhibitions against free trade such as tariffs, quotas, currency restrictions, and other devices which effectively block imports, actually assist the preservation of monopolies or restrictive practices within Britain. But it should by now have been amply demonstrated that the reduction of tariffs and other direct control mechanisms depends upon, and cannot be accomplished without, a solution to the more basic balance-of-payments problem which the United Kingdom faces. Therefore, the problems again interrelate.

The proposals within the National Plan relating to the rationalization of industry reaffirm the government's intent to get rid of restrictive practices and prevent the use of monopoly power, it points out that the government's power should not be used to hinder mergers which would promote efficiency and the establishment of competitiveness of British industry. Indeed, the Plan states that the government should assist in the promotion of such mergers and even take the initiative in bringing them about.

Apart from these international considerations within Britain, anti-competition legislation has taken several forms. Resale price maintenance has theoretically been abolished. Consequently, there have been visible reductions in prices of some of the consumer durable goods formerly subject to such price maintenance agreements.[36] More important, the Restrictive Practices Act of 1956, which is designed to enlarge similar acts passed in 1944 and 1948, established a Monopolies and Restrictive Practices Commission to investigate particular cases of agreements against the public interest. John Heath provides an analysis of the Act. While he finds that some of the purposes of the Act have been fulfilled at the time of writing, he also finds it desirable that the Act should be strengthened in all of its respects. Furthermore, he finds that there are certain limits to which the legal and judicial procedure can go with respect to competition:

. . . Amending the rules of the game whether or not this involves the Restrictive Trade Practices Act can improve business performance; but the effect would be much greater if attitudes changed, if there were a greater sense of enterprise and enthusiasm. A firmer commitment to promote competition may help to change these attitudes but the real problem is much deeper.[37]

In seeking for the real solution, not surprisingly, Heath finds his attention directed to the question of the quality of management, which inevitably becomes central to any approach to increasing British economic effectiveness from whatever point one starts.

Other analysts of the problem have cited the Labour government's tax reforms, noted earlier, designed to stimulate retained earnings, as the antithesis of a true competitive policy. They feel that the distribution of profits rather than their retention would provide the maximum opportunity for those with new ideas and new aggressive methods to get hold of capital and use it more efficiently. That Britain has embarked on serious policies designed to increase competition at all is a step in the right direction. It must be recognized, however, that competition policy is not a matter of occasional

[36] See B. S. Yamey, *Resale Price Maintenance* (London: Institute for Economic Research, Hobart Papers No. 1 1959).
[37] John Heath, *Still Not Enough Competition?* (London: Institute of Economic Affairs, 1963).

measures but rather a continuous campaign based on a detailed knowledge of economic restrictive practices, to develop a sharp and tough competitive climate. That this has value per se is obvious: that it is an indispensible ingredient for success if Britain enters the Common Market places upon effective legislation to stimulate new competition a new imperative.

The effectiveness of competition should not be limited to the formal antitrust type of approach. Other aspects of a competition policy extend into the areas of management and organized labor, although in these areas specific legislation may not be required.

With respect to management, the steps previously outlined to improve the quality of management are themselves in a sense competitive. The selection, the training, and the recruitment of better persons for management is a competitive process. The lessons which better trained managers will carry into industry are essentially designed to increase efficiency and make more effective competition. Bigger earnings for management will also make for competition for managers among firms and for competition among managers for rewards.

The third aspect of a competitive program must extend competitive pressures into the labor market and, indeed, into the very structure of unions. Measures to extend competitive practices to the labor markets and unions are not wholly conservative in origin; but on these matters the National Plan is silent. Michael Shanks, in analyzing the structure of British trade unions, has called them "grotesquely out of date." [38] Restrictive practices, interunion disputes, and the disputes between shop stewards or other local leaders and the trade union hierarchy are aggravated by defects in the trade union structure. For that structure still gives undue importance to craft unions. If craft unions made sense forty years ago, when the only groups of workers with the organizational skill, financial resources, cohesion and solidarity to build up unions and withstand the assaults of the employer were the craftsmen, that division no longer fits the industrial pattern.

The British craft union division is basically horizontal, that is, workers are organized in the unions depending on their degree of skill rather than according to the industry they work in. On the one

[38] *Op. cit.*, see esp. Chap. 4 and 5.

hand are the craft unions, on the other are the two "general workers unions"—the Transport and General Works Union and the
General and Municipal Workers, which represent unskilled workers
in an enormous range of different industries. There are compara-
tively few industrial unions of the type familiar in the United States,
representing all the workers in a given industry, or even in a single
plant whatever their degree of skill. Restrictive practices are more
markedly supported by groups of craftsmen who feel their positions
threatened by technological changes. Craftsmen stand to lose more
than other workers from the spread of automation and technical
skill. They must inevitably act as a force for conservatism in industry, resisting modernization. Andrew Shonfield has argued co-
gently that one of the main reasons for Britain's sluggish economic
growth has been the importance of craft unions in the system.

Since the introduction of new equipment in factories necessarily
makes complete nonsense of the traditional craft divisions and de-
marcations, it is inevitable that a conflict between progress and
unions must ensue from the existing organization. The plant management has the choice between working out a new work arrangement and a new payment structure to fit the new needs, or giving
up the attempt to modernize entirely.

One of the responses to this conflict has been the emergence in
several cases of plantwide bargaining rather than bargaining by
crafts.[39] In this emerging pattern, managements work increasingly
through the shop stewards in agreeing on pay schedules, holidays,
pensions and other elements of collective bargaining in return for a
surrender of restrictive habits. As the quality of management improves and the competitive climate stimulates greater effort, it is
likely that this kind of arrangement will be increasingly adopted of
necessity.

It has been noted earlier that the incomes policy to date has been
ineffective. More damning is the fact that the incomes policy
per se must conflict with plant modernization. In modernization a
management may want to increase earnings for some of its employees by 10, 20, or 25 per cent while pensioning off others. This

[39] For further discussion along these lines see David Howell, "Managing The
British Economy," The Conservative Opportunity (London: B. T. Batsfords,
1965.)

policy cannot prevail in the face of the proposition that wage increases must be limited to the prospective growth of productivity, or something like 3 per cent. Indeed, it is part of the apparatus of restrictionism that union leaders in London can persist in issuing weighty sermons on the need to think about nothing over 3 per cent. "The repercussions of an incomes policy can be decisive in halting precisely the kind of trends in wage negotiations for which every intelligent management and plant labour leader ought to be working." [40]

It may or may not be necessary to supplement the movement toward modernization of the trade union movement with legislation. If a management attempting to modernize its plant offers to the workers blandishments of which the union does not approve, the present government's Trades Disputes Bill gives the unions full legal authority to intimidate via a threatened strike action. In addition to that central piece of legislation, Howell has suggested four more which a government—presumably a new one—might enact to reverse the current trends. First, it can cease to emphasize incomes policy as a matter of economic priority; for when a government focuses on economic dynamism it must forego its blanket incomes policy. Second, it can actively insist on more union mergers and reform of union structures and rules. The very insistence of the government that unions make mergers may well stimulate this development, which most union leaders know in their hearts is needed, anyway. Third, it can make sure that arrangements to facilitate changes of employment—unemployment compensation, retraining programs, and resettlement allowances, among others—are adequate to the point of being generous and really do support all the considerations which victims of technology are likely to face.

Fourth, and perhaps most important, is the question of liability for damages. The trade unions are presently immune from legal action for damages both when they use their collective strength in a genuine industrial dispute and also when that collective strength is used against the individual. As long as that immunity applies in both cases, the unions can use their legal power as a means of resistance against all changes. Howell suggests that the answer must be that while the right to strike in a bona fide industrial dispute must

40 *Ibid.*, p. 103.

be maintained, the right to intimidate (and prevent progress) must not. Whether any government, Labour or Conservative, will have the political courage to insist on reforms of this type even though they fit into an over-all pattern of economic reform and dynamism must remain an open question.

SUMMARY

All of the steps and policy actions which Britain has taken are intimately connected with the goal of improving the British balance-of-payments position.

The present system, for reasons cited in Chapter IV, permits devaluation for a currency in fundamental disequilibrium, which the pound surely is. But as a practical matter, if that currency is a reserve currency, strong external political reasons exist which militate against the use of devaluation. It was apparently these considerations, underscored by the simultaneous weakness of the dollar that decided Britain against devaluation in its 1964 crisis.

In lieu of devaluation, time is needed to make internal adjustments. Time has been bought with loans to provide the liquidity with which the pound can be defended for the time being. The trio of policy groups—the current "stop," the incomes policy to control inflation, and the National Plan designed to achieve structural reform—are all parts of the overall attempt to achieve domestic adjustment. Some would be desirable and necessary even had there been devaluation, or, indeed, were there no balance-of-payments problem. But the urgency of that problem imparts equal urgency to the adjustment steps. Devaluation might have made some of the longer-term policies easier to institute, but is no substitute for other measures designed to raise the growth rate and to achieve price stability.

CHAPTER VI

The Dollar's Dilemma

By mid-1965, the United States had entered what might be called the fourth phase of its postwar balance-of-payments position. The first phase lasted from 1945 to about 1950. In it, the United States, powerful, and undamaged in World War II, earned huge export surpluses as the supplier of goods for European reconstruction, which were partially financed through the Marshall Plan and other aid programs. Part of the American motive was generosity; another part was to establish a strong anti-Communist Western bulwark; at times the motives became so intertangled that no one was quite sure which served as rationalization for which.

The second phase, in which the present concern originated, was roughly the decade 1950–1958. By 1950 the nations of Western Europe, equipped with American-supplied production facilities and know-how, and with greatly devalued currencies, had regained their export potential. In addition, the U.S. involvement in Korea and other commitments to contain communism resulted in a sizable and sustained drain on the balance of payments for military expenditures and aid. By 1950, the American surplus had turned into a deficit, which continued (with the exception of 1957) until the second quarter of 1965, and then resumed. To some, the years before 1958 were thought to be an interregnum in the dollar shortage. In any event, all the new surplus nations were happy to acquire dollars and hold them as reserves. The position of the dollar was thought to be impregnable. The dollar deficits were moderate and were thought to be temporary; with the Swiss franc, the dollar was still the only major convertible currency, and the U.S. gold stock remained near its peak.

The third phase began in about 1958. Americans were still vastly pleased with their grand design, and were congratulating themselves that the economic *Pax Americana* had resulted in the restoration of convertibility among major currencies in Western Europe. But in that same year the United States, still without much concern, incurred a deficit in the balance of payments of some $3.5 billion. The dollar, so sought after earlier was now far less desirable; and indeed perhaps of dubious quality.

Three forces converged about 1958 to make this a turning point in the fortunes of the American balance of payments. The very convertibility of currencies meant that the newly "safe" currencies of the European surplus countries could be freely bought and sold, so that the dollar (and Swiss franc) lost this uniqueness. Second, the same convertibility made possible short-term capital outflows from America, to buy obligations backed by the newly "safe" currencies, with higher interest rates than were available in the United States. Finally, private long-term capital from America was lured to Europe by the launching of the Common Market, with its prospects for growth and profits.

As the United States deficit continued, by 1960 the Europeans began to warn that discipline was in order; even if the rules of the Bretton Woods System were largely of American origin, it too must abide by them. As the Bretton Woods rules impose adjustment primarily on the deficit countries, and as the United States was now the greatest deficit nation, it too must set its house in order. If the U.S. deficit resulted because the European currency devaluations in 1948–1949 had been, in retrospect, excessive, and because American aid had given them the potential to compete, that was history and too bad. The U.S. dollar was overvalued and that was an American problem, insoluble by devaluation lest the system collapse, and so a problem for the Americans to solve internally. If the deficit reflected a continuing American burden in assuming the principal share in aiding the developing nations and providing the military wherewithal to combat communism, that too was too bad, and merely underscored the need for American discipline. The fact that part of the deficit which resulted from vast American private investment in European industry became a particular *bête noir* for many Europeans. While rarely, if ever, denying American corporations the right to invest, they nevertheless complained volubly about the Americanization of European industry, fearing that the smaller European firms would be swallowed whole by their giant American competitors. Indeed, restriction of capital outflow from the United States to Europe came to be a major goal of many European critics, particularly in France, and the United States has partially acquiesced to their desire for the control and inhibition of investment. That surplus nations, too, could make adjustments designed to rectify imbalances had little practical appeal to the Europeans. Tariff reduction, for example, to stimulate imports and turn the surplus of dollars and gold into useful goods, was one path open to the Europeans; as the Common Market gathered momentum, tariffs against the outside world were rearranged, but on the whole not lowered signficantly. Currency revaluations were also possible; but apart from one 5 per cent increase by the Germans and Dutch in 1961, this path was ignored. In the disputes that ensued, the major burden of adjustment remained with the deficit nations.

The fourth and current stage of the American experience is the reappearance of an American surplus in the second quarter of 1965, largely in response to internal American action. Chart 6 below provides a perspective on that surplus, compared to some recent deficits. The action most directly responsible for this turnabout was the imposition of controls over private foreign investment by the Johnson Administration. But these most recent and dramatic American actions were superimposed on others; the Kennedy Administration had initiated the interest equalization tax to reduce the attractiveness of foreign securities, in effect making it more expensive for private American investors to buy shares or bonds of European and Japanese origin. In addition, these controls on capital outflow were superimposed on a conscious dose of the "classical medicine." The United States allowed its unemployment rate to remain very high, and its growth rate to lag. An estimated $30 to $50 billion per year in output has been lost in the process. The government has even, in its "wage-price guidelines," toyed with an embryonic incomes policy.

CHART 6.   U.S. BALANCE OF PAYMENTS
(*annual rate, seasonally adjusted*)

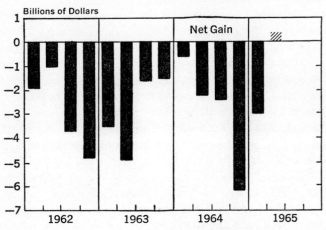

SOURCE: U.S. Department, *Survey of Current Business.*

The key questions that emerge from the fourth phase bear on the fifth, the future. Have the restrictive actions noted above turned the tide? Is their effect sustainable, or do these steps have only temporary effects? By their restrictive acts, have the Americans also diminished the supply of liquidity to the world which the deficit flow of dollars formerly provided? If so, how may it be restored, i.e., what plan for reform can the United States endorse to provide world liquidity without further crippling itself?

By way of preliminary reply to the question of the future, it may be noted that the hopes expressed at the outset of the Johnson Administration's control program in February 1965, that the problem would be solved by these actions, have now given way to a wide consensus to the contrary. Many economists have termed the controls a one-shot affair, capable of large impact but small sustained effect. Henry Fowler, Secretary of the Treasury, now concurs:

There is no sounding of the trumpets that we have reached lasting equilibrium. I expect a slipping back in the third quarter.[1]

Events have proved Secretary Fowler right.

With this background and turn of events, the recent economic history of the United States that bears on and is influenced by the balance-of-payments position again becomes prologue and not archive. Moreover, the positions that have been developed by economists, which eventually in one form or another become the bases for government action, are still relevant for the future.

Perhaps more than in most realms, history and theory blend in this area. Therefore, an appropriate setting within which to consider recent history and, by inference, the future is in terms of the available policy alternatives.

At the risk of slighting many of the important single analyses, ideas, and insights by focusing on whole sets of ideas, we can say that five basic integrated positions have emerged indicating the lines of policy action within the United States.

These five positions exclude those which require international reform on a grand scale for their fulfillment. There may or may not be international reform. In any event, the internal adjustment of the United States to the current imbalance remains an internal problem. True, some reforms might solve the American problem: if the surplus nations, for example, recognize that the "classical medicine" obligates them to undertake fiscal and monetary expansion to eliminate their surpluses, just as surely as it requires the United States or the United Kingdom to deflate to eliminate their deficits, at least half of the internal American problem would disappear. But the use of the "classical medicine" for all is not even proposed as a reform. On the other hand, other proposed reforms probably would not per se solve the domestic problem. If, for example, a new unit (Bancor, CRU) were devised to replace the dollar as a reserve unit, the United States would be freer to act than it is now as the major reserve currency. But freer to act how? In some way, still on its internal costs and prices, directly on its imports, the value of its currency, or the level of its foreign investments and aid, or—in short —in much the same way it must act now without that additional de-

---

[1] "Drain on Dollar Stemmed. . . ." *New York Times*, August 18, 1965, p. 1.

gree of freedom. The question, to which the theories are oriented, remains: how to act now?

The first position questioned the existence, or at least the durability, of any real balance-of-payments problems. By implication, this position considered any major effort on the part of the United States to eliminate its "nominal" deficit as attacking a problem which, for most real purposes, does not exist. Two examples of the manifestation of this posture can be cited. The first is the position taken by the Eisenhower Administration in 1958 and 1959, again by the Kennedy Administration in its early days, and to a much lesser extent by the Johnson Administration. This view was apparently that the deficit was temporary, and even if it was not, a few manipulations and direct controls would restore external accounts to equilibrium, ending the problem. This view has been dissipated, but the fact remains that it had enough status to delay the attack on the deficit for a considerable period.

The second example was to partially define the problem away by using statistical concepts of the deficit other than the Department of Commerce's "over-all balance" which resulted in a smaller deficit figure and evidently therefore a lesser problem. Although it is clear from Table 3 in Chapter II that any of the commonly used concepts will yield a sizable and consistent U.S. deficit since 1958, the "over-all balance" concept yields the largest, and therefore the most pessimistic view of the problem. In the early 1960s, some analysts regarded the huge "over-all" deficit figures as making a statistical mountain out of a mole hill but by mid-1965, this position had been rejected by virtually all students of the questions, including those who held it initially.

The conviction that there is no real problem was satisfying because it is difficult mentally for Americans to accept the changed position. After decades of international strength, and in view of its internal strength, the urge to regard the United States as exempt from foreign pressures was strong.

The second basic position may be associated with the name of John Galbraith. It is, in short, the case for direct controls over U.S. foreign expenditures to correct the deficit. To his great credit, Galbraith has made his case candidly. In brief, he sees the balance-of-payments problem at its basic levels as "the question of long-term

THE DOLLAR'S DILEMMA [145]

capital flows, and even more basic, that of domestic costs and prices, commercial policy, and the overseas operations of the U.S. government."[2]

To remedy international imbalances via direct controls requires certain policies which the United States has in fact already followed to some extent, most notably by its inhibition of private investment abroad. Further, it will require other direct controls to be fully effective. These include a range of peripheral matters—which Galbraith tosses off as "cosmetic or public relations actions"—including such items as limitations on tourism, and on duty-free purchases abroad, the sale of savings bonds to soldiers, etc. But other, deeper, direct controls would include a cut in the expenditures for aid and military programs, an area which Galbraith admits would encounter resistance to action because of vested interests in governmental departments and the military. Moreover, Galbraith would, if necessary, extend the direct controls to the restriction of imports:

In past times the first step of a country faced with balance of payments difficulties was to discourage imports either by tariffs or quotas. This is now highly unfashionable—and it is too bad. Tariffs—the general or selective discouragement of imports by restricting their prices—are in fact the simplest and most straightforward method of dealing with balance of payments disequilibrium.[3]

Those who propose import controls are normally constrained by the recognition that other countries can retaliate with their own import controls with the net result that the world is more autarkic, less free, and poorer into the bargain. Galbraith is under no such constraint because he feels that it would be the United States which is retaliating against relatively high Common Market tariffs in the establishment of its own.

A third position, essentially theoretical in nature, would move in the direction of free markets for foreign currencies as well as for goods. Not surprisingly, it is espoused by Milton Friedman, among many others, and in its ramifications which would end the American support price for gold by A.P. Lerner as well. The case very simply states that the "fundamental disequilibrium" arises because

[2] Galbraith, *op. cit.*, p. 119.
[3] *Ibid.*, p. 120.

exchange rates are pegged at inappropriate levels. If there were flexible exchange rates and, peripherally, if gold were demonetized, an automatic adjustment mechanism would be added which would obviate all of the direct control mechanisms thus far instituted.

We shall deal with a series of objections to this proposal later in this chapter where devaluation is considered; and, more important, with what might be called official contempt against this proposal. Robert V. Roosa, for example, then Under Secretary of the Treasury and the chief architect of American international monetary policy, has written:

Apparently most of the academic effort that could be diverted from the escapist abstractions of fluctuating exchange rates has been intrigued by the search for some new touchstone for liquidity.[4]

A fourth approach is the "classical medicine" of relative deflation for deficit nations. Along with some direct controls, it has been employed by the United States. This approach offers a fundamental theoretical solution, and has implicitly been favored by the American banking community and stanchly advocated by critics in European surplus countries. It is essentially the approach assumed in the admirable analysis and projections of the U.S. balance of payments by the Brookings study.[5] The classical approach and the Brookings study assume that higher rates of price increases in Europe than in the United States will cause an improvement in the U.S. current account which will eventually turn the over-all deficit into a surplus. Depending upon which rate of inflation is assumed for Europe, the United States may achieve a surplus or still be in deficit by 1968. That the Europeans have inflated faster than the United States in the past five years reflects the impact of growth, partly stimulated by American investment in Europe. But inflation has not been a conscious European policy to eliminate surpluses. If inflation threatens European surpluses, European policy may consciously try to inhibit growth, making the American task more difficult. So this mechanism still places the burden of action on the United States to control its level of demand and prices to achieve

[4] Robert Roosa, "Movements of Long-Term Capital and the Adjustment Process," *Review of Economic and Statistics*, May 1964, p. 164.
[5] Walter Salant *et. al.*, *op. cit.*

relative deflation vis-à-vis Europe, while Europe is free to determine its own internal policy with little constraint imposed by the balance of payments.

The Brookings authors are astute and well aware of the tentative nature of their findings, which should be considered hypotheses and not projections. In contrast, some analysts of the problem have, perhaps mistakenly, used the Brookings findings to tranquilize the nation's concern with the problem.

In their conclusions, the Brookings analysts recommended enlarged international liquidity for the United States, to give more time for this "classical medicine" to work:

We believe that, given sufficient time, adjustments can be brought about under a fixed rate system, without sacrifice of high priority objectives, through the normal working of market forces . . . supplemented by governmental policies consistent with a free society.[6]

But if the Brookings assumptions prove wrong, or more time via additional liquidity cannot be borrowed:

We recommend as the best alternative the adoption of a modified flexible exchange rate system.

A fifth and final position is that of acknowledging the deficit and devising ways to finance it without losing more gold while avoiding any of the distasteful means of eliminating it. This position has attempted to create a series of *ad hoc* measures, under which the United States could borrow more from other countries, and thus gain more time to make the basic adjustments. This has been one of the official Washington responses to the balance-of-payments difficulties to date, coupled with the belief that the "classical medicine" buttressed by periodic piecemeal direct controls will work. That this approach may continue and in the interim result in additional piecemeal controls is a possibility for the future upon which few students of the problem look kindly. It is all too apparent to these students that the juggling game may end abruptly when the Europeans refuse to accept additional dollar holdings to finance the U.S. deficits. In such a case all the deficits will result in gold losses, which must ultimately precipitate a more profound solution.

[6] *Ibid.*, p. 262.

THE MAGNITUDE OF THE PROBLEM

The United States has had a deficit in its international payments in every year since 1950 except 1957. This has been true regardless of the concept of the deficit employed (see Chapter II, Table 3) and has been reflected in rather consistent gold losses throughout the period. But prior to 1958, little was heard of the American deficit. Instead, economists were writing of a "dollar shortage" when, in fact, 1958 proved to be the first year of the "dollar glut."

This rapid reversal in the U.S. balance-of-payments position is amply illustrated by some relevant statistics. In the eight years from 1950 to 1957, the United States had a cumulative "basic deficit" (current account plus long-term capital movements) of $12.3 billion, or about $1.5 billion per year on average. This "basic deficit" was the net result of an average $2 billion surplus on current account and a $3.5 billion deficit (an average) in the long-term capital and government aid accounts, reflecting American private investment abroad and aid to other countries. But of the $12.3 billion in deficits from 1950 to 1957, only $1.7 billion (14 per cent) was financed by U.S. gold sales. Instead, the bulk of the deficit was financed by the acquisition of U.S. short-term liabilities by foreign official institutions, which totaled $5.4 billion. The remainder, of course, was accounted for by private short-term capital inflows.

The period beginning with 1958 presents a remarkably different picture, both as to the size of the deficit and the method of its financing. The "basic deficit" for 1958 was $3.7 billion, and for 1958 and 1959 combined, was $7.9 billion; roughly two-thirds as large as for the entire eight-year period preceding. The direct causes of this rapid deterioration in the balance of payments, and subsequent maintenance of a sizable "over-all deficit," can be found in two items in the balance of payments. First, U.S. exports, facing new competition from the rebuilt European industries, fell by $3.2 billion between 1957 and 1959, a decline exacerbated by the end of the Suez crisis, while imports hardly declined at all. Thus the current account balance declined from a $5.5 billion surplus in 1957 to $0.2 billion in 1959. Second, with convertibility restored to European currencies in 1958, short-term capital, including U.S. capital, was free to move in

search of higher interest rates or to speculate against a possible devaluation of the dollar. The result of this freedom began to be felt by
1960, when after two years of large ($3+ billion) deficits, some $2
billion of short-term capital flowed out of the United States just as
the current account was beginning to improve. Since 1960 the current account has continued to improve relatively consistently, but
long-term capital outflows have risen to offset a part of this improvement. Short-term capital movements have been consistently
negative, but fluctuating in magnitude.

With respect to the financing of the U.S. deficit, a sharp contrast
between the 1950–1957 and 1958–1964 periods is found in the percentage financed by gold. In 1958, the United States lost $2.3 billion
in gold, over half of the "basic deficit." From 1958 to 1964, the
U.S. gold stock declined a total of $6.5 billion, or approximately
one-third of the cumulative "over-all deficit" for the period. The remainder of this deficit has been financed by increases in U.S. short-
term liabilities to foreigners. By the end of 1964, those liabilities
totaled over $27 billion.

The combination of gold losses and rising short-term liabilities to
foreigners has impaired the liquidity position of the United States
and raised doubts about the soundness of the dollar. With the dollar
pegged in terms of gold, the ability of the United States to convert
foreign-held dollars to gold at the fixed price of $35 per ounce de-
pends on the supply of gold in the United States relative to the potential demand for it, i.e., the amount of dollars held by foreigners.
In 1950, the gold supply was roughly 200 per cent of the amount of
short-term liabilities, and even by the end of 1957, after seven years
of deficits, the gold stock was almost 150 per cent of the dollar
liabilities. But with the huge deficits beginning in 1958, the gold-to-
liability ratio fell continuously, reaching 60 per cent by the end of
1964. Thus the gold stock was no longer sufficient to meet all the
potential claims against the dollar. The fear that a massive run on
the dollar, by private speculators or by foreign official institutions
would force the United States to devalue the dollar vis-à-vis gold or
let the dollar fluctuate on the foreign exchange market, compelled
U.S. policy makers to take measures to improve the balance-of-payments position and to forestall the conversion of dollars into gold
by foreign countries.

The U.S. deficit has been matched by offsetting surpluses in other countries. Chart 7 plots the payments balance of various countries for the years 1958 through 1964. The "official settlements" definition is used since this concept provides the most consistent basis for international comparison. The chart shows clearly the basic differences in the positions of the United States and the countries of the European Economic Community. Indeed, for virtually the entire period, the U.S. deficit was matched closely by EEC surpluses. Among the EEC countries, France has maintained a consistent and sizable surplus since the devaluation of the franc in 1958. Germany also had sizable surpluses in 1958, 1960, and 1963, while Italy has run consistent, but smaller, surpluses except in 1963.

Since 1960, when the U.S. deficit reached its peak for the postwar period, a noticeable sustained trend toward smaller deficits appears which is reflected in smaller EEC surpluses since that year. This improvement in the U.S. deficit position is the result of a number of forces, including conscious policy actions which will be discussed in detail below.

Because gold and reserves have shifted from the United States to Europe, it is often inferred that all of the U.S. deficit has been with Continental European countries. In fact, the United States has a significant deficit with non-European countries, while Europe has substantial surpluses with the rest of the world. And, of course, large amounts of American military expenditures and aid to developing nations find their way back to Europe and become part of its surpluses. This suggests that if aid and military expenditures were reduced, developing nations would suffer directly, while Europe would find its foreign receipts falling.

The impact of the deficits and surpluses on the reserves of various countries is shown in Chart 8. The gold and foreign exchange reserves (virtually all dollars) are charted for 1950, 1958, and 1964. The American and British postwar balance-of-payments deficits are reflected in the falling reserve totals of each. In 1950, the United States had almost 70 per cent of the free world's monetary gold, but by 1964 only 35 per cent. In 1964, the EEC countries had only $2 billion less gold than the United States, a massive redistribution over a period of fourteen years, most of which occurred in the six years between 1958 and 1964.

CHART 7.   BALANCE OF PAYMENTS OF VARIOUS COUNTRIES, 1958–1964[a]

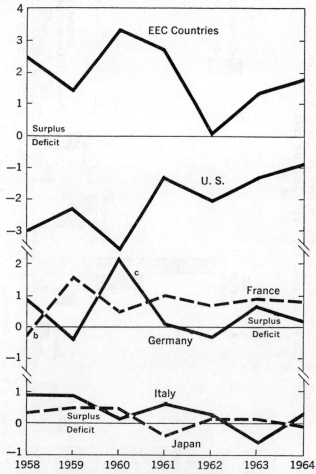

Billions of U. S. Dollars

SOURCE: U.S. data are from Chapter II, Table 3; other countries' data from
   International Monetary Fund, Washington, D.C.
[a] The balance shown here corresponds to the "official settlements" balance,
with minor exceptions where published figures were not available on that basis.
[b] Denotes devaluation of the franc in December 1958.
[c] Denotes revaluation of the mark in March 1961.

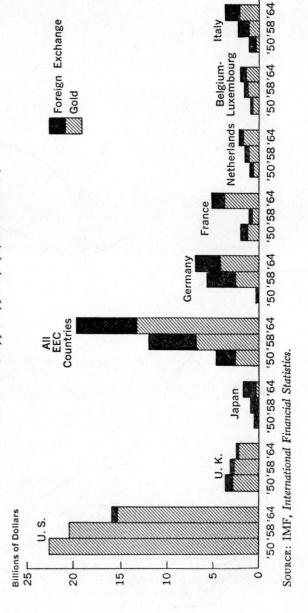

CHART 8. GOLD AND FOREIGN EXCHANGE HOLDINGS, SELECTED
COUNTRIES, 1950, 1958, 1964 (END OF YEAR)

SOURCE: IMF, *International Financial Statistics.*

The chart also makes clear which countries held their reserves primarily in gold and which have accepted foreign exchange, primarily dollars, in settlement of the surpluses. But also important, the chart shows how the surplus countries have divided the additions to their reserves between gold and foreign exchange. This is very significant during the period since 1958 when the U.S. balance-of-payments problem has been acute. Germany, for example, has added roughly $1 billion to her total reserves since 1958, but all of the addition has been in gold while her foreign exchange (dollars) holdings have actually declined. Similarly, the Netherlands has added to her reserves, primarily in gold; and France has added considerably to both gold and foreign exchange holdings, although the campaign to convert additional dollars to gold has reduced France's foreign exchange holdings during 1965. Thus Italy, Belgium, and Japan are the only major countries which hold the additions to their reserves primarily in foreign exchange, thereby alleviating a gold loss by the United States.

THE ROOTS OF THE PROBLEM

It was noted in Chapters I and V that the American and British balance-of-payments problems are very different; Americans earn a formidable surplus on current account which is then expended for other purposes. In contrast, the United Kingdom's trade balance starts in deficit. A more detailed look at the balance-of-payments data for the United States in Table 1 below reveals the magnitudes of several important components of U.S. balance of payments.

From the table it can be seen that in 1964, for example, the United States earned about $7.2 billion surplus on its "balance on private goods and services." Items 3 through 6 in Table 1 show the major items of U.S. gross expenditure. These items are more than sufficient to offset the entire $7.2 billion surplus earned on private goods and services, as well as that from the other receipts not shown in Table 1. If all of the items, shown and unshown, were netted, the $2.8 billion over-all deficit would result.

The interplay between the two major theoretical positions which have been projected—direct controls vs. devaluation or lower domestic prices—can be explained with reference to these data. For, in its

TABLE 1. Major Components of the U.S. Balance of Payments [a]
(*billions of dollars*)

− Denotes payments to foreigners.

	1958	1959	1960	1961	1962	1963	1964
1. Trade balance [b]	3.6	1.3	4.8	5.4	4.4	5.1	6.7
2. Balance on private goods and services [c]	3.1	0.6	4.6	5.5	4.7	4.8	7.2
3. Military expenditures	−3.4	−3.1	−3.0	−3.0	−3.1	−2.9	−2.8
4. Foreign aid (including military)	−2.8	−2.2	−3.4	−4.1	−4.3	−4.6	−4.3
5. Gross U.S. private long-term investment abroad	−2.6	−2.3	−2.5	−2.6	−2.9	−3.7	−4.4
6. U.S. short-term capital out-flow (increase in U.S.-owned foreign assets)	−0.3	−0.1	−1.3	−1.6	−0.5	−0.8	−2.1
7. Over-all deficit (gold sales plus increase in short-term liabilities to all foreigners)	3.5	3.7	3.9	2.4	2.2	2.7	2.8

SOURCE: U.S. Department of Commerce, *Survey of Current Business*.

[a] Expenditure Items 3 through 6 are *gross*, and not reduced by offsetting receipts in these categories. Therefore, Items 2 through 6 will *not* equal 7.
[b] Excludes exports of goods under military grants by U.S. government.
[c] Excludes goods and services rendered under U.S. government grants and loans.

simplest terms, advocates of adjustment of the exchange rate imply that if the U.S. currency were devalued or allowed to depreciate, the value of exports would presumably rise even higher, and the value of imports would decline so that the $7.2 billion surplus would become a greater amount. Ideally, it would be sufficiently larger to compensate for all of the expenditures in Items 3 through 6 and would reduce the "over-all deficit" (7) to virtually zero. Put differently, the overvaluation argument says that in the light of its other overseas commitments, the United States needs a larger surplus on current account. While $7.2 billion is a large amount, it is inadequate to cover the expenditures in other categories.

Another route, the "classical medicine," is designed to do the same thing. Thus, when the United States restricts its level of employment, national income, and internal prices, the presumption is that exports will become cheaper to the world and imports will be slowed, with the result that the U.S. "private balance" will increase, hopefully enough to eliminate the deficit. Table 1 above shows that the U.S. "private good and services balance" (2) has indeed increased, perhaps in response to United States relative deflation. But while the "over-all deficit" is lower than it was in 1958–1960, it still was sizable in 1964.

Those who eschew devaluation, or think the "classical medicine" too slow, uncertain, and costly, would seek balance-of-payments relief by direct controls on Items 3 through 6. A reduction of these items is a relatively simple administrative expedient. It does not involve basic changes in monetary arrangements, nor does it disturb the current reliance of the world on the dollar.

But there are feedbacks with respect to each of these components, which should be made explicit lest it be thought that direct controls over payments for these items are costless and painless.

For example, it is evident that gross private long-term investment (5) has been larger than the deficit and has risen over the last few years.

The major share of U.S. long-term investment abroad is direct investment in capital plant and equipment of foreign subsidiaries. When this type of investment involves the building of new production facilities, these foreign subsidiaries buy a considerable portion of their capital equipment from U.S. suppliers. Thus a part of the negative effect of the capital outflow is immediately offset by the positive effect of an increase in exports. Once the foreign subsidiary is producing, it may take over a part of world markets (in the country receiving the investment) which had heretofore been supplied by exports from the United States, thus reducing U.S. exports and adding to the over-all negative impact of the investment. But, finally, and this applies to all U.S. investment abroad, the foreign investment will return interest and dividend payments to the United States over its lifetime, thereby increasing total foreign receipts in the future.[7] In any normal foreign investment, direct or portfolio, the investor expects to receive more in return (both principal and interest) than the original investment, since the normal expectation of investment is gain. Thus, over the lifetime of an investment, the impact on the balance of payments must be positive, i.e., total receipts as a result of the investment must exceed the payments involved in making it. Those who advocate balance-of-payments improvement by reducing private capital outflows, especially long-term, have in mind only the short-run improvement because the effect will be adverse in the long run.

To a much lesser degree, the same kind of reasoning applies to foreign aid—at least, economic as opposed to military aid. Here the connection between aid and exports is even tighter than with private investment. Under the normal course of events, aid to underdeveloped countries will be spent on imports within a very short period some of which will be U.S. exports. Further, the U.S. aid program has attempted to minimize the negative impact on the balance of payments by increasingly "tying" the aid to U.S. exports since 1960. That is, as a condition for receiving the aid, the recipient country must spend the dollars in the United States. Theoretically, of course, if all aid were "tied," the balance-of-payments impact would be zero, since the added receipts from U.S. exports would be equal to the amount of the aid. However, such cannot be the case in practice. The foreign exchange received by the recipient country as a result of U.S. aid will, indeed, be spent in the United States, but one can assume that some of these expenditures on U.S. goods would have occurred anyway. Thus the aid actually releases other foreign ex-

[7] See Table 3, p. 180, for detail; see also J. Behrman, "The Foreign Investment Muddle," *Columbia Journal of World Business*, Fall 1965.

change which the country can now spend where it pleases, only a part of which may be spent in the United States. Calculations based on past experience estimate that a dollar of U.S. aid will result in a net increase of U.S. exports of between 5 cents and 60 cents, depending on the country receiving the aid.[8] Thus, a reduction in U.S. foreign aid will have an immediate favorable impact on the balance of payments, but not to the full extent of the actual reduction in aid expenditure.

In addition, U.S. aid has tended to move away from outright grants toward low interest, long-term loans to underdeveloped countries. If and when these loans are repaid, the positive effect on the balance of payments will offset the original negative effect of granting the aid. Under these conditions, the ultimate long-range effects of aid could be favorable for the balance of payments.

The expenditure on which the quickest, and perhaps the greatest, controversy can be raised is Item 3, "military expenditures." Feedback measures are not meaningful for military expenditures, since so much of the money is for personnel costs. Military expenditures have in the past been considered exogenous, dependent in quantity wholly on determinations made by the military. It was considered niggardly that a balance-of-payments problem should enter into, or even be a factor in, the government's policy on military expenditures. If these expenditures were desirable in themselves, the balance of payments should not even be considered. However, in advocating direct controls which would cover this element as well as others, Galbraith has again faced the problem squarely:

Military obligations must always be examined in the full context of other policy. We cannot do abroad what we do not have the external resources to pay for. . . . A strong balance of payments is a factor of major importance in international position and leadership. In the past our forced commitment to France and Germany has poured dollars into these countries and, by weakening our balance of payments, weakened our bargaining position vis-à-vis these countries.[9]

[8] Based on the "feedback ratios" published in the Brookings study, Walter Salant *et. al., The United States Balance of Payments in 1968, op. cit.,* Append. to Chap. IV, pp. 275–277.
[9] *Op. cit.,* p. 120.

The American government has chosen to use direct controls and the "classical medicine" of relative deflation to bring about balance-of-payments equilibrium. If some form of devaluation continues to be rejected, it should be apparent that more of the same type of controls may be necessary. What are the arguments against devaluation? Are they likely to hold in the future?

DEVALUATION

When placed side by side, the respective cases for and against devaluation of the dollar are won in theory by the former but as a practical matter are ruled out by the latter.

The case for devaluation flows from observation that the American current account surplus is not large enough, if the United States is to maintain its military and foreign aid commitments at present levels and if American capital investments are to remain free. Devaluation could be the mechanism of adjustment which would make unnecessary not only direct controls, but also the "classical medicine" of deflation and unemployment for which the United States has paid a considerable price in the period since 1958. The extent to which the United States would have to devalue (or depreciate) its currency—assuming no other currency simultaneously devalued—depends of course on the elasticities of demand and supply of U.S. exports and imports.

A number of students, including John Floyd, have attempted to estimate these elasticities for the United States.[10] Floyd concludes that a $3.5 billion improvement in the current account could be achieved with a 4.5 per cent devaluation. This implies a high degree of sensitivity of current account payments and receipts to relative price changes. Since the U.S. deficit was $3 billion on average from 1958 to 1960, a devaluation of the dollar by 4.5 to 5 per cent in 1958 would have eliminated the deficits in every year if capital outflows had been unaffected by the devaluation.

But if, as is likely, the removal of balance-of-payments pressure on domestic monetary policy had resulted in lower interest rates in the United States, more U.S. capital would have been invested

[10] "The Overvaluation of the Dollar: A Note on the International Price Mechanism," *American Economic Review*, May 1965, p. 104.

abroad, making the necessary devaluation greater. Considering these possibilities, Floyd concludes that "the dollar is overvalued by not more than 10 per cent."

The case against devaluation rests on three hypotheses, as well as an important, if often unconscious, psychological assumption. That assumption, which is widely held by the populace, is that national strength and the position of a currency are related. Devaluation is a sign of weakness and since the United States is not weak, why devalue?

The three hypotheses are briefly as follows: First, American devaluation would quickly be offset by competing devaluations of other currencies, so that it would be ineffective. Second, as a practical matter the very way in which the United States is governed would assure massive outflows of short-term capital when advance rumors and discussion of devaluation took place, and thus disrupt the financial system. Third, the role of the dollar as a reserve currency in the modern world effectively eliminates devaluation as a step open to it.

The argument that American devaluation would be quickly rendered ineffective by competing devaluations gives cognizance to the size and importance of the United States in world affairs. It does not suggest that devaluation, as a technique, is not advisable under certain conditions for most countries to remedy a balance-of-payments disequilibrium. Despite the fact that it is often postponed well beyond the time it should be taken, devaluation is and will remain a valuable instrument for smaller countries. But a policy that is applicable to Canada, Chile, or even the United Kingdom is not equally applicable to the United States. What small countries may do vis-à-vis the large ones may be quite different from what the large ones may do vis-à-vis the world. That the United States permitted its European competitors to devalue in 1948–1949 is now history. Indeed, part of the outraged American reaction to European responses to the American position is the recognition of the fact that the Europeans probably would not accord the same advantages to the United States but would devalue to maintain their surpluses. James Tobin, who does not favor devaluation but may nevertheless be used as an example of this type of reaction, has written:

Memories are short, and gratitude is not a consideration respected in international relations, especially when money is involved. But the

United States has and had considerable moral claim on European governments and central banks. . . . During the dollar shortage the United States: gave Western European countries (other than Greece, Turkey and Spain) $32 billion of military and economic aid; lent them $11 billion additional (in spite of defaults of European governments of debts connected with World War I); acquiesced in substantial devaluations of European currencies, without which European exports would still not be competitive. . . . After enabling Europe to overcome the dollar shortage the United States has been expected to adjust to its reversal without the tools that Europe used in its turn.[11]

The virtual certainty that other trading nations would instantly devalue, if the United States did so, knocks the case for devaluation out of U.S. official minds. Other arguments against devaluation are interesting, but supererogatory.

Under a system of flexible exchange rates there could be no countervailing devaluations. In practice, flexible exchange rates may be subject to official jockeying. But the jockeying must be done by other nations, and the United States would be free of the basic balance-of-payments problem which now exists.

It is again Galbraith who has advanced the second argument against devaluation:

As the U.S. is governed, no move to alter parities could be taken without advance rumors and discussion. This would be the signal for massive and massively publicized withdrawals of the very large short-term balances. (One wonders if some balances do not remain here because of the virtual certainty of notice under our system of taking delicate decisions after due public discussion.) This would then seem to force the action. The aspect of political weakness and even helplessness in such a development is obvious. No Administration with any regard for its political reputation would invite it. Those who speak of devaluation either to fixed or floating rates as *serious policy* must show how these manifestations of political disarray and weakness could be avoided.

As a practical matter the United States must correct disequilibrium when it arises within the framework of fixed parities. Devaluation to fixed or floating rates is a course of action vouchsafed only to lesser and differently governed powers.[12]

11 J. Tobin, "Europe and the Dollar," *Review of Economics and Statistics*, May 1964, p. 124.
12 *Op. cit.*, p. 117.

The final and to some most persuasive argument against devaluation is the role of the American dollar as the key reserve currency. In essence a devaluation of the dollar now would mean that all of those countries (and individuals) which have been persuaded to hold dollars as opposed to gold would have been punished for their cooperation with the United States. Even if they should devalue their own currencies correspondingly, they would have lost a possible capital gain had they previously exchanged their dollars for gold. On the contrary, the benefits would go to those who have weakened the dollar by their conversions of dollars to gold, and to the large gold producers and hoarders, including the Soviet Union and South Africa.

The question of inhibitions on U.S. policy due to the dollar's role as a reserve currency raises a host of related questions, about the very desirability of being a reserve currency. If it is crippling to action to be a reserve currency, why be one? When it is pointed out that devaluation might disqualify the dollar for future reserve status, two answers appear. G. Haberler and others answer that devaluation "once in a blue moon" does not (or should not) disqualify a currency from reserve currency status, especially if central bankers match their interest earnings over the years from holding currency obligations against their capital loss from devaluation. Another school will simply reply: Good—who wants reserve status, anyway?

These arguments are usually couched in terms of "the cost vs. the benefit" of being a reserve currency, and apply not only to the dollar but also to the pound, or to any nation's currency that attains reserve status. It may be remembered that no nation in the past has consciously chosen to be a reserve currency country, nor has it been elected to this position; rather, it happens to become one because other countries choose to hold its currency in the settlement of international balances and for the buying and selling of their own currencies.[13]

Being a reserve currency carries with it both benefits and costs.

[13] For more extended discussion of this question see Robert Z. Aliber, "The Cost and Benefits of the U.S. Being a Reserve Currency Country," *Quarterly Journal of Economics*, August 1964, pp. 442–456; and William A. Salant, "The Reserve Currency Role of the Dollar—Blessing or Burden to the U.S.?" *Review of Economics and Statistics*, May 1964, pp. 131–138.

The principal benefit is greater flexibility. In this context flexibility simply means that American deficits can be financed in part through increases in the dollar reserves held by foreign monetary authorities. To the extent that U.S. deficits result in additional dollar reserves of surplus countries, the loss of gold by the United States is smaller than it would otherwise be. One aspect of this advantage is that long-term investments with relatively high rates of return can be and are made while short-term debts costing less are incurred. This is usually profitable.

Much of the action of government officials in the last few years was designed to convince foreign governments that they should indeed hold dollar assets rather than gold. The gain in flexibility which is said to result has been cited by former Under Secretary of the Treasury Roosa and other officials in testimony to Congress.[14]

In summary, this flexibility is said to entail two advantages. First, it means that the United States has more time and scope to deal with its balance-of-payments deficit. This additional time puts off or slows down the "classical medicine" or other restrictive remedies that must be used to get at the roots of the problem; and it allows the United States to take greater risks in adopting economic policies that might have adverse effects on the balance of payments.

On the other side are the costs of being a reserve currency, which of course are constraints on economic policy. When foreign monetary authorities hold large reserves of dollars, they do so without any commitment to keep them in that form. The threat is always present that they will convert these holdings to gold. A reduction of the foreign-held dollars will of course drain gold from the United States and perhaps precipitate the very devaluation which it is feared would shake the entire international system. Moreover, the threat of conversion to gold is a powerful factor in inhibiting the United States from following internal policies aimed at higher levels of employment and economic growth. These policies may prove inflationary or, equally important, foreign governments may think they are going to be inflationary with a consequent worsening of the balance-of-payments position, and a further run on the dollar. Thus, out of

[14] *Outlook for the U.S. Balance of Payments*, Hearings before the Subcommittee on International Exchanges and Payments of the Joint Economic Committee (December 12, 13, and 14, 1962).

fear, they are stimulated to convert dollars to gold before a crisis arises. An analogy may be made between the United States and an individual with reference to this point. Just as borrowing allows a person to spend in excess of receipts, so does the benefit aspect of a reserve currency status allow the United States to avoid putting its balance of payments in order, by reducing the incentive and giving a longer time to do so. But for both an individual and a nation, the obligation to repay debt is an unwelcome and inescapable product of past borrowing. It means that at some time in the future total expenditures must be lower than receipts and a surplus earned in order to repay debt.

To reduce this theoretical argument to historical reality, the United States has actually both enjoyed the benefits and incurred the costs of being a reserve currency in different time periods. Until about 1958 the United States enjoyed the benefits. Other nations were happy to acquire dollar holdings and the American position was thought to be impregnable. However, since 1958, because the U.S. deficits have continued to run at higher levels, and due to the convertibility of European currencies, the United States has faced the costs. The magnitude of additional short-term debt it has incurred and of gold it has lost was discussed earlier. In addition, much of the discontent in Europe, particularly in France, with American policies stems from the dollar's status as a reserve currency. This allows the Americans to run perpetual deficits in their balance of payments. It enables the United States, even in deficit, to export long-term capital with which it can buy out or take over French industry. Moreover, this system is said to "export inflation" to France and other countries. This happens, according to the French, because France, running a payments surplus, is constantly selling dollars on the foreign exchange market. These are paid for in francs which add to the French money supply and drive up prices in France.

American authorities reject this theory. They say the French are attempting to blame their own inflation on the American balance-of-payments deficit and the world monetary system, whereas in fact France or any nation can readily adjust its internal money supply to offset any influence from the balance of payments. Nevertheless, the theory is held tenaciously in France and many other European countries. In response to this theory the Europeans have made demands for "discipline" on the United States to end its balance-of-payments deficit, have demanded a restriction of long-term capital inflows, and have made demands for reform of the system. The favorite de Gaulle theory, a return to the gold standard, would of course eliminate all reserve currencies; other reforms espoused in Europe would replace the dollar as a reserve currency with a new unit.

Jacques Rueff, one of President de Gaulle's economic advisers, has written that the freedom afforded to a reserve currency country to run larger deficits over a longer period is a serious danger, rather than an advantage, both to the reserve currency country and to the world. He holds that this system allowed the United States to live until 1959 or so in a fool's paradise, in which it could ignore the deficit, oblivious of the fact that the day of reckoning, though postponed, would be all the harsher when it came.[15] French Finance Minister Giscard-d'Estaing has made a somewhat similar but more subtle and more modulated point. He has noted that reserve currency countries have obtained credit when they are in deficit, but that they "might not accumulate so readily the currencies of their new debtor" [16] if they should become surplus nations.

THE U.S. RESPONSE

If exchange rate alteration is for all practical purposes ruled out, one or more of the other mechanisms of adjustment *must* be used to correct the deficit. The choice is painful. There is no hard and fast measurable economic criterion to guide the choice. It is, in a sense, a question of establishing a hierarchy of social and political values and eliminating the least desirable. In these areas each man can be his own expert. The difficulty of arriving at a consensus on the proper U.S. approach lies in the different social valuations placed on various goals by various groups. To a military man, the maintenance or even expansion of the military expenditures is a paramount value—to be cut only at great peril; similarly, those involved in aid programs do not desire to see aid cut. To cut internal growth not only hurts all

[15] J. Rueff, "The West is Risking a Credit Collapse," *Fortune*, July 1961, p. 126.
[16] Statement IMF, *Summary Proceeding, the 18th Annual Meeting of the Board of Governors*, September 30–October 4, 1963.

Americans but, since unemployment falls most heavily on Negroes, it exacerbates racial tensions. Every component of the national economy relevant to the balance-of-payments problem has its claimant, and within its own purview every claim seems just.

No one has better stated the dollar's dilemma than Douglas Dillon:

Currency devaluation, import restrictions, exchange controls, substantial restriction of credit . . . or abandonment of our commitments for protection of the free world are all out of the question.[17]

If all these things are out, what is in? Dillon ticked off every mechanism of adjustment—exchange rate variation, direct controls, the "classical medicine" (restriction of credit). True, he has omitted incomes policy, but since inflation is not a major part of the American problem, this device has not been significant in any event.

Despite Dillon's statement, which accurately reflects what most Americans would like to do, the United States has taken some steps from each of the available mechanisms of adjustment (except devaluation). The American response falls under three broad heads, two designed to reduce the balance-of-payments deficit, the third to gain time without further loss of gold to allow the first two steps to be effective. The "classical medicine," in the form of relative deflation, and certain direct control measures comprise the first two steps; a group of borrowing devices designed to induce Europeans to hold dollars in lieu of gold comprises the third.

RELATIVE DEFLATION

There is no question that, from 1958 to at least 1964, U.S. economic policy has tolerated greater unemployment and less growth than would have been sustained without a balance-of-payments problem. Three distinct time periods appear to emerge with reference to this question. The Eisenhower Administration was at best only peripherally concerned with the balance-of-payments problem. Its penchant for deflationary policies flowed from its generally conserva-

[17] Testimony before the Joint Economic Committee, "The United States Balance of Payments," Part 1, *Hearings Before the Joint Economic Committee*, July 8–9, 1963, p. 17.

tive posture, and its concern with internal inflation which, in retrospect, proved unnecessary. The Kennedy Administration recognized the importance of the problem. It was also deeply concerned with domestic stagnation, and took the first steps to attempt to reconcile expansionary policies and the limitation imposed by a deficit in the balance of payments by some direct controls on the international payments side, coupled with expansionary budget policies internally. President Johnson's masterful legislative abilities have put into law a new and full range of policies for internal growth. But as internal growth will probably further deteriorate the international position, the conflict between internal and external needs again comes into sharper focus.

Since economic policy is, thus, a mixture of motives dictated by conflicting internal and international desires, it is impossible to assess *how much* of the restrictive economic policies reflect the balance-of-payments objective alone. It is clear, however, that the restrictionism was greater than it would have been without the problem and, furthermore, the attack on stagnation was probably delayed for this reason.

The extent to which economic growth was suppressed may be measured quantitatively. Restriction entails lost production, employment, profits, government revenues, and in general a shrunken income stream. A convenient summary of these relationships is found in comparisons between the actual output of goods and services (GNP) and potential output. When actual is less than potential, output and income have been lost; the gap shows how much.

Chart 9 shows the Council of Economic Advisers' estimate of this lost output—and real income. While prior to 1958 the gap was relatively small—indeed, negative at times—it widened appreciably in 1958 and has stayed high since.

The gap between actual and potential output as estimated in the chart assumes that the latter includes a 4 per cent unemployment rate. On this assumption, real GNP (in 1964 prices) *lost* due to unemployment and slow growth averaged over $35 billion per year from 1957 to 1964.

R. Musgrave [18] has converted this estimate of the "GNP gap" to

[18] R. Musgrave, "Measuring Fiscal Performance," *Review of Economics and Statistics*, May 1964, p. 217.

CHART 9. ACTUAL AND POTENTIAL GROSS NATIONAL PRODUCT
AND UNEMPLOYMENT RATE

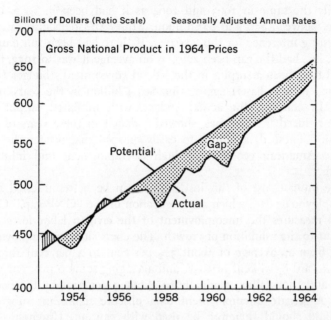

Billions of Dollars (Ratio Scale)   Seasonally Adjusted Annual Rates

Gross National Product in 1964 Prices

Potential

Gap

Actual

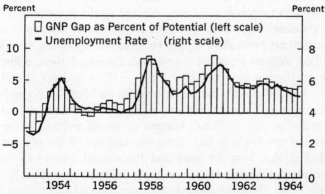

Percent   Percent

☐ GNP Gap as Percent of Potential (left scale)
▬ Unemployment Rate   (right scale)

SOURCE: *Economic Report of the President, 1965* (Washington, D.C.: U.S.G.-
P.O., 1965), p. 82.

current prices, and the loss of GNP on this basis from 1957 through 1962 was about $190 billion, again on the average a loss of some $35 billion per year.[19] Chart 9 indicates that the gap continued to be roughly the same in 1963 and 1964 as it had been in 1962, or in dollars between $30 and $35 billion. Musgrave's data also carry an interesting inference for the taxpayer. If there had been full employment, i.e., had the gap been zero, as on average it was to 1953, there would have been a surplus in the federal government's budget (on a national income basis) aggregating $64.4 billion in the years 1957–1962. In contrast, the actual budget, with inhibited output and hence reduced tax revenues, showed a deficit in these years of $4.9 billion.[20] These data reduce to easily grasped magnitudes the cost to the American economy of high unemployment and inhibited growth.

The human cost of this lost output can be better inferred from unemployment data which are a reflection of the "GNP gap." Chart 9 also measures the unemployment of the civilian labor force consequent to the inhibition of growth. The chart shows unemployment rising from an average of about 3½ per cent to 4 per cent through 1957 toward 8 per cent in 1958, and averaging some 6 per cent until 1962, and then falling gradually to about 5 per cent by the end of 1964. Aggregate unemployment data obscure significant subgroupings, and should therefore be used with caution. Unemployment "pockets" in certain regions can, because of the immobility of labor, exist simultaneously with shortages elsewhere. More significant, certain skills may be in short supply (e.g., secretaries or engineers) while unskilled workers remain unemployed. Given all these refinements, however, there is no doubt that the inhibition of demand and hence output has fallen with particular severity on Negroes. Since Negroes in general have less education and skills, because there are restrictions and prejudice against them, because as recent arrivals in the industrial-urban centers they lack seniority, and for all the other reasons, the fact is that between 1958 and the second quarter of 1965 the Negro unemployment rate was at all times at least double that of whites. With the continued strong expansion of the economy since

[19] Musgrave's measure of the GNP loss (in billions of dollars): 1957, $14.5; 1958, $39.5; 1959, $26.6; 1960, $32.2; 1961, $43.1; 1962, $32.0.
[20] Musgrave, op. cit., p. 217.

1961, the Negro unemployment rate finally fell to less than double the rate for the entire labor force in the second quarter of 1965 for the first time since 1957. With the economic expansion since 1962, the drop in Negro unemployment has been faster than in white unemployment.

It should be noted in passing that there has been some misinterpretation of the reasons for the high unemployment figures from 1957 to 1964. Some labor economists said that the *major* cause of unemployment was technological progress; the unemployed were "unemployable" because they did not have the skills required by the rapidly advancing technology. Retraining programs have been instituted to upgrade skills, and they are indeed valuable for the future. But service jobs still exist, including such mundane tasks as cutting lawns and washing dishes. It seems clear from the recent trend in the statistics that the unskilled depend far less for their jobs on retraining than on the aggregate level of demand, whatever may be their future fate. Those analysts who looked with skepticism on the technological structural hypothesis, feeling instead that the root of the problem was in the failure of aggregate demand to keep pace with productive capacity, seem to have been vindicated by the developments in 1965.

Beginning in 1961, under the Kennedy Administration, the United States commenced an economic expansion that has proved to be the longest in any peacetime period. While this expansion has not closed the gap, completely, it is quite clear that it is tending in that direction. Given the sentiments of the Johnson Administration toward fuller employment and social reforms—toward the "Great Society"—and given the ability of the Administration to obtain legislation to effect what it wants, continued expansion may soon begin to result in advancing price levels. Thus the United States, like the United Kingdom, is subject to the conflict between faster growth and stable prices. These Administrations have attempted to keep wage increases within the Council of Economic Advisers' "wage-price guidelines," i.e., to keep wage (and hence cost) increases within productivity increases for the whole economy, so that there will be no cost pressures on the average price level. But the movement of wages and costs in the unorganized industries such as personal services where little increase in productivity occurs will undoubtedly place further upward pressure on the price level as demand continues to expand even if the wage guidelines keep other prices the same.

That U.S. stagnation and relative deflation, whatever their inspiration, have resulted in a decline in American prices relative to those of Europe may be seen in Table 2 below, which compares trends in consumer prices since 1958. The rise in the U.S. consumer price index from 102 in 1960 to 109 in 1965 is the lowest increase among the major nations. As the policy emphasis shifts to fuller employment, it is dubious that the American price advantage, which accounts in part for the vast U.S. surpluses on current account, can be maintained to the same extent in the future.

TABLE 2. CONSUMER PRICES IN VARIOUS COUNTRIES, (1960–1965)
(Index: 1958 = 100)

	1960	1961	1962	1963	1964	First half 1965
United States	102	103	105	106	107	109
United Kingdom	101	104	109	112	115	120
France	110	114	119	125	130	133
Germany	102	105	108	111	114	116
Italy	102	104	109	117	124	128
Netherlands	103	105	108	113	119	120
Japan	105	111	118	127	132	140
Canada	102	103	104	106	108	110

SOURCE: IMF *International Financial Statistics*.

MONETARY-FISCAL POLICY

Part of the theory of the "classical medicine" requires a reduction in aggregate demand, and hence in income by means of higher interest rates and budgetary surpluses. Since 1960 the United States has, so to speak, split its approach and attempted to separate monetary from fiscal policy to accomplish two objectives at once. It has attempted to use fiscal policy to stimulate economic expansion. But monetary policy, including interest rates and debt management, has been designed to reduce capital outflows so as to improve the balance-of-payments position, while at the same time allowing the expansive fiscal policy to be effective.

The government's expansive fiscal policy has concentrated on taxes rather than expenditures, and has involved three major steps. First, the government has granted a 7 per cent tax credit to business for investment in plant and equipment. Designed to accelerate modernization of production facilities, it has also increased the demand for producers' goods. Actually, an important part of the sustained economic expansion from 1961 has reflected the increased demand for capital goods. Business capital spending, in part stimulated by this tax cut, has risen from a level of $50 billion in 1962 to approximately $65 billion (annual rates) by 1965, and is still trending upward. Second, depreciation allowances were liberalized in 1962 so that the costs of new capital equipment and plant could be written off more quickly and tax deduction achieved earlier. This step, in conjunction with the first, has had the effect noted above. Third, and most important, the reduction in personal and corporate income tax rates in 1964 has added an estimated $20 billion to the income stream; further adjustments were made by the reduction of federal excise tax on many items in 1965. By mid-1965, economic analysts were beginning to question the ability to sustain the economic expansion without further stimulus. As questions were raised, further tax cuts were being proposed in Congress. Rising expenditures for the Vietnam conflict have vitiated the need for such tax cuts. In any event, the point has been made that the government will not administer to the American economy a dose of the "classical medicine" sufficient to eliminate the balance-of-payments deficit, but will rely on other devices. Economic expansionism has achieved a priority over other considerations. If there were any doubt as to the validity of this priority in the minds of the American people, the 1964 elections should have settled it. But economic expansionism cannot fail to act with some degree of adversity on the balance-of-payments position in the future.

Monetary policy has been used for a different purpose as can be seen from Charts 10 and 11 below. Chart 10 compares American *long-term* interest rates with those of other countries. Long-term government bond yields are used as an indicator of other long-term interest rates. It is apparent from Chart 10 that American rates are still below most other countries (except Switzerland). Chart 11, which compares short-term interest rates of the same countries, shows that American rates have risen more rapidly than those in other countries, although in 1965 they were still below some of the European's.

CHART 10.   LONG-TERM INTEREST RATES IN VARIOUS COUNTRIES, 1958–1965

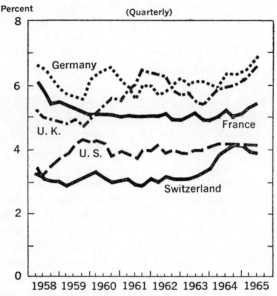

SOURCE: IMF, *International Financial Statistics.*

When the two charts are read together the policy described as "operation twist" may be seen. The purpose of "operation twist" was to keep the U.S. long-term interest rates low, so as not to depress internal economic expansion. At the same time, by raising the short-term interest rates, the attempt was made to keep short-term capital from going abroad in search of higher interest rates or even to attract short-term funds to the United States, so as to improve the balance of payments. In order to make "operation twist" effective, the Federal Reserve authorities discarded their self-imposed limitation to the "bills only doctrine" and now feel free to extend open-market operations to the entire maturity range of government securities, rather than to Treasury bills only which had been the previous policy.

Monetary analysts have raised a number of questions about the

CHART 11. SHORT-TERM INTEREST RATES IN VARIOUS COUNTRIES, 1958–1965

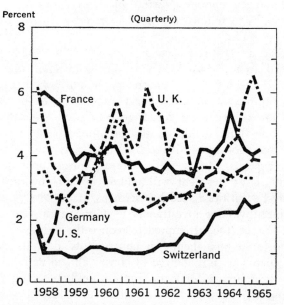

SOURCE: IMF, *International Financial Statistics.*

schism between fiscal and monetary policy. Thus while U.S. long-term interest rates have remained fairly constant, there has been a rise despite the high unemployment levels. To further increase long-term interest rates would probably not affect the balance of payments significantly, since the principal long-term outflow of capital is direct investment in the subsidiaries of U.S. corporations and not capital outflow in search of an interest rate advantage. But while international capital movements are no doubt more sensitive to short-term than to long-term rates, the latter also have an impact on long-term portfolio investments and bank loans. It is for this reason that the Treasury requested the interest equalization tax, which in effect reduces the interest return on private portfolio investment in Europe or Japan. Furthermore, these analysts point out that there is communication between sectors of the capital market which limits the range within which long-term and short-term yields can be separated. Put differently, they feel that a continued increase of short-term rates must eventually force the long-term yields up, to the detriment of internal economic growth. One objective of the direct control program is to remove the *need* to resort to such interest rate rises.[21]

The American task has been partially eased by certain policy actions abroad. In 1964 both Germany and Switzerland took measures to discourage the inflow and encourage the outflow of private capital. For example, in February 1964, new issues of bonds of the Federal German Republic could be purchased only by German residents. The Bundesbank has also prohibited payment of interest on time deposits of nonresidents, and raised reserve requirements on foreigners' deposits. Moreover, the German government imposed on nonresidents a 25 per cent withholding tax on any income from fixed interest securities issued by Germans. It has also provided certain tax incentives for investments by Germans in less developed countries. France, too, attempted to reduce the inflow of capital by prohibiting interest payments on nonresidents' deposits. Moreover, French residents are not allowed to borrow abroad without approval of the Bank of France for loans over one million francs. Thus, the surplus countries have made some efforts to reduce their surpluses, but most revolve around capital inflows, and to these there is attached a degree of self-interest in that they are attempting to reduce

---

[21] Discussions of interest rates are often fraught with emotional overtones. Advocates of the "classical medicine" and European advocates of "discipline" in the United States inevitably recommend higher interest rates. It has been contended that the banking community, which also seems always to favor higher interest rates, does so with an eye to its profits as well as to the welfare of the nation. On this Galbraith has written (*op. cit.*, p. 118):

"The rate of interest in the United States can only be understood as the one price that has been, in some sense, consecrated. Producers of wheat, copper, cotton, and even steel are assumed to prefer higher prices for the larger revenues they return. Those who lend money, in contrast, are permitted to urge higher interest rates not for the greater return but as a selfless step designed to protect the nation from the evils of soft money, loose financial practices, and deficient economic morality. An economist who sees the need for a higher weekly wage may well be suspected of yielding to the unions; one who urges an increase in the rediscount rate is, however, invariably a statesman. This should not keep anyone from penetrating to the fact. There is a lively, insistent, and durable preference by the money-lending community for high rates of return; this is related to an intelligent view of pecuniary self-interest. It would be astonishing were it otherwise. . . ."

the liquidity of their banking systems which represents a potential inflationary threat.

In summary, the "classical medicine" is designed to reduce domestic prices and costs so that American exports will be competitive abroad and to reduce the incentive for capital outflows. It is apparent that this effort has resulted from, or at any rate been accompanied by, huge losses of potential output and employment which could otherwise have been enjoyed by the American people. While official pronouncements have denied any conflict between domestic goals and balance-of-payments needs, the United States has obviously altered its policy to meet the latter, at least in so far as interest rates are concerned. However, by mid-1965, as the sustained economic expansion brings the American economy closer to a full utilization of its resources, a more stringent test may be at hand. Probably the earlier relative deflation will continue to provide the United States with a price advantage over Europe, even if U.S. prices begin now to rise in response to the expansion. More important, however, are the direct controls, which affect many categories of the balance of payments and which are designed to operate in conjunction with, or if necessary as a substitute for, the price advantages gained by the American use of the "classical medicine." It is to these controls that we now turn.

DIRECT CONTROLS

Since 1962 the United States has increasingly resorted to direct controls and *ad hoc* measures to improve its balance-of-payments position. Following Galbraith's colorful terminology, the controls to date may be divided into two classes: those with "cosmetic" or "public relations" value, and those more basic. The economic impact of the former is impossible to assess, but is probably not great. The more basic steps have had a considerable economic impact, but leave at least two key questions unanswered: Are they adequate? And since, as indicated earlier, the answer may be negative, what next?

"Cosmetic" controls include a number of devices, some of which are here used as examples, with no pretense to completeness. In 1963 the U.S. Department of Commerce undertook an export sales promotion drive consisting of U.S. trade fairs abroad, the provision of information on possible markets for individual exporters, etc. The program was not vigorously pursued, largely because it would hardly have been worth its cost. Similarly, the stimulation of tourist travel to the United States, attempts to *discourage* American tourism abroad, the reduction of duty-free imports from abroad by tourists, campaigns to sell savings bonds to soldiers abroad or to inhibit the travel of their dependents (while civilians remain free to travel), attempts to "persuade" Japan and even Hong Kong to reduce their textile and other exports to the United States, all of which are *ad hoc*, humiliating to Americans, restrictive of American freedom, and unable even in the aggregate to alter the fundamental balance-of-payments position. On the contrary, the measures have been criticized because each contains elements of self-delusion, and false tranquilization of the public may merely postpone more relevant action. A further danger is the ever present temptation to extend such measures. It was recently proposed to Congress, for example, that Americans should forcefully be prevented from living abroad, presumably on the theory that Manhattan, Carmel and East Hampton are tolerable substitutes for Paris and Capri.

However, it is not on these or the many other "cosmetic" actions that the government has relied for its effective policy. In 1963, the government brought into the battle its heavy artillery in the form of a number of direct controls aimed at bank lending, at inhibition of corporate investment abroad, and similar steps. These are in effect exchange controls, although they have never been so labeled openly. The first was the interest equalization tax, first requested in July 1963, with retroactive effect. It was a hurried response to the large capital outflows then taking place. Its provisions impose a tax on purchases of long-term foreign securities of up to 15 per cent of the purchase price, depending on the maturity of the security. In effect, the tax was designed to raise the interest cost of foreign borrowing in the United States by about 1 per cent per year and thereby to remove the incentive for the sale of foreign securities in the United States, and thus reduce the capital outflow. When it became law in September 1963, it exempted Canadian securities issues in U.S. capital markets as well as borrowings by underdeveloped countries.

The interest equalization tax had an important impact on capital outflows from the outset. New issues of foreign securities in the

United States declined from $1.9 billion in the first half of 1963 to $0.6 billion in the second half. Simultaneously, trade in outstanding securities switched from a $302 million outflow in the first half to a $204 million inflow in the second. In 1964 these low rates were maintained. But loans by U.S. banks for terms longer than one year, seeking higher interest rates abroad began to substitute for the foreign security issues as a source of capital outflow. From the first half of 1963, when long-term bank loans amounted to $322 million, they rose to over $1 billion by the third quarter of 1964. Thus, substitute capital facilities were found and tapped by foreign borrowers.

In criticizing the interest equalization tax (which in August 1965 was extended to run through 1966), Galbraith contended that it was inadequate; it did not touch direct investment of American corporations, which is the largest part of private capital outflows. He proposed instead

A more effective procedure . . . to establish a capital issues committee, authority for which exists under Section 5(b) of the Trading with the Enemy Act of 1917. Subject to appropriate exemptions, it would control access to the issues market. Under the same authority, it would also authorize expansion and take over investment by American corporations involving substantial commitment of dollars abroad.[22]

In February 1965, President Johnson announced a "voluntary program" to further limit private capital outflow, but did not go as far as the capital issues committee. Instead, (1) the interest equalization tax was extended to bank loans (under the provisions of the Gore amendment to the September 1963 act); and (2) "guidelines" were established for foreign lending by banks and other financial institutions and for total foreign payments and receipts by business concerns.

Under the Gore amendment provision, banks also paid the interest equalization tax, which reduced the effective yield on loans abroad by approximately 1 per cent, or closer to American levels.

Under the "guidelines," the banks were to have loaned during 1965 not more than 5 per cent more than their total outstanding at the end of 1964. This meant that the rapid rate of increase in bank lending would be reduced. Although voluntary, the program was to

22 *Ibid.*, p. 119.

be administered by the Federal Reserve System. It involved receiving reports from a relatively small number of banks, about 150, of which no more than 20 do the vast bulk of foreign lending.

The effects of this program on bank lending were phenomenal. During the first half of 1965, the growth in foreign loans and investments by banks was reduced to an annual rate of less than $100 million from a record of $2,500 million in 1964. Financial intermediaries other than banks (for example, insurance companies), which in 1964 had increased their credits and investments abroad by $1 billion, held their expansion in the first half of 1965 to less than $150 million. During the April–June quarter of 1965, the banks actually returned $380 million to New York. Chart 12 below indicates the changes in the volume of lending abroad during 1964 and the first half of 1965.

CHART 12.   THE BANKS RESPOND

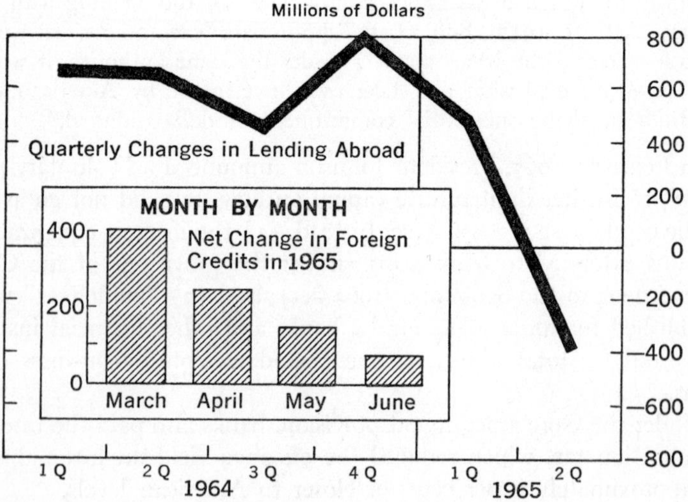

Millions of Dollars

SOURCE: *The Economist*, September 4, 1965, p. 911.

With reference to corporate investment abroad, it has been noted earlier that much of it is for the purpose of expanding subsidiaries or increasing production facilities of American-owned companies. The outlays return vast amounts of earnings to America over the years, in the form of interest and dividend payments. The data relating to investment and return are seen in Table 3 below.

Table 3 compares investment and income from investment since 1958 in three categories. Items 1 and 2 tabulate *all* private (excluding government) long-term investment abroad. (Long-term means investments with a repayment period—maturity—which exceeds one year.) This total consists of two subtotals: first (Item 3), direct investment, which in the main means corporate spending for plant and equipment abroad with funds obtained in the United States and excluding funds obtained abroad through retained earnings or foreign borrowings; second (Item 5), other investment, including the purchase of stocks and bonds (portfolio), long-term bank loans, and other items noted.

Focusing on direct investment (Item 3) for the moment, its significant rise—doubling from $1.2 billion in 1958 to $2.4 billion in 1964—attests the increasing desire of corporations to tap foreign markets, for both production and sales. Perhaps more important, however, is the extraordinary return on past direct investment, which was $3.7 billion in 1964, and in 1965 is running at an annual rate of some $4.5 billion. Clearly, this results from past investment, to which new investment adds greater future potential return, and clearly also, this is one of the great sources of strength in the U.S. balance of payments. The sharp cut in the rate of investment in the second quarter of 1965 reflects the direct control program on corporate investment. The income will not fall immediately because of the backlog of earning power. But to continue to inhibit investment in future will surely cut this income and weaken the future balance-of-payments position.

With respect to Items 5 and 6, the investment return ratio is not as high, for a number of reasons: the rapid increase in loan extensions by banks, the slower repayment time of portfolio as opposed to direct investment, and so on.

The combined income from these sources, which equaled $5 billion in 1964 and is running at a rate nearly $6 billion in 1965, enters the balance of payments as a "service receipt," and is thus part of the "balance on private goods and services," Item 2 in Table 1 (p. 154). This is the United States largest service income item, and should

TABLE 3. U.S. PRIVATE LONG-TERM INVESTMENT ABROAD: OUTGO AND INCOME
(*billions of dollars*)

	1958	1959	1960	1961	1962	1963	1964	1965 [b] (1 Q)	(2 Q)
1. Total private long-term investment	2.6	2.3	2.6	2.6	2.9	3.6	4.4	1.7	0.9
2. Income on all private investments	2.5	2.7	3.0	3.6	3.9	4.1	5.0	1.4	1.4
3. Direct investment	1.2	1.4	1.7	1.6	1.7	2.0	2.4	1.0	1.0
4. Income from (3)	2.1	2.2	2.3	2.8	3.0	3.1	3.7	1.1	1.1
5. Other private long-term [a]	1.4	0.9	0.9	1.0	1.2	1.6	2.0	0.7	-0.1
6. Income from (5) and short-term investments	0.4	0.5	0.7	0.8	0.9	1.0	1.3	0.3	0.3

SOURCE: U.S. Department of Commerce, *Survey of Current Business*, various issues.

[a] Includes portfolio investment, long-term bank loans, trade in outstanding foreign securities, and other.
[b] 1965 data are preliminary.

be built, not repressed. In contrast, in the same account, travel, meaning tourism, cost the United States $1.1 billion in 1964, as Americans spent $2.2 billion abroad while foreigners spent $1.1 billion on U.S. tourism. On transportation (mainly shipping and air transport) the United States spent $2.5 billion in 1964, but earned (thanks mainly to airlines) $2.3 billion, holding the loss on this account to $200 million. A comparison of other items in the "service" account with investment income (Item 2 of Table 3) underscores the importance of the latter; if it is reduced, it is difficult to see what type of income of the requisite magnitude could conceivably compensate for the loss.

The immediate response of the American corporations to the President's "voluntary program" was to repatriate liquid funds held abroad. In the first quarter of 1965 this repatriation amounted to $240 million, and it was continuing at a reduced pace in the second quarter. The corporations, in order to cooperate, have canceled or postponed some investment projects. But this contribution—a little over $100 million—amounts to, in the *Economist's* term, "a flea bite." Furthermore, the attempt has been made by some companies to raise capital for their foreign expansion in overseas capital markets. By September 1965, however, the plans to borrow had totaled a modest $300 million.[23] It had been hoped that the "voluntary" restriction program would induce corporations to reduce their investments abroad. However, in the first half of 1965 corporations invested some $2.0 billion, only $400 million less than the whole 1964 figure; for 1965 as a whole the figure promised to be about $1 billion in excess of 1964. Moreover, the hoped-for increase in exports did not materialize, adding only 1.5 per cent to the 1964 rate. By September 1965 it had become apparent that the voluntary program to restrict corporate investment abroad was not working in sufficient magnitude to have the desired effect on the balance of payments. It is therefore logical that the more severe controls in this area were enacted for 1966. This further underscores the tendency to "drift toward controls" in lieu of a more adequate adjustment mechanism.

There are several possible reasons why the United States decided to attempt to stanch the outflow of dollars, and hence of gold

[23] See "Volunteers, under Protest," *The Economist*, September 4, 1965, p. 911.

through a reduction of private capital spending abroad. The most obvious is that it is a large figure and relatively easily controlled. Those who favor direct controls had recommended restriction of the capital outflow prior to its initiation. Another reason, suggested previously, is the American acquiescence to European demands in this respect. The campaign to restrict American corporations was mounted initially in France, where newspaper stories reflecting the sentiment of French businessmen and government officials continually cite such facts as General Motors' annual sales are larger than the Netherlands' gross national product, and that General Electric's turnover is more than six times that of the entire French electronics industry. The campaign is said to be directed by the French Employers Association, the Conseil National du Patronat Francais.[24]

An analysis of "Le Patronat's" actions and motives asserts that French businessmen are trying simultaneously to reduce American competition, and by focusing on the dangers of it, to minimize the action of the antitrust provisions in French law and in the EEC's Rome Treaty so that they may themselves establish larger units; and, additionally, to win more backing in their opposition to the tariff cuts being proposed in the "Kennedy round" of trade negotiations. These desires fit President de Gaulle's political aim of reducing European dependence on the United States and so are supported by the French government. "Le Patronate" is a pyramid of business organizations, operating through trade associations, which claims to speak for 900,000 French companies. The views of "Le Patronat" are expressed by Georges Villiers; they are not in every sense "Gaullist" but run strongly to a Europe without Britain, and with a minimum of American competition.

These fears are reflected in various other countries in varying degrees, in most cases far less vociferously. However, the Federation of Catholic Employers in the Netherlands reflects "Le Patronat's" views and has warned that the financial strength of U.S. companies is so great that the competitive relationships can be completely distorted unless the Americans maintain the necessary self-control. Germany's automobile manufacturers have agreed to cooperate to meet competition from General Motors and Ford which together

[24] "U.S. Capital Stirs Fears in Europe," *Business Week*, December 5, 1964.

control nearly 40 per cent of the German market. On the other hand, Belgium continues to offer investment subsidies to American corporations.

The fear of American penetration focuses on specific types of enterprises including computers, ball bearings, home appliances, chemicals, and oils. The competition of American giants has stimulated mergers in France and other European countries. While the Common Market's antitrust laws are severe, it is doubtful that they apply to mergers. EEC vice-president Robert Marjolin has said, "I am for company mergers which will enable European firms to attain the dimensions of their American counterparts, but I am against cartels." [25]

While the American government has restricted capital investment, and business is cooperating with the government to do so, the cooperation is restive and promises to be short-lived. Most American economists accept our acquiescence in this part of the government's program only as a necessary and short-term expedient, to be abandoned as quickly as possible. P. B. Kenen has argued that U.S. capital outflows to Europe, as well as to less developed countries, are justified on theoretical grounds. Europe lags behind the United States in two important capital-intensive categories—housing and consumer durable goods. A sizable portion of each is financed by credit, and U.S. capital investment in Europe provides a source of credit which releases funds to finance these rapidly expanding expenditures. European economists, as noted in Chapter I, are ambivalent about the reduction of American investment in Europe, as it has fueled a good part of Europe's growth. Despite these fears, the aggregate ownership of American manufacturing capacity in Europe is still relatively small, some 3 to 4 per cent of the European total.

With reference both to bank (and other intermediaries) lending and to direct investment, the spectacular initial success of the President's program seems to have reflected a one-shot adjustment. Its impact did convert the American deficit to a surplus in the second quarter of 1965, but many of its effects are likely to be nonrecurring, and it is no doubt for this reason that Secretary Fowler correctly expected a new deficit in the third quarter. Undoubtedly, part

[25] *Ibid.*

of the voluntary restraints are effective out of fear that they might be made law, or out of fear that banks which failed to cooperate might meet with something less than cooperation in tapping the discount window of the Federal Reserve. However, even if all the cooperation was purely patriotic fervor, there is ample evidence now that both banks and business would like to be freer in these matters. Thus George Champion, chairman of the Chase Manhattan Bank, is quoted as being fearful of "government by guideline" which is leading to federal domination behind "a façade of friendliness." [26]

The reduction in U.S. capital outflows from all sources in 1965 had an initially adverse effect on European liquidity. One of the indications that the U.S. deficit has provided the liquidity for much of the rest of the world is the Euro-dollar market.[27] In this market U.S. dollars (as well as some few other foreign currencies) are deposited with foreign banks. These deposits are normally time deposits, earning interest at a higher rate than can be earned in the United States on comparable forms, and supplied by American and foreign holders of dollars. Repayment and interest is denominated in dollars. Foreign banks hold these deposits, in turn lending them to foreigners. The bankers earn interest on them in excess of what they in turn pay the depositors. The Euro-dollar market is relatively large, totaling $5 billion in 1963 (plus an additional $2 billion of other currencies). This has been an important source of credit abroad. Its importance as a marginal credit source for European and Japanese borrowing is hardly reflected even in its sizable volume. Euro-dollar loans have been instrumental in providing liquidity (secondary reserves) for European banks as well as a source of credit for financing capital and trade. In a very important sense, Euro-dollars are another manifestation of the reserve status of the dollar, substituting for gold reserves and acting as an international medium of exchange and a standard of deferred payments abroad.

When the President's program was announced in February 1965, the impact on the Euro-dollar market was severe and quick. Identified withdrawals of short-term funds by American banks, business

26 *The Economist*, June 5, 1965, p. 1,146.
27 See A. Holmes and F. Klopstock, "The Market for Dollar Deposits in Europe," Federal Reserve Bank of N.Y. *Monthly Review*, November 1960.

corporations, and financial intermediaries from Canada and Europe over the first half of the year totaled over $600 million, most of it after March 1965. In the Euro-dollar market a sudden spectacular hardening of interest rates occurred. Further data show a $300 million drop in dollar liabilities of London banks during April—June 1965. By September 1965, however, the interest rate impact was over. Rates on Euro-dollar deposits had come back down very close to the levels prevailing earlier. To some extent this occurred because British and Canadian banks, in Secretary Fowler's words, "refilled the pool by withdrawals of funds from American banks." But in addition, a large number of dollars held on the Continent, including a large supply from the German Bundesbank, came into the Euro-dollar market.[28] This squeeze on European liquidity, which has in fact proved very temporary, has nevertheless furthered concern about the problem of liquidity in the event of an American surplus. By September 1965, as the American surplus seems again less imminent, the fear of a liquidity crisis appears so too. Thus the impact of the "voluntary program" and that of European illiquidity were simultaneous, and seem to have worn off at about the same time. Despite the focus of attention on steps to improve world liquidity, this problem seems now far less important than the continuing internal problems raised by the American balance-of-payments deficit.

MEASURES TO REDUCE THE LOSS OF GOLD

Another group of measures have been employed to minimize the gold loss which are, in one sense, designed to give the United States more time to eliminate its deficit—i.e., to remove the need for severe restraint and allow the measures outlined above to bear fruit.

These measures were primarily engineered by former Under Secretary of the Treasury Roosa, and may be grouped into three categories: (1) raising short-term interest rates to make dollar asset holdings more attractive relative to gold, (2) arrangements for credit facilities to stave off a run on the dollar (or other currency), and (3) measures to neutralize foreign official dollar holdings by turning them into longer-term assets ("Roosa bonds").

The first measure, raising short-term interest rates, has been dis-

28 See *The Economist*, September 4, 1965, *op. cit.*

cussed earlier as part of "operation twist." This has the double effect of tending to reduce U.S. short-term capital outflows, and thus reduce the deficit, and to make more attractive foreign short-term investment in the United States, thereby reducing the gold drain, which was the original objective. In 1962, the Federal Reserve sanctioned a rise in the interest rate paid to foreign official institutions on time deposits at commercial banks. Later, the general rise in short-term interest rates made possible higher return on all foreign-held short-term dollar assets. Thus, to convert dollar holdings to gold would have cost more in lost interest income than before. This has not entirely inhibited foreign countries from converting dollars to gold, as the "soundness" of the dollar has declined, the magnitude of conversions by France, Germany, and others has been earlier noted.

The second group of measures constitutes means of extending credit to deficit countries with weak currencies. These indications of international cooperation include the "General Arrangements to Borrow," in which the Group of Ten countries grant short-term credits to the IMF which in turn lends to a country whose currency is weak, such as the United Kingdom in late 1964 and again in September 1965. The United States has not utilized these *ad hoc* facilities as yet, although it has borrowed from the IMF on occasion.

Another device which the United States has employed frequently is "currency swaps." This involves the temporary exchange of the currencies of two countries. The "weak currency" country (United States) then uses the foreign exchange received in the swap to support its own currency on the foreign exchange market temporarily, with the idea of repurchasing the foreign exchange for dollars when its own currency regains strength. The swap can then be reversed. The United States has entered into currency swaps with Canada, France, the United Kingdom, Germany, and other countries on a number of occasions since 1962. At mid-1965 the total amount available under outstanding "swap" agreements is in excess of $2 billion. Since 1962, the United States has drawn almost that amount at one time or another, although most of these swaps have been reversed.[29]

The other main approach to financing the deficit is the sale of

[29] See C. A. Coombs, "Treasury and Federal Reserve Foreign Exchange Operations," Federal Reserve Bank of N.Y. *Monthly Review*, September 1964. Periodic reports on such operations appear in this publication.

"Roosa bonds" to foreign governments. These bonds are inter-mediate-term U.S. government securities (maturities of between one and two years), and are sold for dollar holdings of foreign official institutions. Most "Roosa bonds" are denominated in foreign cur-rencies, thus eliminating any possible loss to holders through U.S. devaluation; but repayment by the United States requires that it earn the foreign exchange necessary to repay the bonds before their maturity. The sale of these bonds has no effect on the balance of payments, since this only exchanges one type of U.S. liability (short-term) for another ("Roosa bond"). They do, however, neutralize for the term of the bond foreign-held dollars which might have been used to buy gold. Thus they are merely a device for buying time.[30] These bonds have been sold to a number of countries, especially Switzerland, Germany, and Italy. Sales of such bonds amounted to $702 million in 1963 and $375 million in 1964.

It will be readily apparent that while these measures all have a degree of ingenuity, and serve a short-run expedient purpose, they do nothing to improve the basic imbalance on international ac-count. Nor—in fairness—are they designed to. The role assigned to Treasury technicians in this context limits them to this type of "jug-gling," while the basic attack on the balance-of-payments problem must proceed on a deeper level. This attack cuts across the bounda-ries of politics and economics, and draws into the vortex of discus-sion the whole range of modern governmental responsibility, includ-ing full employment, world power, and the freedom of the citizenry. And as the discussion starts with unresolved questions about these basics, so it must end there; for there is yet no clear, and certainly no easy, resolution of the dollar's dilemma.

THE PROSPECTS

It is apparent from the foregoing that the American response to the balance-of-payments problem has been eclectic. No single pos-ture has been assumed or carried to its logical conclusion. Thus, some of the "classical medicine" has been used to reduce relative costs

[30] For a discussion of these bonds by their originator, see the testimony of Robert Roosa in Joint Economic Committee Hearings, "The United States Bal-ance of Payments," Pt. 1, July 8–9, 1963, pp. 96–101.

and prices in the United States, but not enough to do the whole job, and under the Johnson Administration the further use of this medicine is unlikely. Some controls have been instituted, but not the full range proposed by Galbraith, including import restrictions and a capital issues committee.

The restriction of capital export now bears the major burden of adjustment. It is a program admittedly detrimental to the balance of payments in the long run, but is necessary because of short-run pressures to reduce the U.S. deficit. But even in the short run there is doubt that capital restriction may give rise to new problems, perhaps leading to new controls. The "voluntary" program has been made more stringent for nonfinancial corporations in 1966, and the restriction on bank lending and the interest equalization tax have been extended in time. Leaks have appeared, since capital markets are interconnected. United States corporations borrowing abroad drive up European interest rates and thus short-term capital may flow out. United States investors can earn more on American-guaranteed bonds issued abroad than can be earned at home, so foreign portfolio investment may rise too. The balance of payments is weakened in the long run and in the short run will improve only if these leaks are not large and can be controlled. May this sequence not call forth still more and greater controls?

Exchange rate adjustments have not been used. However, critics of the steps that have been taken are fond of pointing out that some controls are in fact devaluations of the dollar for specific, spot purposes. Thus the interest equalization tax, by deducting 15 per cent from the dollar's value when it is used to purchase foreign securities, is in fact a 15 per cent devaluation for that purpose; similarly, the policy of purchasing supplies for the Armed Forces within the United States rather than abroad, if American prices for the relevant goods do not exceed 150 per cent of their cost abroad, is a devaluation of up to 50 per cent for that purpose.

Taken together, the eclectic and partial steps used do not seem to have solved the problem, so that in the fall of 1965 the United States remains with the deficit. True, the deficit is less, but this is a temporary respite from a problem crying for more profound solution.

One of the more confusing aspects of the American position is the American penchant for worrying about other nations' problems *if* the United States were in surplus, when in fact it has not solved the key problem of getting itself into surplus, or into tolerable proximity to it. This confusion manifests itself in what some critics have called a tendency to "technical escape" under which vast effort is expended in concern about the world's liquidity if the United States ended its deficit. It is noted in the discussion of the plans for reform (Chapter VII) that several of the plans for increasing world liquidity, including the Bernstein (or Composite Reserve Unit), Triffin, and now the Roosa plans start from this premise. Per se, none of these plans offers any solution for the U.S. deficit, and in fact they are not designed to do so.

One of the paths increasingly often suggested is for the United States to reduce its military and aid commitments. This is often phrased as "tailoring our burdens to our resources." What is really meant, however, is that by these steps the United States should reduce its burdens to its available foreign receipts, which are different from its resources. Factual comparison of American aid to developing nations with that of other industrial countries belies the opinion that the United States is giving excessive aid. In dollar amounts U.S. aid is greater, but as a percentage of its GNP, the United States during the period 1956–1962 gave an average of .5 of 1 per cent, compared with .6 of 1 per cent for France, .4 of 1 per cent for Japan, .3 of 1 per cent for Germany (a figure increased in 1963 and 1964), and .4 of 1 per cent for the United Kingdom. The average aid figure of all Western bloc nations is .5 of 1 per cent, just equal to the U.S. figure.[31]

Military expenditures are, however, a different story. For here the United States does bear a disproportionately large share of the total, in the aggregate and in foreign expenditures. Again, using the 1956–1962 total as a percentage of GNP, the United States spent 9.7 per cent; France, 3.5 per cent (prior to the cessation of war in Algeria); Germany, 3.2 per cent; Japan, 1.4 per cent; and the United Kingdom, 6.7 per cent. Therefore the argument that expenditures should be tailored to resources (or surpluses) really bears most heavily on the military. One of the obvious means to improve the U.S. balance of payments would be to obtain a

[31] Data from S. W. Rousseas, *The Political Dilemma of American Captialism* to be published in 1966.

more equitable sharing of the military burden among the Western nations. Since this could also involve a sharing of power, this approach faces important politico-military barriers, which may preclude it.

Two suggested solutions for the American problem have been made by important political groups. The report of the Republican Coordinating Committee, a study group established to "solve" the balance-of-payments problem, is, as might be expected of the outs, very critical of the policies of the Democratic ins. Rhetoric aside, its basic suggested solutions are: (1) monetary-fiscal policy which might be described as more relative deflation by higher interest rates and smaller budgetary deficits; and (2) reductions in both military and aid programs. With reference to troops abroad, the report says "the time has long since arrived for a substantial reduction of our excessive military establishment in Western Europe." With respect to aid, the government should "reduce the cost of foreign economic aid programs, especially by confining assistance to those countries which maintain a hospitable climate for private investment capital." The report condemns the Johnson Administration's program of voluntary controls over lending and investing abroad as "ultimately self-defeating," "artificial," and "expedient." [32]

Second, the Congressional subcommittee on international exchange and payments of the Joint Economic Committee, which consists of five Democrats and three Republicans, headed by Representative Henry Reuss, has unanimously offered its "Guidelines" for monetary reform in a report dated September 1965.[33]

Much of the report focuses on the question of international liquidity. It advocates that new monetary reserves be created through the IMF, but makes no firm choice among the available plans for doing so. It distinguishes clearly, however, between the international problems of additional liquidity and internal problems of adjustment: "no amount of liquidity would suffice if payments imbalances were not brought to an end." Of major interest in the Reuss report is the im-

[32] "The Balance of Payments, the Gold Drain, and Your Dollar," Republican National Committee (Washington, 1965).
[33] "Guidelines for Improving the International Monetary System," Report, Subcommittee on International Exchange and Payments of the Joint Economic Committee, Congress of the U.S.A. (Washington: U.S.G.P.O., 1965).

pact of international reform on internal policy, i.e., on ending imbalances:

International financial reforms, however desirable, are not sufficient. Substantial improvements are needed in the adjustment process which brings international imbalances to an end.

The Committee makes two major recommendations that bear on this question: first, that international monetary and fiscal policy should be "harmonized" to create rules of the game, particularly in regard to capital controls, which do not exist now; and, second, that the time may now be ripe for a complete study of an evolutionary step in the system to allow "a modest broadening of the present limits of exchange rate variations," i.e., fluctuating exchange rates within reasonably narrow bands.

With respect to international harmonization, the Committee notes that some surplus nations have increased their interest rates and even reduced taxes when they should have reduced interest rates to discourage capital inflow and encourage capital outflows and raised taxes to curb inflationary pressures. These inappropriate policies have greatly intensified the difficulties of adjustment in the United States because they have offset the intended effect of the raising of American interest rates.

Part of the harmonization required is to institute some type of code of national behavior with respect to restriction of capital movements for balance-of-payments reasons. The report notes that

there may be circumstances when restrictions on capital movements are the best—least worst—response to a difficult problem . . . but the long-run objective must be to continue to seek freedom for international capital transactions as well as for trade.

This the Committee feels can best be done by achieving agreement among nations on the principles governing the restrictions on capital movements, pointing out that the focus of past effort, reflected in the GATT agreements, has been on freeing trade movements. But the IMF does not regulate restrictions on capital movements. While some progress toward agreed-upon rules of conduct has already been achieved through the liberalization of capital movements negotiated within the OECD, this work, the report indicates, should be extended to the establishment of general principles and priorities to govern the use of restrictions on capital movements.

The second point made—the recommendation of more flexible rates is probably the Committee's most important. While the report is technically asking the Johnson Administration to *study* the problem, it is quite obvious that the Committee has thought about the problem a great deal and is actually asking the Administration to show why this position should not be adopted. The report cites the advantages, both historical and at present, of broadening the limits of permissible exchange rate variation.

It asks:

What are the disadvantages of broader exchange rate limits? Are there any, or is it simply that the idea is at variance with the current preferences of central bankers? We do not seek change for the sake of change, and would not lightly recommend that current practices be altered. But if inconsistency with current practices were sufficient reason to oppose change, we would never progress.

The report reminds its readers that in 1964 and again in 1965 the Joint Economic report had asked the Administration for a study of the feasibility of more flexibility. Moreover, the Banking and Currency committee of the House in its April 1965 report also endorsed consideration and study of broader limits of exchange rate variation. These requests for study have been ignored. It is interesting that in Germany, in the United Kingdom, and in the United States there has appeared something of a schism between academic economists—and now the Joint Committee—many of whom have favored some form of exchange rate flexibility, and government officials who have treated these recommendations with such contempt that they did not even bother to rebut them. Wider bands of fluctuation would, for both the United Kingdom and the United States, result in depreciating currencies at the outset, which would presumably enable these countries to increase their balance on current account.

Exchange rate variations were made a part of the original IMF agreements. Indeed, a rereading of the basic papers of Keynes and White makes it clear they were a *sine qua non* for the system to work. The provision of the IMF agreements which allows exchange rate variations could not be followed by the deficit countries because of the fear of the consequences for and from their reserve status. The IMF rules also provide that variation of spot rates are to be no more than 1 per cent on either side of parity. In practice the European countries limit their rate variation to plus or minus .75 of 1 per cent. Some adopt even more restrictions.

Having taken a vast amount of learned testimony and having boxed the compass, so to speak, from every point of view, it is significant that the report sees in flexible exchange rates the method by which the balance of payments may seek some inherent adjustment, without superimposing further the panoply of controls and other devices which must be onerous to anyone who continues to believe in the values of free trade and free capital movements.

In all of the twists and turns of policy-fixing, it is all too easy to lose a basic sense of what this is all about. It is therefore a welcome affirmation of first principles in the Report that:

It is one of the ironies and inconsistencies of modern life that, to protect fixed exchange rates—the means—we have compromised freedom of capital movements and, to some extent, of trade—the ends which the fixed rates are intended to serve.

CHAPTER VII

Plans for Reform

THE previous two chapters have attempted to show how costly and difficult adjustments within the existing gold-exchange system have been for the United States and the United Kingdom. In the case of Britain, inability to adjust has almost brought down the international payments system. Indeed, only an *ad hoc* reform of the system, the extension of massive credits to the United Kingdom under the Group of Ten's "General Arrangements to Borrow," has saved the system, perhaps temporarily.

One of the major mechanisms of adjustment, exchange rate variation, has been denied to the United States and United Kingdom, despite their persistent deficits and fundamental disequilibrium, for a variety of reasons of which reserve currency status loomed most important in Anglo-American minds. The plight of the reserve currencies alone, and its implicit threat to the system would be sufficient reason to evoke consideration of reform of the system. There are others.

Since the inception of the Bretton Woods system discontent has been expressed with the highly evolved gold-exchange standard it established. This discontent has multiplied since 1958, when the major European currencies restored convertibility and the United States developed chronic and sizable balance-of-payments deficits. The free flow of capital permitted by relatively free convertibility of currencies, the sizable dollar outflows and gold losses of the United States, and the recurring balance-of-payments difficulties of the United Kingdom have all placed unexpected stresses on the Bretton Woods system. A growing consensus doubts the ability of the existing system to meet these, to say nothing of likely future problems, without serious breakdown.

Broadly speaking, two types of reform have been proposed. One would improve the adjustment mechanisms of the system. The other would increase and regularize the supply of liquidity. Until mid-1965, official American opinion favored the latter type of reform, although there persisted within both the United States and the United Kingdom an academic "underground" of opinion that the former was in more serious need of repair. The inspiration for the official American position was twofold: a genuine concern that the system would lack liquidity and suffer shrinkage when American deficits became surpluses; and an inversely related belief that additional liquidity creation would somehow permit persistent deficits, as some of the additional liquidity would accrue to the deficit nations.

While the initial urge for reform came from Europe, the United States has now concurred it is necessary. Secretary Fowler has asked a major conference for the purpose of reforming the system. There is some indication too, as noted in Chapter VI, that at least semi-official American thinking in Congress has shifted its focus from liquidity as the sole desideratum to both adjustment and improved liquidity creation.

Problems under the Existing System

The world monetary system set up under the Bretton Woods agreement (1945) is a fixed exchange rate system. The rates of exchange between currencies are stable, for they are fixed within 1 per cent limits around the par value. The par of a country's currency can be altered only when its balance of payments is in fundamental disequilibrium. Ordinarily balance-of-payments deficits are met out of a nation's reserves which consist not only of gold, but of reserve currencies (dollar and pounds) and IMF automatic drawing rights (the gold tranches). If these owned reserves prove insufficient, a country may borrow reserves from the IMF "pool of currencies," or through other devices which have been developed to facilitate lending by surplus countries to deficit countries. An essential ingredient of the system is that national currencies (primarily the dollar and pound) serve as part of the reserves of other nations, and the supply of this component of reserves depends on the balance-of-payments deficits of the reserve currency countries. In general, this system depends on shifts of international reserves rather than exchange rates to meet international payments imbalances.

The deficiencies of this gold-reserve currency system, for which reforms are sought, can be conveniently grouped into three broad categories.[1]

First, the balance-of-payments adjustment mechanism to eliminate imbalances is inefficient under the present system. Changes in exchange rates are seldom used; and even when they are used they tend to be postponed as long as possible so that a currency crisis first develops. This is particularly true of the reserve currency countries with respect to devaluation, but neither have the chronic surplus countries revalued their currencies upward sufficiently to eliminate their surpluses.

Without appropriate exchange rate adjustments, payments disequilibriums must be eliminated in the long run by domestic deflation or inflation, or in the shorter run by direct controls over trade and capital movements. The use of relative inflation and deflation often creates conflicts in economic policy between domestic economic goals and balance-of-payments objectives. Direct controls result in distortions of trade and capital movements, and are antithetical to the world movement toward freer trade and capital markets.

Furthermore, the primary burden of adjustment is placed on the deficit countries which must deflate or devalue to stop the loss of reserves. Surplus countries are not forced to inflate or to revalue their currencies, or to undertake greater aid and other foreign expenditures to reduce their surpluses; apparently, they can go on accumulating reserves without adjusting their domestic economies.

[1] Fritz Machlup, *Plans for Reform of the International Monetary System,* Special Papers in International Finance, No. 3 (Rev.) (Princeton: International Finance Section, 1964), pp. 13–19. See also Robert Triffin, *Gold and the Dollar Crisis* (New Haven: Yale University Press, 1961) especially Pt. I, Chaps. 3–7.

Second, world reserves and liquidity will not grow fast enough to finance future international payments imbalances. The major sources of reserve growth, new gold production and deficits of reserve currency countries, provide haphazard increases in reserves. Gold production alone is not sufficient; and reserve growth stemming from U.S. and U.K. deficits must be severely limited if doubts about continued convertibility of these currencies into gold and consequent currency crises are to be avoided. A universal increase in the price of gold (devaluation) to multiply the value in national currencies of present and future gold holdings has usually been ruled out since losses and gains from such action would be inequitably and inefficiently distributed among nations and, in any case, would not provide the steady growth in reserves thought necessary.

Third, the first two deficiencies create a condition in which the international monetary system is inevitably prone to collapse. If the deficits of the reserve currency countries, especially the United States, should be permanently eliminated under the present system a shortage of world liquidity and reserves would soon develop. With inadequate world reserves, trade and investment would be retarded; a reversion to direct controls, competitive currency devaluations, and other beggar-thy-neighbor evils to accomplish balance-of-payments equilibrium would likely occur.

But if, on the other hand, the deficit-reserve currency countries cannot stop their deficits, confidence in the continued convertibility between their currencies and gold will be lost, and runs on these currencies could force devaluation or crisis application of exchange restrictions, gold embargos, or other autarkic measures. The system seems damned if it does and damned if it does not (experience an end of the reserve currency country's deficits).

While this brief diagnosis of the international financial system may be overdrawn, it does point up the logical contradictions which, if not mitigated, could result in severe disruption in international finance, trade, and capital flows. The plans discussed below are prescriptions to forestall such disruption if not to prevent it in our time. However, note that the various plans seek solutions in very different ways, focusing more closely on one type of deficiency and less closely, or completely ignoring, others, preferring one technical means to another, and implying very different degrees and forms of international cooperation and organization. Division of the plans into two broad categories is useful.

1. Some plans focus on improving the deficient *adjustment mechanism*, thus greatly reducing the need for liquidity and reserves. Plans in this category will be examined first. These are:

   a. A *return to the gold standard* championed mainly by French economist Jacques Rueff. In sharp contrast, although not attacking the same adjustment problem, are proposals to eliminate gold from the monetary system completely; these plans too will be examined briefly.

   b. The adoption of fully *flexible exchange rates* or plans allowing exchange rate changes to occur in greater magnitude than the present fixed system although restricting that flexibility to limits specified in advance.

2. The second major group of plans are those which would *increase world reserves and liquidity* thus allowing more time for countries to adjust to balance-of-payments disequilibria while leaving the adjustment mechanism basically as it is. These proposals also fall into two main subgroups:

   a. The creation of an expanded International Monetary Fund (XIMF) as an *international agency* to hold and *to create international reserves* along lines similar to national central banks. The Keynes plan proposed before Bretton Woods is the father of these plans and was briefly discussed in Chapter IV. The Triffin plan and current variants of it will be examined in more detail.

   b. The establishment of a *"composite"* or *multiple reserve unit* system through which reserves could be increased, but which would still be based upon national currencies. These plans propose to extend the system of reserve currencies to include national currencies other than the dollar and the pound as a basis for reserve creation, within the IMF (Composite Reserve Units) or outside it (multiple reserve currencies).

Although our discussion focuses principally on the economic and institutional implications of each plan, political considerations cannot be ignored. Some plans favor certain countries within the present international environment, and national interests help to explain the advocacy or rejection of particular plans in certain circles. The degree of international cooperation required under the various plans not only is relevant for evaluating the prospects of a specific plan being adopted but also helps in understanding and even predicting the positions taken by various negotiators in official discussions for reform. Brief reference will be made throughout to the political implications of the various plans.

RETURN TO THE GOLD STANDARD

The advocates of a return to a semiautomatic gold standard are, as one would expect, primarily Continental Europeans. It represents the main portion of the over-all plan of Jacques Rueff, its most vocal advocate.[2] A "return to gold" would impose more discipline on the principal deficit countries, the United States and the United Kingdom, to force them to do the adjusting necessary to get out of the current predicament.

The appeal of the gold standard, beyond the fact that it smacks of the "golden age" of the last century when many of our present problems did not exist, is to be found in its automaticity. It sets a standard and procedure by which international maladjustments can be ironed out without tinkering and mending by mere monetary authorities. Balance-of-payments problems presumably would be eliminated automatically in an orderly manner as a result of following the rules of the (gold) game. All international payments imbalances would be settled by gold transfers since official holdings of foreign exchange would be eliminated. The system would be introduced by mutual agreement among the advanced countries. The United States and United Kingdom would pay off all official dollar and pound liabilities with gold, immediately or over a period of time. Each nation's currency would be made convertible into gold at a fixed price, and gold could be held by individuals as well as governments and central banks.

2 The views of Rueff can be found in Jacques Rueff and Fred Hirsch, *The Role and Rule of Gold: An Argument*, Essays in International Finance, No. 47 (Princeton: International Finance Section, 1965) and in his "Gold Exchange Standard, a Danger to the West," *The Times* (London), June 27–29, 1961. See also M. A. Heilperin, "The Case for Going Back to Gold," *Fortune Magazine*, September 1962. The latter two articles are reprinted in Herbert G. Grubel, ed., *World Monetary Reform: Plans and Issues* (Stanford: Stanford University Press, 1963), Selections 18 and 19.

The automaticity of such a system can be simply explained in theoretical terms. The domestic money supply would be determined by a country's gold holdings. A loss of gold due to a balance-of-payments deficit would reduce the money supply while the surplus country would gain gold and its money supply would expand. The rising money supply in the surplus country would create easy credit conditions, lower interest rates, and higher prices and incomes. The opposite reactions would occur in the deficit country: Capital would tend to flow toward the deficit country, its exports should rise and imports fall, thus reversing the deficit. Meanwhile the surplus is reduced by a similar process in the surplus country. The proposal requires that the domestic money supply move in the same direction as the changes in the country's gold reserves and that the change in the money supply be no smaller than the change in reserves. To accomplish the latter task, sterilization of the effect of gold flows on the money supply by central bank action, which occurs under the existing system in every country, must be ruled out. The gold system would work best if there were 100 per cent gold backing for the money supply. Once there is less, i.e., once a fractional reserve system exists, central banks cannot be allowed to manipulate the ratios of gold to money to counteract the more upsetting effects of gold movements or for any other, say, domestic, purpose.

Gold-standard advocates see the reserve currency component of international reserves as the source of the fundamental difficulty of the present system. The strength of their position rests on noting the dilemma of a reserve currency system: Reliance on deficits of reserve currencies to increase reserves necessarily undermines confidence in these currencies and undermines the system as well, because certain countries are enabled to avoid balance-of-payments adjustment for extended periods. Thus the stage is set for currency crises and eventually for large and disruptive changes in prices and exchange rates. It is alleged that a system based on a continually rising ratio of liabilities to gold for the reserve currency countries must eventually fail. If gold were the only international reserve, countries could not avoid adjustment.

Furthermore, the other reform proposals are unacceptable to the "gold" reformer. Despite the automaticity of freely fluctuating exchange rates in eliminating surpluses and deficits, fluctuating rates would not impose adequate discipline against inflationary or deflationary domestic policies that politically minded policy makers might pursue. Without the restraint of limited international reserves, governments could undertake dangerous inflation to achieve the politically palatable goal of full-employment. A worldwide inflationary bias would be the result. This argument assumes governments do not view domestic price stability as a high priority goal, and that unless the discipline of gold is imposed from outside, inflation will result. Involved here are unproven assumptions concerning the behavior of policy makers and underlying basic world economic trends. Of course, the other usual arguments against flexible exchange rates are also employed, arguments concerning the possibility of destabilizing speculation, disruption of trade and capital movements, etc.

The gold-standard advocates also reject those plans which would provide more time to adjust to balance-of-payments problems. Plans for multiple reserve currencies and international lending devices presumably compound the inadequacies of the present system while not eliminating the essential adjustment problem. The dangers of holding national currencies as international reserves remain. Similarly, plans for an international reserve-creating agency, while correcting world reserve deficiencies, do not touch the central problem. Transference of reserve creation to an international authority does not assume better performance than the existing system of national authority reserve creation unless an integrated economic policy among nations is achieved. A central reserve-creating agency also carries with it the possibility of too rapid expansion in world reserves which would permit worldwide inflation to occur.

The primary disadvantage of this full-gold system which effectively removes it from serious consideration is that it requires that each country give up control of its money supply to the vagaries of its external balance. The fact is that conditions in industrial countries make this virtually impossible. When a deficit country loses gold and its money supply declines, prices are presumed to fall so that exports become more competitive. It is only in the old "quantity theory" of money and not in the real world that prices change in proportion to money supply changes. In response to restrictive domestic policies it is not prices but incomes and employment that fall readily; and modern societies will hardly allow such dire domestic consequences to arise from a deficit in the balance of payments. The political and economic costs of a return to gold are too great. Thus, unless some means to institute relatively painless downward flexibility in prices and wages is found, so that the level of employment can remain relatively steady while a balance-of-payments deficit is reversed, a return to the gold standard can hardly be taken seriously. Indeed, the gold standard was abandoned in the first place because its effectiveness required too much unemployment in the deficit countries. During periods of general depression or recession, such medicine has proven to be intolerable. The postwar emphasis on full employment and growth policies indicates that the current climate is even less conducive to gold-standard conditions than was the case in the 1930s.

Associated with the desire to return to a gold standard in current discussion, and an integral part of Rueff's plan, is the idea that gold should also be revalued; that is, that its price should be increased from $35 to say $70 per troy ounce. This, it is alleged, would provide the world with a new supply of liquidity since everybody's gold hoard would be twice what it is now. No currency would be affected more than others since in effect all Western currencies would be devalued by 50 per cent. But the further suggestion is made that countries should pay off all of their outstanding obligations in gold. This political posture is popular in de Gaulle's France, because it is directed against the United States and Great Britain. For while "les Anglo-Saxons" like everyone else would increase their liquidity by doubling the values of their gold hoards, they could not keep it. The total effect of the proposal on the United States is that its gold hoard would be raised in value from approximately $15 to $30 billion which in turn would be used to pay off approximately $13 billion in official dollar holdings to other nations, and perhaps another $10 billion to other holders of U.S. liabilities. This would leave the United States with about $7 billion of gold and the present U.S. creditors with the rest. In the case of England the suggestion makes no sense in any event since even if one doubled England's gold stock it still could not suffice to retire the foreign short-term liabilities against it. In any case, a large part of the liquidity increasing effects of devaluation will be offset by the liquidity decreasing effects of retirement of the reserve currency holdings.

The return to gold even after devaluation does not automatically provide for increased international reserves. However, gold revaluation would tend to increase gold production by making gold more valuable in general purchasing power and might pull gold from private hoards where it has been lodged in expectation of just such a profitable price change. The real issue is whether such a secular increase in gold will provide a sufficient rate of increase in international reserves when gold, and gold alone, and no reserve currencies are in use as reserves. Dislodging of hoards, moreover, would only happen if the speculators were convinced that further currency devaluations would not be forthcoming. This the advocates of the gold system are very willing to guarantee. But can they? Such a guarantee presumes that as world production and world trade rise in volume the gold supply will keep pace. Since all money supplies will be based on gold holdings, future output rises must be accompanied by new gold supplies. Otherwise, prices must fall, or the rate of turnover of money increases. Since prices are inflexible downward, and monetary velocity changes very slowly in the long run, a slow rate of increase in gold supplies may well impose a deflationary drag on output unless periodic upward revaluations of gold occur. This is hardly the neat, automatic system which the gold advocates picture for us.

Besides, any gold revaluation which is necessarily worldwide in application will apply in part the perverse principle: Reward one's enemies and punish one's friends. Upward revaluations in gold benefit the gold producing countries, such as South Africa and the Soviet Union; it also benefits those countries which hold most of their international reserves in gold. It would penalize those countries which in cooperative good faith have kept most of their reserves in pound and dollar balances. The return to gold would be unjust as well as inefficient. But in any case it seems politically impossible.

In contrast to a return to the gold standard, it has been advocated that gold be removed altogether from its central position in the world monetary system. The link between gold and the world monetary system is the U.S. dollar. The dollar serves as the international unit of account and shares with gold the store of value and medium

ANTI-GOLD SOLUTIONS

of payment functions of international money. The fact that national currencies are convertible into dollars at fixed prices gives the world fixed exchange rates, but the U.S. obligation to maintain convertibility of foreign official dollar holdings to gold ties the exchange rate system to gold. Since the Gold Reserve Act of 1934, the U.S. Treasury has dealt in gold with foreign treasuries and central banks at the official price of $35 per ounce. Although this policy of gold-dollar convertibility was at the administrative discretion of the U.S. Treasury until 1945, the Bretton Woods Agreements Act, which became law in 1945, made it the *legal* obligation of the United States to maintain the $35 per ounce gold price. Thus foreign monetary authorities can exchange gold for dollars automatically, and vice versa. Gold remains the ultimate means of settling international payments deficits and surpluses between countries.

The continued reliance on gold as an international money was called a "barbarous relic" by Lord Keynes. The affinity for gold probably rests on an irrational desire for an automatic monetary system and on the fear that, unless gold imposes its discipline on the domestic monetary management of nations, inflation is the inevitable result. Historically it is true that countries have more often created excessive amounts of paper money than too little, and devaluations of currencies vis-à-vis gold are much more common than upward revaluations. As a result, gold is often deemed a better store of value than assets denominated in national currencies, even though the interest earned on such assets held for a period of years would offset the gain from a sizable devaluation of the currency. But whether rational or not, hoarders hold gold to defend themselves against, or to gain through, currency devaluations. Private gold hoards increase when currency devaluations seem more possible.

In recent years, many private hoarders have sold dollars and bought gold (or stocks of mining companies) in the hope that this action would further weaken the dollar, force its devaluation, and thus create a capital gain for the hoarders as the value of gold rose. At time this speculation has become feverish. This has caused some students, mainly Americans, to seek to relieve such pressure by cutting the gold-dollar tie, which would in effect introduce the chance of loss into this one-way speculation in gold.

Two basic plans have been advanced to cut the tie of the dollar to gold. One involves the withdrawal of the obligation of the United States to *buy* gold at $35 per ounce; the other would eliminate both the *buying* and *selling* obligation, i.e., would end any convertibility between gold and the dollar.

The first proposal, to remove the guaranteed *buying* price of gold,[3] is a partial step toward demonetization of gold. This proposal simply requires that the United States announce that it will continue to sell gold to foreign monetary authorities at $35 per ounce but will not buy gold at any set price, and perhaps not at all. Thus, the United States would set the maximum price of gold, but there would be no minimum, and the price of gold could, and perhaps would, fall relative to the dollar. Instead of a devaluation of the dollar, there would be a devaluation of gold.

This proposal originally was intended to dampen the impact of gold speculation on the U.S. balance of payments. Beginning in 1959, short-term capital outflows accounted for a significant portion of the U.S. deficit. The evidence suggests that much of this U.S. capital outflow, as well as some foreign capital, was used to purchase gold. The attractiveness of this gold speculation resided in the expectations of capital gains if the United States should devalue its dollar relative to gold while no possible capital loss by the speculator is risked; the only costs are interest income foregone and transaction charges, if the United States did not devalue; speculators need not fear a revaluation of the dollar upward. When the United States was running sizable deficits (1958 to 1964), the falling gold stock and rising short-term liabilities which could be mobilized for gold conversion made dollar devaluation plausible. Some dollar holders converted their dollars to gold in the hope of a capital gain when they later sold the gold after devaluation; even though the United States did not devalue, they lost very little on their *one-sided* speculation.

By eliminating the obligation of the U.S. Treasury to buy gold at $35 per ounce, but retaining the obligation to sell at that price, gold speculators would face the possibility of capital loss as well as gain since the United States would then buy gold only when it saw fit.

[3] See Howard Piquet, "Some Consequences of Dollar Speculation in Gold," *Factors Affecting the United States Balance of Payments* (Joint Economic Committee, 1962), pp. 305–324; and Abba Lerner, "Let's Get Rid of our Cross of Gold," *Challenge*, April 1964.

This might very well dampen speculative demand for gold, and also lead to sales of gold from private hoards held in such countries as Switzerland and India. If gold could fall in value relative to national currencies, its attraction for hoarding would be reduced. Indeed, Abba Lerner's proposal would *force* the price of gold to fall. He suggests that not only should the United States not buy gold, but should sell its existing gold stock, either rapidly or over a period at successively lower prices. Then, past speculators would incur capital losses and the prospect of further losses if they continued to hold gold. With removal of the support price for gold, private speculators and foreign official institutions would have to choose between dollars (or other national currencies) whose value derives from what they will buy and gold whose value without the guaranteed price in dollars might well be allowed or forced to fall.

If this innovation were made, what would be the effects? Confidence of private speculators in gold might be shaken, and gold hoarding and gold speculation would be reduced, thereby benefiting world reserves and the U.S. balance of payments.

But what would be the response of foreign governments? Would they keep their currencies tied to the dollar, or would they attempt to assume the role of the United States and fix the price of gold? If they kept their currencies fixed in value to the dollar, then the fixed exchange rate system would remain intact, but all currencies would fluctuate with respect to gold, and the world would be very close to the dollar standard. On the other hand, if one or more countries attempted to support the price of gold in terms of their own currencies and were successful—which is by no means certain because of their relatively thin gold reserves—the outcome would be unpredictable. Should the United States then continue to run a deficit, the U.S. gold stock would continue to be drained, but if the United States became a surplus country, the dollar would appreciate vis-à-vis other currencies and gold. Thus, the full implications of unilaterally removing the fixed buying price of gold are uncertain. The status of gold thereafter depends on the reactions of other governments and the future balance-of-payments position of the United States.

The second major suggestion for "tinkering with gold" also would require unilateral action by the United States. This involves the complete demonetization of gold by the United States by removing both the buying and selling obligation so that dollars would no longer be convertible into gold. Such action would require other nations to make the choice as to whether to keep their currencies tied to the dollar or to gold. Should they maintain fixed exchange rates between their currencies and dollars, the existing exchange rate system would remain but gold as a source of world liquidity to finance deficits would be effectively eliminated. The world would then depend even more on the dollar as a reserve currency, and should the U.S. deficit disappear, one wonders where the needed liquidity would come from. But if the U.S. deficit did continue, other countries would be *forced* to hold dollars rather than gold, and thus the U.S. deficit would be financed by short-term lending by surplus countries, and the lenders would have no alternative but to lend if the pegged exchange rates were to be maintained.

On the other hand, if other nations chose to fix the prices of their currencies in gold, rather than the dollar, the United States would have a flexible exchange rate and its external accounts would be automatically balanced, while other nations would be tied to gold and continue with payments imbalances. It seems unlikely that the other nations would opt for gold if the world's largest trader eliminated its own ties to gold. Maintaining a fixed rate with the dollar is probably more important to most countries than a fixed gold price, and it is doubtful if any country has sufficient gold reserves to support the price of gold without severe limitations on its domestic policies.

While these proposals may appear immediately attractive from the U.S. point of view, the long-run implications surrounding them make their adoption most unlikely. The chief benefactor of these unilateral actions would be the United States, either through a suppression of the adverse impact of gold speculation on the balance of payments, or alternatively through the economic power to force surplus countries to finance the U.S. deficit should it continue. Should it not continue, there would result a decline of world reserve growth. For the world as a whole, these proposals suffer from the basic defect that, while it may be rational to remove gold from its throne, unilateral action by one country in which nothing is offered to take gold's place is a thoroughly irresponsible solution. Removal of gold from its central position requires that further basic reforms be agreed upon by the interested nations, including a rational and manageable substitute for gold. Whatever the short-term rewards of such a plan for the United States, American officials have displayed great zeal for international cooperation and responsibility, which in effect rules out this solution.

FLEXIBLE EXCHANGE RATES

The economists who advocate flexible exchange rates form an impressive group.[4] But the reception that flexible rate proposals have received from central bankers, government treasury authorities, and the IMF can at best be described as cool. Indeed, in international discussions of proposals for reforming the international payments system, rate flexibility has been effectively dismissed as a relevant alternative.

Yet the appeal of flexible exchange rates for many academicians persists. The root of its appeal lies in two areas. First, balance-of-payments adjustment under flexible exchange rates is automatic. Potential surpluses or deficits are automatically eliminated by exchange rate changes emanating from changes in the supply of or demand for foreign exchange in the foreign exchange market. Under a flexible rate system, the price, or exchange rate, adjusts so as to keep supply equal to demand without any, or only minimal, official sales and purchases. Thus balance-of-payments equilibrium is insured.

Second, this automatic adjustment occurs without the traumatic changes in domestic prices, incomes, or commercial policy associated with fixed exchange rates. With flexible exchange rates, few international reserves are needed since the primary function of reserves is to finance a deficit at a fixed rate of exchange. With no defiit to

[4] The standard case is made in Milton Friedman, "The Case for Flexible Exchange Rates," *Essays in Positive Economics* (Chicago: University of Chicago Press, 1953), pp. 157–201, and Egon Sohmen, *Flexible Exchange Rates: Theory and Controversy* (Chicago: University of Chicago Press, 1961). Positive proposals for exchange flexibility can also be found in James E. Meade, "The Case for Variable Exchange Rates," *Three Banks Review*, September 1955, pp. 3–27; W. M. Scammell, *International Monetary Policy* (London: Macmillan, 1957), pp. 82–108; and G. N. Halm, "Fixed or Flexible Exchange Rates?," *Factors Affecting the United States Balance of Payments* (Joint Economic Committee, 1962), pp. 253–266. In addition, the position has some Continental support. A committee of economists appointed by the German government to investigate the question has recommended this solution; however, the German government has ignored its recommendation.

finance, reserve losses cannot compel domestic deflation; therefore economic policy is freer to pursue domestic objectives. In the simplest terms, flexible exchange rates cut the ties between the external balance and reserves, which in turn frees the domestic economy from the classical discipline. Thus, while the gold standard too would make balance-of-payments adjustments automatic, flexible exchange rates offer the added advantage of divorcing domestic policy from direct influence of the balance of payments.

More than one type of flexible exchange rate system is possible. At the extreme, the exchange rate may be allowed to seek its own level without *any* intervention by governmental authority; i.e., a completely *free* foreign exchange market. In this situation, international reserves serve no function; gold would lose its "international" role and become simply another metal. On the other hand, governmental agencies, while allowing the exchange rate to find its own level, may smooth exchange rate movements through official purchases and sales of foreign exchange in the market. This practice was followed by Canada (1950–1962) when that nation allowed its dollar to float. If official intervention is the practice, some reserves (of gold or foreign currencies) are necessary to carry out the official operations. (In the ensuing discussion, we treat the completely free and the minimal official intervention system as equivalent since the arguments raised about flexible rates apply to both systems.)

To install a world system of flexible exchange rates would require an international agreement among the major countries to the effect that no country would interfere in the market for foreign exchange, or, at least, the agreement would set standards to limit intervention. In addition, a procedure for liquidating some or all of the present holdings of gold and foreign exchange reserves would have to be provided so as to minimize the distortions of exchange rates that otherwise would result from liquidation of excess reserves. Furthermore, either the International Monetary Fund would be eliminated or its function would be reduced in magnitude, e.g., to assist underdeveloped countries with their foreign exchange problems.

It is possible for one country to adopt a policy of flexible exchange rates unilaterally, although this would be in violation of the IMF articles. In such a case, the country would refrain from foreign exchange market intervention (or intervene only on a limited scale), or in the case of the United States, would refuse to buy and sell gold at a fixed price.[5] The international repercussions of individual countries opting for exchange flexibility would depend on the magnitude of the involvement of each country in international financial relationships. In what follows we assume that flexible exchange rates would be adopted as a system by agreement among many countries.

But still another prerequisite concerning the behavior of countries is necessary if flexible exchange rates are to prove beneficial. Given a relation between political power and international economic prestige, political pride could play a role in a flexible exchange rate system. The "strong currencies," which normally means those of surplus countries, have a big voice in international matters, and the weak currencies sometimes speak in muted and humble tones despite, as in the case of the United States, considerable economic power. Pride might dictate that the United States and United Kingdom have currencies which do not depreciate vis-à-vis the foreign currencies. This very political pride would impose some sense of discipline on the deficit countries. It is thus possible that political pride (in a "strong dollar") would require the same kind of discipline (internal deflation) required today under the gold-exchange standard. In this case, flexible exchange rates will have lost most of their economic value from the viewpoint of a nation's internal policy since the policy measures followed would be essentially those required of a country with fixed exchange rates and limited reserves.

On the other hand, if pride is less a factor, and if the pound and dollar are freed, certainly the pound, and probably the dollar, would decline in value vis-à-vis other currencies. In this event, there would be no gold outflow and no need to inhibit growth; but there would be a political "crisis" in the sense that the dollar and the pound would become cheaper. How great a crisis depends on how much pride. At the same time, the international cheapness of the dollar and the pound would equilibrate the balance of payments of the United States, the United Kingdom, and the surplus countries as well.

For all their apparent virtues, flexible rates are not popular with

[5] But even if the U.S. unpegged the price of gold, flexible exchange rates between the dollar and other currencies would still depend on the actions of foreign governments. See above, pp. 207.

traders, bankers, or the IMF—in short, with "practical" people. The most common criticism involves the fact that exchange rate fluctuations introduce another element of risk into foreign transactions and migh tend to retard trade and capital movements. For example, an exporter not only has to cope with the domestic currency price of his goods, but also with the price of foreign exchange in domestic currency when he receives payment. Of course, such a risk arises to a degree under the present system because exchange rates may vary within 1 per cent on each side of the par rate. At the present time, short-term exchange risks may be hedged in the forward exchange market by the purchase or sale of foreign (or domestic) currency to be delivered in the future, at a price set now. The cost of cover—the difference between the spot price of foreign exchange and the price of foreign exchange for future delivery—is the explicit cost of foreign transactions. With flexible exchange rates, the spot rate can fluctuate, theoretically without limit, and presumably (although by no means certainly) the cost of cover would be higher, thus tending to make foreign trade more costly. In addition, foreign investment of a longer-term nature could not be covered for exchange risk, since limited forward markets in foreign exchange exist for maturities over one year. Even so, this element of risk is fairly small. The advantage of a 1 per cent higher rate of return on a twenty-year foreign investment can be offset only by a large exchange rate change.

Thus, analysis of the argument that flexible exchange rates by increasing trade risks would reduce foreign trade and investment is not very convincing. Furthermore, its impact depends on the degree to which a country depends on foreign transactions for its economic welfare. Certainly this argument is more forceful for Great Britain and the Netherlands than for the United States or France. But where international transactions are a large part of total business, and businessmen *think* that fluctuating exchange rates involve substantial additional risk, it is likely that their introduction will disrupt business decisions and the domestic economy.

A second common argument is that short-term capital movements will be destabilizing and will cause violent movements in the exchange rate, thus distributing capital gains and losses at random and disrupting trade. This argument is based on historical episodes. In the rush away from free convertibility which occurred during the monetary collapse of the early 1930s,[6] flexible rates fluctuated widely because of the massive capital flows. (A similar episode occurred soon after World War I.[7]) The argument runs that since short-term capital movements were destabilizing with respect to exchange rates during the only occasions they have been attempted on a broad scale, such will be the case if they are tried again. But this argument presupposes that flexible rates were the cause of the capital movements, when in fact a fairly solid case can be made that the international environment of depression, Hitler, uncertainty, and exchange rate manipulation, was actually the major cause of the "hot" money flows of the 1930s. In fact, all evidence suggests that they were the cause of the abandonment of fixed rates rather than vice versa. The appeal to unusual historical experience is no basis for rejecting flexible rates, say its advocates. The Canadian experience in contrast actually suggests that private short-term capital movements were stabilizing, and cushioned exchange rate movements rather than accentuated them.[8] Whether destabilizing capital flows in the present international environment would prevail in a system of flexible rates can hardly be determined in advance. The fact remains that the existing system also induces disruptive "hot" money flows during currency crises, necessitating costly rescue operations, as with the pound sterling in 1964. Is this any worse than one would expect if the pound had been free to seek an equilibrium level?

Another common argument is that flexible exchange rates will allow and validate inflationary domestic monetary policies. That is, the discipline of limited international reserves is removed and countries will be free to pursue rapid growth and high employment policies without consideration for the effects on domestic prices. As a result, the country's currency will depreciate, raising the prices of imported raw materials, which in turn will induce further price rises and wage demands to offset the new higher cost of living. As increasing costs of production and prices spread throughout the economy, i.e., as inflation spirals internally, the currency spirals downward

[6] The classic interpretation of this period is Ragner Nurkse's study, *International Currency Experience, op. cit.,* esp. pp. 140 ff.
[7] Triffin, *The Evolution of the International Monetary System, op. cit.,* p. 21.
[8] See T. L. Powrie, "Short-Term Capital Movements and the Flexible Canadian Exchange Rate, 1953–1961," *Canadian Journal of Economics and Political Science,* February 1964, pp. 76–94.

externally. To add to the problem, the prospect of a continually depreciating currency causes capital flight and compounds the exchange rate decline.

However, there are several weak assumptions implicit in this sorry process. First, the argument assumes that the fear of losing gold or other international reserves is required to induce the monetary managers to control inflation. But there is no *a priori* reason why price stability will be abandoned as a goal simply because flexible rates are adopted. Actually, fear of a falling currency value may act as a similar prod. Second, it is assumed that the rest of the world controls inflation, while the country in question does not. It is only in the event of significantly different rates of price change among countries that exchange rate depreciations induce cumulative upward pressure on domestic prices. Indeed, one of the advantages of flexible exchange rates is that changes in international cost-price relationships are equilibrated automatically, rather than requiring domestic adjustments in income and prices, or prolonging the maladjustment until an exchange crisis or devaluation occurs, as is the case under the present adjustable peg system. Nevertheless, fear persists that these runaway trends may prevail if the flexible system is tried. For this reason, some advocates of flexible rates have suggested that limits of flexibility be set. (This proposal, known as the "band" proposal, is discussed below.)

A somewhat more fundamental criticism of the flexible exchange rate system charges that inefficient reallocation of economic resources will be induced. If the exchange rate varies by substantial amounts periodically, such as over the course of the business cycle, there will be an incentive to move resources into or out of the export industries and those industries which compete in the home market with imports. For example, if the domestic currency should depreciate in an expansion, the profitability of export and import competing industries would be expected to rise vis-à-vis the industries producing for the domestic economy, and labor and capital would tend to move toward the profitable industries. A subsequent appreciation—in a recession—would reverse the process.

Reallocation of resources is costly. Costs are incurred just to move resources from one industry to another, and if the incentive for the movement reverses itself later, two costly movements may be made.

Reversible exchange rate movements cause temporary market disruption domestically and impair economic performance. An extension of this argument is even more damaging. If businesses find their profits fluctuating in an unpredictable way, the incentive for new plant and equipment expenditure to modernize production processes may be retarded. Thus, the country may lag behind the technological and productivity growth of its trading partners.

While these arguments are basically sound, they assume that the exchange rate undergoes sizable up and down fluctuations. Even if such large changes did occur, the opponents of flexible rates must demonstrate that an alternative fixed rate system would not produce similar resource misallocation. If reserves are large enough, a fixed rate country running a deficit simply uses its reserves to ride out the deficit. But if reserves are small relative to expected deficits, as for example the United Kingdom's have been, a deficit and reserve loss causes policy makers to adopt "stop" policies, i.e., to deflate domestically in order to achieve external balance. Here, not only does one have the adverse cost required by a temporary reallocation of resources, but in addition the country pays a further price by inhibiting the growth of the whole economy. The "stop" policy stops all industries; only to turn to "go" policies as the deficit is reduced or eliminated. Thus, in the case of the United Kingdom and in other cases which could easily be assembled, the alternative to flexible rates may be more wasteful than flexible rates themselves.

One final reservation concerning flexible exchange rates is of prime importance. This argument is that internal and external economic matters are so inextricably entwined, that even flexible exchange rates will not insulate the domestic economy from happenings abroad, over which no single nation has control. The argument underscores the need, under *any* financial arrangement, for international cooperation.

When international movements of capital flow freely, changes in the domestic level of interest rates relative to those abroad affect the volume and direction of capital flows. Most capital movements also affect the supply or demand of foreign exchange and therefore the level of the exchange rate which, in turn, affects the current account balance. Consider a country "A" in "internal balance" with full employment and reasonable price stability. If interest rates abroad rise, capital outflows from country A to foreigners will increase. This causes a depreciation in country A's currency. The depreciation in turn causes an increase in net exports, thereby raising demand in country A and inducing inflation. The country's monetary policy *must react to* the exchange rate movement to stop the inflation. In other words, the domestic policy of country A is *not* independent or isolated, but must be coordinated in a very basic sense with policies abroad over which A has no voice or control. While flexible exchange rates may *increase* the freedom of domestic policy, it cannot completely insulate it from foreign developments. No international financial system can eliminate the need for international coordination of economic policies.

Opponents of flexible exchange rates generally use one or more of the above arguments to show that flexible exchange rates will be "unstable" exchange rates. Indeed, flexible rates *can* be unstable rates. Since the demand and supply of foreign exchange depend on among other factors, relative international prices, relative rates of growth in national incomes, and international interest rate differentials, a prolonged movement of one or more of these variables for a country which is out of step with the rest of the world will introduce prolonged one-way movements in the demand (or supply) of foreign exchange and of the exchange rate. Once it is clear that the movement in the exchange rate will be in one direction only, private speculators will line up on one side of the market only, forcing a more rapid and destabilizing movement in the rate which can only be stopped by massive contra-speculation by the country's monetary authorities and by fundamental changes in domestic policies. But the advantage of flexible rates lies in meeting once-and-for-all changes in international relationships. To cope with a bout of inflation which is eventually stopped in the country of origin, a flexible exchange rate will realign international price relationships *without* a deflation of equal magnitude to bring the foreign balance back into equilibrium.

It appears, then, that so long as a country's prices, growth rate, and interest rates do not get flagrantly out of line with those of its trading partners, a flexible exchange rate will be a basically stable one, and will ease the adjustment to once-over changes with economic conditions abroad. But coordination of economic policies with those abroad is a necessary factor in keeping the exchange rate stable. The stability of the Canadian dollar during its period of flexibility from 1950 to 1962 is a case in point. The most cogent explanation of that stability is that Canadian economic performance was similar to that of the Unied States during the period and that Canadian monetary and fiscal policies did not diverge greatly from those in the United States. Since the United States is Canada's major trading partner as well as the source of most of her foreign capital, conditions were such as to keep the fluctuations of the Canadian dollar within narrow limits.

But the basic issue remains. If, even with flexible rates, international coordination and internal restraint are still necessary, why adopt flexible rates? The answer must lie in the lesser *degree* of coordination necessary, a degree tolerable even to nations unwilling to surrender much sovereignty. Moreover, this is the only system that will restore appropriate international price relationships automatically when they get out of line without inducing domestic price changes.

Aside from the basic economic arguments against flexible rates advanced above, there remain a number of operational complexities and practical problems attaching to a system of flexible rates among a number of countries. First, a *system* of flexible rates would pose the problem of many currencies fluctuating against each other, theoretically without limit, thus making calculations of the cheapest way to make international payments a complicated procedure. A simplified example will illustrate. If France, England, and the United States each had flexible rates, there would be a $/£, a $/fr. and a £/fr. rate in New York with which to contend. In addition, a trader or speculator would have to consider these same rates in London, Paris, and other international money centers which need not be the same as in New York. Furthermore, for each of these "spot" rates, there would be one or more "forward" rates for each currency to be considered, all fluctuating against each other, with no limits to the range of fluctuation. If *all* world currencies were so cross-connected, foreign exchange dealings would become complex indeed. It is true that even under the present system there are similar considerations, but the rates are fixed within narrow limits and the loss (or gain) from a miscalculation cannot be large. In addition, most international transactions today are carried out in one of two "vehicle" currencies which serve as international units of account. It is possible, but not certain, that this convenient device would continue under flexible rates. Moreover, private speculators will give traders the opportunity to hedge foreign exchange transactions—at a cost—and it may well be that more sophisticated forward exchange markets would develop and reduce the fluctuations of currency cross-valuations.

Second, should a flexible exchange rate system be adopted in which official institutions engage in operations to smooth exchange rate movements, the very important possibility exists that two countries' operations would be at cross purposes and either cancel each other out or compound the amount of intervention. Thus, if both the pound and the dollar were appreciating, the United States might find itself buying pounds for dollars while the United Kingdom was buying dollars for pounds. To avoid this, a high degree of coordination between central banks (or other institutions) would be necessary.

Third, for a country with heavy involvement in international transactions, fluctuating prices of foreign exchange may prove to be intolerable to traders and others. If the foreign sector of the economy accounts for a large part of total business, the uncertainty associated with flexible rates affects a large percentage of total transactions. Since business likes stability and predictable future conditions, fluctuating foreign exchange rates would impose a real burden which the business community would actively resist.

From the points made above, it is clear that flexible exchange rates are no panacea for solving all of the world payments problems, and that there is much which remains questionable about how such a system would operate in practice. However, the system is theoretically appealing in that the need for international reserves, and their increase, would be greatly reduced, and some greater independence in domestic economic policies would be possible. But is greater *national economic* independence good or bad? If we assume as a world goal the greater integration of the national economies with the eventual objective of an all-encompassing international economic unit within which free trade, free capital and labor movements, and close cooperation in economic policies will prevail, the adoption of flexible exchange rates may well be viewed as a step backward to economic nationalism. To use an analogy, it would be rather naïve to recommend that the Common Market, while moving toward free trade and capital movements, adopt flexible exchange rates between the currencies. Since the original goal was economic, and eventually political, unification, one may assume that it can best be furthered by a unified or common currency. The old group of national economies would behave as one unit and balance-of-payments problems would not arise. If international integration and cooperation can be extended to the (free) world, it is hard to find a place for flexible exchange rates. Indeed, most of the economists who argue in favor of them tacitly presume that the national economy is the unit that is important. They either fail to consider the subsidiary effects which such a system would have in retarding a general movement toward economic internationalism, or do not believe this to be a practical possibility.

Aware of the potential parochialism and the latent nationalism of their arguments, flexible exchange advocates make two significant points. First, they remind us that nationalism is not their invention, but seems to be the present and foreseeable status quo, and that it is better for the monetary affairs of a nation to be run by its elected officials than by a remote "House of Lords" of central bankers over whom the electorate has no control. Second, they insist that another type of internationalism, consisting of *really* free trade—unfettered by partial remedies such as tariffs, exchange controls, quotas, etc., which are the concomitants of the present system—will be possible *only* under a flexible exchange rate system.[9]

Modified Versions of Flexible Exchange Rates

An almost infinite variety of exchange rate systems are possible between the extremes of completely fixed rates and completely flexible rates. The gold standard, which is very close to the complete fixity extreme, and completely free rates, the other extreme of unlimited, unmanaged flexibility, have been discussed. Of those possible arrangements along the continuum of increasing flexibility in exchange rates, two systems have gained a number of adherents and

[9] See A. P. Lerner, *The Economics of Employment* (New York: McGraw-Hill, 1951) for a particularly lucid exposition, which points out the pitfalls of "sentimental internationalism" and of basing a policy on what one wishes were so but is in fact not.

deserve some consideration. The first which we shall call, for short, "bloc flexibility" involves fixed exchange rates between countries within a particular grouping, but flexible rates are used between the several groups in the world. The second, the "band" proposal involves flexible exchange rates within wider limits than the 1 per cent on each side of parity allowed by the present system but not yet wholly free or unlimited in range.

Bloc Flexibility. The currency groupings or bloc flexibility proposal is a combination of fixed and flexible exchange rates based on geographical divisions. The geographical lines should, however, be based on economic and historical criteria. Theoretically, a currency bloc would include countries with close trade, capital, and cultural ties. R. A. Mundell has outlined the basic theory of employing completely fixed exchange rates within a relatively homogenous area, but with flexible exchange rates among areas, as an optimum means of maximizing economic welfare and minimizing balance-of-payments problems.[10] R. I. McKinnon has gone further and attempted to derive operational criteria for setting the bounds of the currency blocs.[11]

The rationale of currency blocs is relatively simple. By keeping fixed rates of exchange between the currencies of countries which are the major trading partners of each other, the problem of the risk of exchange rate change is minimized. In addition, countries with close economic ties will find it less difficult to coordinate economic policies with each other—which they may already be doing anyway—and thus the cost in that area is minimized. By letting the exchange rate between one bloc's (primary) currency and others' fluctuate, basic differences in economic developments will not be allowed to cause balance-of-payments problems between blocs. In effect, we would have fluctuating exchange rates, but based on much more rational groupings than existing national boundaries.

If this type of flexible exchange rates were to be adopted, three major "blocs" or "areas" would seem likely to evolve.[12] That the

[10] R. A. Mundell, "A Theory of Optimum Currency Areas," *American Economic Review*, September 1961, pp. 657–665.

[11] See especially R. I. McKinnon, "Optimum World Monetary Arrangements and the Dual Currency System," *Banca Nazionale del Lavoro*, December 1963, pp. 366–396.

[12] This system is, in essence, advocated in the Brookings report should the U.S. be unable to solve its payments problem or the world its liquidity problem. See Salant *et al.*, *The United States Balance of Payments in 1968*, *op. cit.*, pp. 258–262.

Western Hemisphere would remain tied to the dollar can hardly be doubted. Likewise, Continental Europe would probably become one currency area with which ex-colonies in Africa and Asia would align themselves. Whether the British would join the dollar or European currency area, or go it alone with the sterling area is open to question. This type of organization leaves room, so to speak, for the later incorporation of an East European, Russian, or some such future bloc into the world system of trade and monetary arrangements.

For the period since 1958, this system would have been extremely helpful. The dollar and the pound would have tended to depreciate vis-à-vis a European currency unit, making the rather distasteful policy actions in England and the United States unnecessary or considerably less extreme. This proposal has some appeal in that it parallels actual political developments in the world, rather than trying to impose on political realities some ideal arrangement designed to solve only its monetary problems.

The "Band" Proposal. The "band" proposal would merely widen the permissible limits of exchange fluctuation under the existing system.[13] Thus, exchange rate changes would do part of the adjusting to changes in the international economy. Indeed, if such changes were small, exchange rate changes would absorb the entire adjustment. For drastic, or persistent, national divergencies, the rate would move to the lower or upper limit, and international reserves would then be lost or gained to keep the currency within the band.

The proposal to widen the "band of fluctuation" is in conception not new; it parallels proposals to widen the gold export-import points under the gold standard. A considerable number of economists have proposed a widening of the existing 2 per cent band under the IMF system as a useful and rather innocuous means of achieving more exchange rate flexibility.[14] In addition, the Joint Economic Com-

[13] For an extended discussion of the "band" proposal see George Halm, *The "Band" Proposal: The Limits of Permissible Exchange Rate Variations*, Special Papers in International Economics, No. 6, (Princeton: International Finance Section, 1965).

[14] For example, Peter B. Kenen, Philip Bell, and George Halm each suggested a widening of the bands in testimony before the U.S. Joint Economic Committee. See *Outlook for the United States Balance of Payments*, Hearings of the Joint Economic Committee of U.S. Congress, December 12, 13, and 14, 1964 (Washington: U.S.G.P.O., 1965), pp. 127, 143, and 181. A number of English economists have also written to this view. Probably the most interesting views

mittee of the U.S. Congress has given favorable airing to the "band" proposal. Although it has not specifically recommended adoption of the proposal, it has directed that the administration carefully consider the merits as well as the disadvantages.[15]

The "band" proposal is admittedly a compromise between the views of advocates of flexible rates and those who desire to maintain the present relative inflexibility. Besides the gain in more effective balance-of-payments adjustments which a widening of the band would achieve, other advantages are claimed by its advocates.

For example, an advantage in controlling international capital movements is claimed. If capital flows among nations in search of higher interest rates, it is likely that the foreign investors are hedging their currency transactions in the forward exchange market. If this is the case, it is the covered interest rate differential, i.e., the interest differences between countries minus the discount (or premium) on forward foreign exchange, which induces the capital flow. The discount or premium on forward foreign exchange can be influenced by official sales or purchases of forward foreign exchange. This, in turn, changes the "covered" interest rate differentials which influence the capital flows. Under present circumstances, where the limits of exchange rate change are 1 per cent on each side of par, the price of forward exchange cannot be pushed past the limits for spot exchange since the buyer could wait and buy spot exchange at a future date for that price. Thus, the width of the band effectively limits the ability of a central bank to influence the forward discount or premium, and, hence, the covered interest differential. With this limit, sizable interest differentials cannot be offset, and the ability of the central bank to influence capital movements is also retarded. With a wider band, a greater interest differential could be offset, thereby allowing more freedom for a country to influence capital movements without altering its own domestic interest rates.

This, of course, is no different from the situation under completely flexible exchange rates except that there is a limit imposed on the

---

are those of J. E. Meade, "The International Monetary Mechanism," *Three Banks Review*, September 1964, modifying his earlier advocacy of freely flexible rates; see "The Case for Variable Exchange Rates," *Three Banks Review*, September 1955.

[15] *Guidelines for International Monetary Reform, op. cit.*

degree of fluctuation. A more basic difference is that par values are still maintained for currencies. These would govern all dealings with the IMF and perhaps even all official dealings between countries. It offers an effective and *automatic* substitute for the adjustable peg—within the limits imposed—without giving up the concept of the peg.

Another advantage of the proposal is its evolutionary nature; it amends the status quo without radical alterations or new schemes and yet offers substantial aid in the solution of current problems. Little alteration in the IMF agreement would be necessary. Furthermore, a gradual widening of the band could be negotiated as central bankers gained experience and private traders and investors became accustomed to dealing with the wider fluctuations. For example, the band might be widened 1 per cent per year to some maximum, such as 5 per cent or 7½ per cent on each side of parity. Thus the transition would be gradual and the ultimate 10 or 15 per cent (approximately) permissible fluctuation would absorb a considerable amount of international adjustment, assuming that effective forward exchange operations made short-term capital movements stabilizing in nature.

The limits of the band would require a nation's central bank to stand ready to support its currency in unlimited amounts when the "price" of its currency reached the limit. Thus the need for international reserves would not be eliminated, but would be reduced considerably. But perhaps at least as important, the movement of the currency within the band would be an indication of the country's conformity to world economic developments. As a nation's currency fell toward the lower support limit the need for restrictive economic policies would become apparent, and the country would be able to undertake adjustments before the bottom limit was reached. Thus while additional freedom in domestic (monetary) policy is provided for, clear criteria to guide a nation's monetary managers toward appropriate deflationary (or inflationary) policies would also be provided so that action could be taken before the situation became critical.

But what happens when a country's currency falls (or rises) to the limit and reserves are lost (or gained)? In short, what about chronic deficit or surplus countries? They must still adjust internally to attempt to return toward the center of the band. The proposal to widen the bands is generally accompanied by a proposed guarantee that the peg (center of the band) will not be altered except for catastrophic changes. If the center of the band could be changed at will, then the destabilizing currency speculation of the present system will not be eliminated by rather worsened; for the same criteria that guide the money managers are also understood by speculators. Thus the "band" proposal can improve the adjustment mechanism, but it cannot make it completely automatic. Balance-of-payments discipline would still be necessary, but the price mechanism, through exchange rate changes, would reduce the load placed on domestic policies, and more time would be available in which internal adjustments could be undertaken.

To put the "band" proposal into practice, each country would have to agree to widen the support points of its currency by equal percentages. The width of the band would be flexible. At present, the bands would have to be fairly wide, e.g., 5 to 7½ per cent around the center peg. But if the world economy became more integrated, the bands could be narrowed or even eliminated at some time in the future.

Plans to Increase World Liquidity

While the return to the gold standard or the adoption of flexible exchange rates would increase the speed with which balance-of-payments disequilibriums are eliminated by automatizing responses to disequilibriums, the plans to be discussed next would leave the adjustment mechanism largely unaffected. They would, instead, increase the available supply of liquidity, i.e., of reserves and borrowing power, and hence the period of time over which balance-of-payments adjustment can be made. By increasing the amount of reserves available to a deficit country, it may be enabled to ride out its deficit, without making price and income changes—the disequilibrium may not be fundamental and may reverse itself in time. At the very least, if price and income changes prove necessary, the extra reserves will make those changes relatively less painful by stretching them out over a longer period of time.

Most of the innovations introduced into the Bretton Woods system have been along these lines, i.e., liquidity increasing. For example, currency swaps and lending by the Group of Ten are means of temporarily placing additional reserves into the hands of deficit countries. Likewise, "Roosa bonds" are a means of formally shuffling reserves from surplus nations to the United States, a deficit country.

But there is opposition to liquidity increasing schemes. One school argues that, all things considered, the existing system has worked quite well. This school maintains that the existing supply of reserves and liquidity is sufficient and the existing system can cope with future liquidity problems. Not surprisingly, this tends to be the position of IMF officials and staff. Others argue that the creation of excess liquidity, as a substitute for a more efficient adjustment mechanism, is dangerous. Excess reserves are said simply to delay crises, and to make them worse when they finally arrive. This type of criticism is most often offered by supporters of flexible exchange rates whose main focus is on adjustment rather than liquidity.[16]

Nevertheless, preoccupation with plans to increase the future supply of world reserve persists. In good part this path is chosen because it is more difficult (and perhaps more dangerous) to attempt to make a major change in the adjustment mechanism. And some reform would seem to be inevitable. Thus, assuming that the present "adjustable peg" exchange rate system will continue largely as is, with less rather than more adjustments in exchange rates, some other change in the present system is necessary to remedy its increasing operational deficiencies. Two deficiencies receive particular attention by those who would increase reserves. First is the reserve currency anomaly: World reserves grow faster when reserve currency countries run a deficit, but running persistent deficits undermines confidence in the quality of the (reserve) currency. But when the deficit is eliminated, slower growth in world reserves, and perhaps reserve scarcity results. Of such dilemma are international monetary crisis spawned. Second, without a new source of reserve growth, future reserve inadequacy will increase the pressure for more restrictive measures against free trade and capital flows, or for more drastic income and price adjustments when paced, orderly adjustments are needed.

[16] See, for example G. Haberler, *Money in the International Economy* (London: Institute of Economic Affairs, Hobart Paper 31, 1965), pp. 36–38.

The various plans for "liquidity" reform to meet these problems can be grouped into two categories. The first involves essentially the creation of a super central bank with the power to create international reserves. The second category includes multireserve currency plans which encompass less drastic modification of the existing IMF system.

The Triffin Plan

Organizational Features. The Triffin plan is reminiscent of the Keynes' Clearing Union proposal. But the Triffin plan has been developed to fit into the institutional arrangements of the IMF, whereas Keynes worked on a clean slate, for the world at that time had no international monetary institutions. The Triffin plan would create new reserves in the form of deposits for the various nations in the XIMF (expanded IMF). The XIMF would create these XIMF deposits by lending to member countries and by undertaking investment in specified securities. These are similar, but are not completely comparable, to the techniques commonly associated with national central banks, such as the Federal Reserve.

The implicit politics of the Triffin plan are almost the opposite of those of flexible exchange rates. Triffin would move further toward internationalism and international consultation or multilateral surveillance and away from nationalism. It is in this sense an extension of international sentiments (or sentimental internationalism) which prevailed at Bretton Woods and in the formation of the United Nations at about the same time. Moreover, the Triffin plan would replace the dollar and pound, or any one nation's currency, as a *reserve* currency with the new unit called by the old name "Bancor." Those Europeans who see the importance of the dollar and pound as symptomatic of Anglo-American political domination should be pleased by this replacement, although as later noted, they have other grounds for concern about Triffin's plan. By the same token, some Anglo-Americans might be displeased with the dethroning of "English-speaking" money. The Bancor unit would be equivalent to a specific amount of gold and each nation's currency, in turn, would be fixed in value relative to Bancor. Bancor would become a new unit of account in transactions between nations and the XIMF, and presumably between the official institutions of member countries.

To implement the plan, Triffin would require each member country to acquire XIMF deposits equal to at least one-fifth of its total reserves of gold and foreign exchange.[17] These deposits would be purchased with gold or foreign exchange holdings from the present reserves of the participants. Each country would also agree to accept Bancor deposits in settlement of future payments imbalances and, in case of a deficit, would settle the deficit by a reduction of its own Bancor account. Thus, Bancor would become a new medium of international payment among official institutions. Its function is initially to supplement and eventually to replace the present national reserve currencies.

When the plan is instituted, the XIMF would receive primarily dollars and pounds or, more precisely, short-term liabilities of the United States and United Kingdom from other countries, and gold from the United States and United Kingdom, in payment for their minimum Bancor balances. This, of course, would reduce the total official holdings of pounds and dollars, but would not completely deplete the dollar and pound holdings of other governments. But the elimination of pounds and dollars held as reserves, and their replacement by Bancor, is one of the primary objectives of the Triffin plan. To accomplish this, Triffin proposes that all of these pound and dollar assets except working balances of central banks be converted to Bancor deposits. Although this would inflate the XIMF's holdings of these currencies, provision would be made for their gradual liquidation.

To make Bancor more attractive than gold as reserves, the XIMF would pay interest on its Bancor liabilities. Whether Bancor would be more attractive than pound or dollar obligations, which also pay interest, remains to be seen. But Triffin's expectation is that the gold and exchange value guarantees attached to Bancor deposits will make them preferable to national currency reserves.

[17] *Gold and the Dollar Crisis, op. cit.*, pp. 104–107. This ratio could, of course, be set at any level by international agreement. In fact Triffin has recently suggested that a ratio of 60 per cent gold to 40 per cent credit reserves may be more appropriate under present conditions to ensure that "excess Bancor" acquired in return for dollars and pounds would not be used to drain gold from the XIMF or from the United States. In addition, he suggests that it may not be necessary to *require* countries to maintain that ratio in the beginning. See "International Monetary System," *Moorgate and Wall Street*, summer 1965, pp. 32–33.

The XIMF unit would be fixed in terms of gold, and each nation's currency would be fixed in terms of Bancor. But there is no presumption that exchange rates must be fixed for eternity. The Triffin plan allows for exchange rate adjustment under conditions of fundamental disequilibrium in a country's balance of payments. The XIMF is protected from loss through such a currency devaluation, for each nation would guarantee the gold value of its currency which the XIMF held. This provision is presently part of the IMF rules, and so imposes no new burden on nations. Thus, a devaluing country would be required to pay into the XIMF such additional securities or gold as is needed to preserve the value of its liabilities to the XIMF.

If a country accumulates Bancor deposits in excess of its minimum required ratio to gold, it has the option to purchase either foreign exchange or gold from the XIMF with that excess Bancor. In this respect, the Triffin plan retains a direct tie to gold; indeed, this represents one of the major problems with the plan.

Reserve Creation. The major objective of the Triffin plan is the *programed* increase in international reserves. In large measure, the Triffin plan is inspired by fear that, since gold production cannot be predicted, nor can reserves long continue to be comprised of deficit country obligations (U.S. and U.K. liabilities), sooner or later the *supply* of reserves will diminish and tend to strangle world trade. This fear was voiced long before the current U.S. program to curb its deficit had started, perhaps in anticipation of such a move. Ideally, reserves could be made to grow at a rate determined from time to time, in the light of current needs, by the XIMF managers. But to reduce the arbitrary power of the managers, Triffin has proposed that the rate of reserve increase not exceed a predetermined rate (3 to 5 per cent) per year.

By planning the increase in reserves, both inflationary and deflationary excesses are to be avoided. When world reserves expand too rapidly, an inflationary bias is imparted to the system. Surplus countries have no check on inflation; and because they do not fear that their reserves will be depleted, deficit countries also can pursue unrestrained inflationary policies. Thus a surfeit of reserves is accompanied by little pressure on deficit countries to deflate. On the other hand, if reserves increase too slowly relative to trade and capital movements, deficit countries must react quickly with deflationary policies, while surplus countries will resist inflation in order to conserve and accumulate reserves. Here, the bias is toward general deflation.

Somewhere between these two extremes is a middle ground of reserve expansion which will require balance-of-payments adjustments but which will not be unduly harsh on the deficit country. Similarly, the middle ground will remove the conditions under which all (or most) countries try to increase reserves by running surpluses at the same time. It is this middle ground that Triffin seeks with his proposal that reserves increase no more than 3 to 5 per cent per year; the growth of world trade in the past has been in this range. Triffin's fear, as noted, is that neither gold production nor additions of new reserves through the deficits of reserve currency countries can do the job. Thus a reserve-creating agency is needed. But as the agency will be run by fallible men, their *maximum* reserve-creation powers should be set to avoid inflation-creating conditions.

How is this steady growth in reserves to be achieved? First, the XIMF could grant temporary credit to deficit (borrowing) countries by lending them Bancor, much as the IMF lends foreign exchange to its members now. Such loans, although initiated by the borrowing country, would be relatively short term, and subject to the approval and therefore the conditions set by the lender, the XIMF. Second, by purchasing securities the XIMF would create Bancor deposits in final payment for the investments. These investment operations would be taken at the initiative of the XIMF and are similar to the way the Federal Reserve creates bank reserves through open purchases. Thus the two procedures are roughly parallel to rediscounting and open-market operations of national central banks.

In Triffin's proposed world, total reserves could increase by three means: new gold production, XIMF loans to deficit countries, and XIMF investments. Since the XIMF would control its own investment operations, it could adjust these purchases to offset any level of reserve increase from the other two sources, and thereby achieve the desired rate of increase in world reserves.

Criticisms of Triffin's XIMF. While Triffin's plan is analytically sound and appealing, a number of problems and questions attach to the methods by which the XIMF would create reserves. With respect to the credit facilities for a nation which wishes to borrow, the problem is straightforward: It is basically a political one. It cannot be denied that the lending potential of the XIMF to deficit countries would be increased and currency crises thereby more effectively combated. But these credit facilities would have to be restricted to short-term balance-of-payments problems and not used for prolonged financing of balance-of-payments deficits or for development loans to underdeveloped countries. To remove this possibility, XIMF loans would have to be made contingent on approved policies to restore long-run equilibrium in the borrower's balance of payments as is the case with IMF drawings under existing arrangements. There would be continuous XIMF surveillance of the internal economic policies of borrowers, and in this sense, some national sovereignty in the form of conditional lending would be surrendered to the international central bank. Fear of the loss of national sovereignty is a major factor in the rejection of the Triffin plan by some national officials. A conflict of interest between "safe" lender's criteria and domestic economic growth policies is only too possible.

With respect to the international open-market operations, the problems are considerably more complex and largely unanswered. Even Triffin has been unclear on this score. The essential questions are: What kinds of securities are to be purchased? Where will they be purchased? Such investments would not be purchased from a government directly, but would involve purchases of a government's securities in national capital markets with the permission of that government. The selection of the country in which to purchase is not at all neutral as to the benefits conferred by the XIMF. First, the country in which the purchases of securities takes place will receive the Bancor deposit adding to its international reserves; other countries will receive no such addition. Second, the securities purchased must be guaranteed in gold (or Bancor) value, a guarantee that is hopefully enforceable. Third, the purchases should be so directed as not to disrupt the capital market in which they are made.

Triffin originally advocated the purchase of securities—presumably, government securities—in markets "whose need for capital was greater than in the U.S. and U.K." Furthermore, "a portion of such investments might be channelled into relatively long-term investments for economic development through purchases of IBRD (World Bank) bonds. . . ." [18] However, his view has since changed. He still advocates the purchase of some marketable obligations of international institutions (IBRD) but the remainder of the purchases should be made in short- and medium-term securities in major financial markets such as the United States, the United Kingdom, and a few European capital markets.[19] The purchases of widely traded securities of highly developed nations has two advantages. First, the provision of a gold guarantee which must be attached to such securities presents few problems. Second, a ready market exists should the XIMF desire to sell such securities, which it would want to do if international reserves increased by too much in any given period. For example, if XIMF made loans to deficit nations which, in the aggregate created reserves totaling more than the 3 to 5 per cent increase allotted for the year, it could *reduce the aggregate* of international reserves by selling some of its securities in the open market. The buyer of these securities (assuming he were an American) would pay dollars, which the XIMF could redeem in equivalent value of Bancor; by retiring the Bancor, the XIMF would be reducing international reserves.

The fact that the XIMF, by the latter-day Triffin doctrine, will be purchasing securities in the largest markets poses a problem, if as in the past, these markets are in deficit countries. Since the XIMF in its open-market operations would supply new reserves to the country of purchase, it could help finance their deficits. With this aspect Continental Europeans can hardly be expected to be sympathetic. If, on the other hand, securities of surplus countries are bought by XIMF, their holdings of reserves, including Bancor, are simply increased further.

The Triffin plan does not improve the efficiency of the balance-of-payments mechanism. A deficit country would still lose reserves (Bancor) and it cannot do so indefinitely. To the extent that a deficit country is assisted by XIMF loans or investment operations, the deficit country gains time to make internal adjustments, but they must still be made, presumably by relative deflation. The Triffin plan may therefore be expected to encounter many of the same objections

[18] *Gold and the Dollar Crisis, op. cit.,* pp. 118–119. See also Oscar L. Altman, "Professor Triffin, International Liquidity, and the International Monetary Fund," in Seymour Harris, ed., *The Dollar in Crisis, op. cit.,* pp. 261–265.
[19] "The International Monetary System," *op. cit.,* p. 37.

the present system does, but the reserve currency problem would be effectively solved, and the supply of world reserves would not be subject to haphazard influences as it now is.

Variants of the Triffin Plan

A number of other plans which are essentially variations on the Triffin plan have been proposed.[20] A number of these proposals suggest that the participants not be statutorily required to hold a minimum percentage of their total reserves in XIMF Bancor deposits as is the case with the Triffin plan. Instead, the inducement of interest earnings on the Bancor deposits and the desire to hold working balances in Bancor are relied upon to keep the XIMF operating.[21]

The Angell Proposal. A more fundamental revision proposed by James W. Angell—one-way convertibility of gold—attempts to meet the "gold leak" possibility under the Triffin plan.[22] Since the Triffin plan permits surplus countries to convert their "excess" Bancor into gold, the XIMF could conceivably act as a channel to pass gold to chronic surplus countries, thus reducing its own gold supply. If enough gold were lost, the demand for gold might be switched to the deficit countries themselves. This would approach the possibilities under the existing system should foreign governments attempt to convert their dollars to gold. Angell proposes that gold be used to buy Bancor deposits, but not vice versa. In addition, transfers of gold between member countries or between members and the XIMF would not be required, but could be arranged only by mutual agreement. But XIMF members would be required to accept Bancor deposits from other member countries in settlement of deficits. Gold as a medium of international exchange would be eliminated except where mutually convenient. The XIMF would be a true central bank creating Bancor deposits in exchange for gold and the foreign exchange holdings of members and making "direct" loans to a deficit nation. Triffin's provision for making investments to create Bancor is omitted.

[20] See Machlup, *Plans for Reform of the International Monetary System, op. cit.,* pp. 47–61.
[21] *Ibid.,* pp. 50–51.
[22] James W. Angell, "The Reorganization of the International Monetary System: An Alternative Proposal," *Economic Journal,* December 1961, pp. 691–708.

The elimination of the obligation of the XIMF to sell gold, plus other features of Angell's plan are more similar to Keynes's "clearing union" than to Triffin's XIMF. Thus a surplus country which acquired the currency of a deficit country could convert this foreign exchange to Bancor deposits. Likewise, the lending provisions of the XIMF would allow the deficit country to buy Bancor (borrow) with its own currency. But such financing of deficits by the XIMF would be specially limited and subject to an interest penalty as well as other sanctions which the XIMF could enforce should its holdings of the currency exceed stated limits. Sanctions could also be applied to surplus countries to stimulate adjustment to eliminate the surplus, when the Fund's holdings of such currency fell below certain limits. Thus, the Angell plan attempts to set out precise operational criteria to achieve many of the objectives of Keynes (and Triffin) while moving the world away from its dependence on gold.

The Stamp Plan. Basically different from the variant plans already discussed is the plan devised by Maxwell Stamp. This plan does not centralize international reserves in XIMF deposits but does have a mechanism for "reserve" creation.[23] The Stamp plan ties reserve creation to loans for underdeveloped countries. This is a central purpose of the Stamp plan, whereas such loans are peripheral in the Triffin plan. Briefly, Stamp would have the IMF distribute certificates (of deposit) to underdeveloped countries which would use them to pay for imports from developed member countries. The developed countries that acquire them would hold these certificates of IMF deposits as international reserves and use them in their own balance-of-payments settlements. In the revised (1962) version, these certificates would represent fifty-year loans to the International Development Association, which would, in turn, lend to the underdeveloped countries. Limits would be set on the amount which any developed country would be asked to absorb and hold.

While this plan is ingeniously designed to achieve the twin objectives of getting more capital to developing nations and increasing reserves at the same time, its chances of adoption seem remote. One criticism is that aid to underdeveloped countries and additions

[23] See Maxwell Stamp, "The Fund and the Future," *Lloyd's Bank Review* (1958). For a modified version see his "The Stamp Plan—1962 Version," *Moorgate and Wall Street*, Autumn 1962.

to world reserves are not alike and should not be mixed; aid should be based upon the ability to use it effectively, and this may not be equal to the need for additions to world reserves. But more important, the acceptability of the certificates among developed countries and the value of the certificates as bona fide reserves would be in doubt, if a question arose as to the ability of the underdeveloped countries to repay IDA. Thus, the essential criticism is that the quality of IMF assets would be lower under this scheme than under the existing IMF or under Triffin's plan.

Potential Innovations within the IMF. Actually, under the existing IMF rules, members can borrow new reserves in the form of foreign currencies if not Bancor or some central reserve unit, but the borrower is restricted in his ability to borrow and must face conditions imposed by the IMF if new reserves are actually created. A member country even now may automatically draw foreign exchange from the IMF equal to 25 per cent of its quota (gold tranche), and therefore this amount is normally considered a part of each nation's reserves. But if a country borrows in excess of this amount, the excess may be deemed a reserve creation and to this portion the IMF conditions of multilateral surveillance are applied. It has been proposed [24] that the borrowing of the other 75 per cent of its quota (credit tranche) be made automatic or at least be subjected to less stringent conditions. This rather minor revision of IMF could increase the potential reserve-creating capacity without setting up a super central bank. But Triffin's central objective—to increase the total supply of reserves at a rate which would be compatible with world trade needs —would not be achieved. Nor would an annual increase of IMF quotas per se assure a steadily growing quantity of reserves. An increase in quotas only creates lending capacity; to transmute this potential into actual reserves requires borrowing by deficit countries. In short, to make the whole credit tranche automatically available would still leave the initiative wih the member countries while Triffin would shift the initiative to the XIMF managers.

But there is evidence that the IMF is willing to consider additional means of reserve creation. Official consideration has already been

[24] For example by Edward Bernstein in testimony before the Joint Economic Committee. See *Outlook for U.S. Balance of Payments*, U.S. Congress, December 12, 13, and 14, 1962, pp. 205–240.

given to increasing the "automatic" drawing rights of a country above the gold tranche position. But more important, the *Annual Reports* of the IMF in 1964 and 1965 [25] have examined somewhat sympathetically schemes to increase "unconditional liquidity" or claims on the IMF through investment operations by the IMF. Needless to say, this is not far removed from the essentials of the Triffin plan or its variants.

MULTIRESERVE CURRENCY PLANS

Reforms of the system less revolutionary than a return to gold, the establishment of flexible exchange rates, or the creation of a super central bank have been advocated widely, particularly in the United States. These reforms focus on further evolutions of the present IMF system to ease the tasks of the two reserve currencies and to increase cooperation among central banks so as to enhance the capacity and willingness of surplus countries to lend to deficit countries.

The very existence of a reserve currency system involves the granting of credit by surplus countries to deficit countries, since the surplus countries' official institutions hold the short-term liabilities of the deficit countries—to date, dollars and pounds. But the granting of credit has advanced beyond the narrow framework of reserve currency holdings to include numerous *ad hoc* arrangements (currency swaps, Roosa bonds, Group of Ten credits, etc.) which have been discussed previously.[26]

But it is more and more widely thought that *ad hoc* arrangements are necessarily tentative, leaving the international monetary sysem constantly guessing about the next piece of "ad hoccery," and hence inherently unstable. Moreover, reformers say that *ad hoc* arrangements have not solved the inherent contradictions that reside in the system, and that the IMF cannot resolve these contradictions within its existing powers.

A number of plans have been advanced which would *require* greater central bank cooperation in extending credit to deficit coun-

[25] International Monetary Fund, Chap. 4 of 1964 *Report*, and Chap. 2 of 1965 *Report*.
[26] See above, pp. 224.

tries. Many of these would rely on loans by the surplus countries *to the IMF* which would in turn make credits available to deficit countries for the continued financing of their deficits.[27]

Roosa's Plans for Long-Term Loans

In addition, Robert Roosa has proposed that long-term loans be granted on a formal basis to weak currency countries by surplus countries under three sets of conditions.[28] The first proposal would only extend the issuance of "Roosa bonds" to all future reserve currency countries. The United States has sold intermediate-term bonds which are convertible to dollars to surplus countries for some of their official short-term dollar assets. By so doing, the liabilities of the reserve currency country (the United States) are transformed from short term to intermediate term, giving temporary respite from gold loss. Roosa would formalize and extend this practice. Second, to "consolidate" their obligations, *long-term* bonds might be issued by the United States and United Kingdom to foreign official holders of their short-term liabilities. This procedure would attempt to reduce the pressure on the current reserve currencies by soaking up a major portion of their short-term official liabilities for extended periods and allowing time to make basic balance-of-payments adjustment without constant concern over possible currency crises or renewal of existing credits. Finally, long-term loans for "monetary reserve purposes" could be made by strong currency, surplus countries to particular countries who "had outgrown the scale of their present reserves."[29] The intent here is to provide reserves on a longer-term basis for a country in need of additional breathing space to accumulate earned reserves by balance-of-payments surpluses. Examples of potential recipients of such lending are the United Kingdom and Japan, whose owned reserves are thin in relation to actual and potential balance-of-payments deficits. This proposal's

---

[27] This is essentially the institutionalization of the "General Arrangements to Borrow," making it a permanent and normal mechanism. This is the arrangement proposed by Xenophon Zolotas, *The Problem of International Liquidity* (Athens: Bank of Greece, 1961).
[28] Robert Roosa, *Monetary Reform for the World Economy* (New York: Harper & Row, 1965), pp. 100–109.
[29] *Ibid.*, p. 105.

purpose parallels the apparent objective of the recent credits to the United Kingdom and additional standby credit authorized by the Group of Ten (excluding France) in September 1965.

The new feature of this fuller "Roosa plan" is that the countries making long-term loans (buying the bonds) would consider these assets as part of their "secondary reserves." Roosa's proposal includes the hope that means will arise by which the lenders can shift these (secondary reserve) bonds to other lenders in return for more liquid currencies when the lender needs them. For example, the proposal suggests that if France were an original lender but began running a deficit before repayment, France could call upon other lenders to take over the loans in return for foreign exchange (reserves). In short, if a lender found its balance of payments turning into a deficit before the bonds were redeemed, the bonds could be "rediscounted" or used to acquire "primary reserves" which in turn could be used to finance the deficit.

Although these arrangements would increase world liquidity by formalizing and extending the borrowing facilities of deficit countries, they are hardly sufficient to fulfill world liquidity needs should the U.S. deficit disappear for an extended period. But such is not the intent of this proposal. Plans which are specifically designed for this eventuality rely on multireserve currencies. These are the "multiple reserve currency" and the "composite (or collective) reserve unit" proposals.

Multiple Reserve Currencies

The Procedure and Requirements for Reserve Creation. The multiple reserve currency proposal is designed to finance the deficits of developed countries by expanding the reserve currency system to include currencies other than the dollar and the pound, which surplus countries will acquire and hold as reserves.[30] The plan, in simple outline, would merely require that surplus countries acquire the short-term liabilities of the deficit countries in at least partial settle-

---

[30] In the strictest sense, the essential ingredient of this system already exists in that some countries hold foreign exchange in addition to pounds and dollars. But for all practical matters, the pound and the dollar are the acknowledged reserve currencies.

ment of the deficit, and agree to regard these foreign exchange holdings as part of their reserves. In this manner new reserves can be created since the deficit country does not lose reserves (of gold, dollars, or pounds) equal to its deficit, but instead increases its liabilities to the surplus countries; in effect, it borrows from them. Actually, this is precisely how the U.S. deficit has created reserves. Foreign official institutions have added to their stocks of U.S. short-term assets, rather than converting all of them to gold. In other words, the United States has borrowed short term which increased the dollar reserves of foreigners, while U.S. gold reserves declined by substantially less than the full extent of the deficit. Multiple reserve currencies would simply apply this procedure to many currencies rather than restricting it to the dollar and the pound.[31]

In large measure, the multiple reserve currency proposal is designed to offset the shortage of world reserves and possible liquidity crisis that might threaten when the U.S. deficit becomes a surplus. That the focus of the plan is basically limited to an eventual U.S. surplus may explain the failure of the plan to deal sufficiently with the long-run problems which may well arise, such as how to cope with the chronic deficit country or the declining ratio of reserve currencies to gold as total reserves grow. The multiple reserve currency plan is a short or medium-term expedient to preserve the present system, while postponing basic reform concerning which there is no current consensus of world opinion. Furthermore, under this plan the United States will retain its central position, not as a supplier of reserves through deficits but as a holder of reserves through surpluses. Since the United States is the world's largest trader, it would presumably be the largest holder of currency reserves too.

The plan contemplates reserve currency status for most of the major currencies, in addition to the pound and dollar. This means that any nation which happens to be in surplus, including the United States, would extend credit to any country in deficit. At

---

[31] Perhaps the major academic advocate of this plan is Friederich Lutz. See *The Problem of International Equilibrium* (Amsterdam: North-Holland Publishing Co., 1962) and *The Problem of International Liquidity and the Multiple-Currency Standard*, Essays in International Finance, No. 41 (Princeton: International Finance Section, 1963).

present there exists a one-way extension of credit, essentially from Europe to the United States and United Kingdom. The objective, of course, is to allow the deficit countries to finance their deficits *without* losing reserves, or at least losing less reserves than the total amount of the deficits, so that they may undertake slow and orderly internal adjustments to eliminate the deficits.

For example, if the plan were in operation, each country would hold in addition to gold a number of foreign currency assets as reserves, acquired when it was in surplus. Now suppose that France incurs a deficit to other countries while the United States has a surplus of approximately the same size. The French deficit and the U.S. surplus may be settled in one of three ways, or some combinations of them. First, the United States could use its accumulated francs to buy gold, thereby reducing the reserve stock of France and increasing the reserve stock of the United States. A given quantity of gold is simply shifted from France to the United States, and the aggregate supply of reserves in the world monetary system stays constand. But this mechanism is already inherent in the existing system and involves no reserve creation. Second, the United States could retire dollar assets owned by France which France had earned while she was in surplus and the United States was in deficit. In this case France's reserves in dollars would decline while U.S. reserves remain unchanged; total world reserves would decline. Again this procedure is inherent in the present system and actually occurred in the first half of 1965. Third, and this is the procedure contemplated by a multiple reserve currency system, the U.S. Federal Reserve System could hold as reserves the francs which the United States earns by its surplus. Then, the United States would have additional foreign exchange reserves (its old stock plus the new francs) while France would have no decrease in her reserves, but an increase in liabilities to foreign official institutions, in this case the U.S. Federal Reserve. Thus the crux of the multiple reserve currency system lies in its ability to finance deficits by reserve increases on a global basis rather than restricting such finance to the United States and United Kingdom as is now the case.

By increasing the number of currencies which nations will agree to call "reserves," a subsidiary objective of the plan is to reduce the load placed on the present reserve currencies to make them less susceptible to speculative runs. The short-term liabilities of the United States to foreign official institutions are only slightly less than the U.S. gold stock, while such liabilities of the United Kingdom greatly exceed her gold holdings. If total short-term liabilities to all foreigners (both official and private) are considered, they exceed the combined U.S. and U.K. gold holdings by at least 50 per cent. On the other hand, the official liabilities of countries other than the United States and United Kingdom are virtually nil, while their holdings of gold and foreign exchange reserves are high compared to earlier periods. It is this feature which places speculative pressures on the pound and the dollar but not on other currencies. Under a multiple reserve currency system, other countries, finding their official liabilities rising relative to their reserves when they incurred deficits, would develop into true reserve currencies. By the same token, should the United States and United Kingdom run surpluses, their foreign exchange reserves would increase while their liabilities to foreign official institutions would remain the same, or even fall. Thus, the plan could bring about better balance among the reserves-liabilities relationships of the countries and eliminate the unique problem of the pound and the dollar.[32] However, this aspect of the design presupposes that the United States and United Kingdom eliminate their deficits.

Although a U.S. surplus might allow it to introduce the system unilaterally by holding foreign exchange as reserves instead of calling for settlement in gold, an agreement among the major trading countries obviously is preferable. Such an agreement would provide that the monetary authorities of the various nations gradually acquire a reserve mixture of a number of currencies and gold. Since it is doubtful that this would take place unless each currency were convertible to gold on demand, each country would agree to buy and sell gold at a fixed price against their currency held by foreign officials. Thus, gold convertibility of all of the major currencies would be achieved and is likely to be a *sine qua non* for the plan to be effective.

In addition, each country must agree to provide short-term credit instruments suitable for foreign monetary authorities to hold as re-

[32] Lutz, *op. cit.*, pp. 247–249.

serves.[33] One of the reasons why the pound and the dollar have emerged as reserve currencies is the highly developed money markets in the United Kingdom and United States and the easy availability of short-term credit instruments such as treasury bills, time deposits, etc.—which are convertible to demand deposits, quickly and without risk. Such is not the case in many European countries, and reserve currency status presupposes that these will exist, for countries will be reluctant to hold as reserves the currency of a country lacking a supply of short-term credit instruments and the facilities for readily converting them to cash.

Finally, it is usually proposed that each nation attach a gold value guarantee to its liabilities held by foreign official institutions to induce nations to hold foreign exchange as reserves instead of gold. This guarantee would protect the country that holds a nation's currency as reserves from any loss in terms of gold should that nation devalue.

The institution of the multiple reserve currency system depends greatly on the elimination of the U.S. deficit, and perhaps less so on the U.K. balance of payments. Should these countries remain in deficit while most of the European countries remain in surplus, the plan is academic. The United States (and United Kingdom) would not be able to acquire foreign exchange except by currency swaps. Likewise, the European countries would find it difficult to acquire any currency reserves except dollars and pounds. New reserve currencies could be created only to the extent that some countries other than the United States and United Kingdom ran deficits, which the surplus nations are willing to finance, i.e., to consider as part of their reserves. It is also likely that only if the United States becomes a surplus nation and thus a major holder of foreign exchange reserves would the system be able to create a sizable volume of new reserves. If the United States does not become a surplus country, the principal reserve creation will continue to be the acquisition of dollar liabilities, or barring this, the U.S. will continue to lose gold. That is, the existing system with its deficiencies will remain.

If the United States does become a surplus country—the condition

---

[33] See F. Machlup and B. G. Malkiel, eds., *International Monetary Arrangements: The Problem of Choice* (Princeton: International Finance Section, 1964), pp. 89–92.

on which the plan seems to be premised—its successful operation requires that the United States accumulate and hold the currencies
of the then deficit countries as reserves, instead of relying almost
totally on gold as in the past. This, of course, would be a reversal
of the situation since 1951, and requires that the United States be
the future short-term lender to deficit countries. The power which
the United States will thereby acquire over the deficit countries
will be significant, for there would necessarily be limits on the
amounts of a deficit nation's currency which a surplus nation would
have to hold as reserves before it could demand gold instead in
settlement of the deficit. If the U.S. surplus is large enough, its
holdings of other nation's obligations as additional reserves would
be at the discretion of the United States. Its power will derive in
part from the threat to convert to gold, once the limit is reached.
Furthermore, if the U.S. surplus turns out to be relatively large, it
will virtually control the amount of reserves to be created and the
speed with which deficit countries will be required to adjust their
balance of payments; the United States could exercise such control
by varying the amounts of foreign exchange it acquires relative to the
gold it buys. For example, should France incur a sizable deficit and
the United States a surplus, the United States will be in a position
to choose whether to hold francs or convert to gold, which in turn
governs the pressure on France for domestic adjustments. Thus, in
a sense, the United States will still be the focus of power under
this new system, if the conditions for the system's implementation—
a U.S. surplus—are achieved. The United States has played the
banker role before when it voluntarily extended large long-term
credits in the 1940s and early 1950s, and would be required to adopt
that posture again under this system, but this time as a short-term
creditor. However, there may be pressures inside the United States
less charitable than those which prevailed in the earlier period; for
when the Europeans had achieved their surpluses and growth with
American help, they proved to be not very benevolent when the
pound and dollar ran into trouble. In addition, the Communist
threat no longer shapes U.S. relations with Europe as in the earlier
postwar period. These factors raise the question as to whether the
United States will—or perhaps should—finance Europe's deficits
should they arise again.

All the same, this plan has been favored by American officials.[34] It is in nature evolutionary and American officials have favored no radical departures from the status quo. Further, the United States would still be left in a key position in international monetary arrangements, reflecting its overwhelming economic importance in the Western world. Moreover, the plan meets certain European objections to the status of the dollar as a reserve currency, by elevating other currencies to that status, and at the same time sharing with them the responsibilities inherent in that status. The plan also incorporates measures to overcome the feared liquidity shortage, and may provide a continued source of growing reserves to meet world trade and capital needs.

Possible Disadvantages. There are two things it does not provide, however, which many reformers would like: There is no specific provision for assistance to developing nations in the plan and no improvement is made in the adjustment mechanism. Indeed, through its gold-guarantee provision, the plan may well tie world currencies tighter into the fixed exchange rate pattern, and make adjustment by devaluation even more difficult for more nations.

The criticisms of the plan are basically those of the present system: It cannot cope with a chronic deficit country. Indeed, the operation of the system is seldom examined beyond the time when the United States becomes a surplus country. Some versions of the proposal attempt to deal with the chronic deficit problem requiring each country to hold (within minimum and maximum limits) a fixed proportion of foreign exchange reserves to gold reserves.[35] In this manner, a surplus country could not wantonly convert foreign exchange to gold and contribute to currency crises, nor could a deficit country continually have its deficit financed by surplus countries without losing gold.

Some basic problems arise with respect to negotiated limits on the ratio of gold to foreign exchange. First, it is not clear how these limits can be set in the beginning so as to be the same for all coun-

---

[34] Robert V. Roosa, "Assuring the Free World's Liquidity" reprinted in Grubel, *op. cit.*, pp. 261–274. Roosa has also retained this plan in his more complete recommendations. See *Monetary Reform for the World Economy, op. cit.*, p. 57.
[35] Machlup and Malkiel, *op. cit.*, p. 42.

tries. For example, the United States would have to run a sizable surplus for a number of years before its currency-gold ratio reached the level of, say, Italy or Germany. And it would be wholly accidental if the configuration of future deficits and surpluses should make the attainment of comparable ratios among the countries easy to achieve.

Second, even if attained, relatively fixed ratios of currency to gold reserves would be difficult to maintain. To finance a deficit by creating greater liabilities of the deficit country to other nations keeps the deficit country's currency-gold reserve ratio constant, but raises the ratio for the surplus country. Thus to stabilize the ratios, some combination of currency reserve increase plus gold transfer is required; this would be difficult to accomplish in a multicountry, multireserve currency environment.

Third, if countries agreed to maintain a fixed reserve currency—gold proportion, aggregate reserves could increase only at the same *rate* as gold protection unless alterations were made in the currency-gold ratios; this would require periodic negotiation and agreement among the countries.

It is evidently because of these problems that many multiple reserve currency advocates take a relatively short-run view and do not explicitly recommend a fixed reserve currency-gold ratio.[36] The plan is most often viewed as a means of avoiding the liquidity crisis which could result when the United States cures its deficit. Beyond that event it is evidently presumed that further evolution based on new experience will provide a solution.

A more basic criticism remains—chronic deficits or surpluses—whether a fixed currency-gold reserve ratio is attained or not. A chronic deficit country will either have a rising volume of short-term official liabilities or a falling level of currency and gold reserves. Doubt will arise about the ability of the country to maintain the existing exchange rate; as the quantity of a currency held by other nations rises, its quality becomes dubious. The normal reaction will be for the other countries to sell the deficit country's currency from their portfolios of reserve currencies or at least not to accept further holdings, i.e., refuse to continue to finance the deficit by lending. The gold guarantee will temper the actions of the foreign holders—since if the guarantee is honored they cannot lose—but, when the

[36] Lutz, *The Problem of International Liquidity* . . . , *op. cit.*, esp. pp. 247–249.

official liabilities of the deficit country exceed their gold reserves, can the guarantee be honored? Furthermore, the gold guarantee only extends to the official holdings of other nations. What about private holdings? Private foreign holdings of the deficit country's currency to which no gold guarantee is attached will run the risk of capital loss. Speculative runs on the currency, originating in the private sectors, could force devaluation or necessitate *ad hoc* loans to the deficit country in trobue. This is quite familiar. These are some of major problems of the present system.

Thus, there are serious limitations to multiple reserve currencies as an over-all reform plan. A rather broad range of issues must be agreed upon to make it operative but, even then, the system contains major deficiencies, characteristic of the present limited reserve currency system.

Composite Reserve Units (CRU)

The Composite (or collective) Reserve Unit proposal is an extension of the multiple reserve currency system but still a less fundamental change in the IMF system than the Triffin plan. The CRU plan is superimposed, so to speak, on the existing system of national reserve currencies and the *ad hoc* arrangements existing among IMF members and national central banks. In this sense, the CRU is intended to be an addition to the existing system, rather than a replacement of it.

The CRU proposal, originated by Edward M. Bernstein, has been considered sympathetically by the Group of Ten in its 1964 *Report*. In addition, there is evidence that the CRU proposal is gaining some sympathy in European countries as well as from officials in the United States and United Kingdom.[37] Thus the proposal is among the front runners of the plans for reform, particularly with the world's monetary negotiators.

The CRU and Reserve Creation. The plan would require that each country in the participating group (the Group of Ten plus Switzerland, presumably) place specified amounts of their own na-

[37] See *New York Times*, July 6, 1965, p. 47. Likewise, the CRU's are an integral part of the Roosa plan, but in a slightly altered form. See Robert V. Roosa, *Monetary Reform for the World Economy, op. cit.*, pp. 73–100.

tional currencies with the IMF, which in turn would create composite currency units equal in value to $1.00, but representing fixed percentages of the eleven currencies paid in by these nations. In the latest Bernstein proposal the IMF would create $1 to $1.5 billion in CRU's in each of five years. The countries would pay into the IMF an aggregate equivalent of $5 billion in their own currencies. The reserves thus created would be owned by the contributing countries in the form of a CRU deposit allocated to each country pro rata its contribution.[38]

In addition Bernstein suggests that it might be desirable to have the IMF itself acquire some of the CRU's created for its own account rather than crediting all the CRU's created to the accounts of the participating countries. This could be accomplished if for each dollar of national currencies paid in, the member receives only 75 cents in CRU's while the IMF retains the other 25 cents for its own account. The IMF could make more loans (allow more drawings) and thus be able to channel greater reserves to deficit countries where they are needed. This aspect of his plan has effects similar to selective IMF quota increases for the participating countries in the current system.

How is each country's contribution or quota determined? Either by negotiation or, as the Group of Ten suggested, in accordance with the gold holdings of the country relative to the total gold holdings of the Group. In any event, each country would agree to hold CRU's in some fixed relation to its gold holdings.[39] In the normal course of events, a deficit country would transfer a fixed proportion of gold *and* CRU's to a surplus country which had previously accumulated the currency of the deficit country.

The CRU proposal is obviously designed to achieve several objectives, but the major one is to provide a means for increasing world monetary reserves. While $1 billion is the presently slated annual increase in reserves, this could be raised simply by requiring the purchase of more CRU's with national currency; that is, by raising the CRU-gold ratio in the future. Thus, steady growth in world

[38] See E. M. Bernstein, "Further Evolution of the International Monetary System," *Moorgate and Wall Street*, summer 1965, pp. 59–65.
[39] *Ibid.*, *p.* 62; and *Report of the Study Group on the Creation of Reserve Assets* (the Ossola Report) (The Group of Ten, 1965), pp. 26–28.

reserves could be achieved. In the process, a subsidiary and potentially politically important institution is created: the new international unit of account—the CRU. It supplements dollars, which would still remain the main reference currency and reserve currency as well.

One of the principal purposes of this proposal is to create a "safe" reserve unit. The CRU, backed by the IMF and behind this by gold guarantees attached to the currencies paid in, should not be subject to the same challenges with respect to quality that sporadically plague current reserve currencies. But with CRU creation limited to the rate of $1 billion per year, CRU's cannot replace and therefore will merely supplement the dollar and pound as reserves. The total $5 billion of CRU creation suggested by Bernstein can be compared to the $13 billion of U.S. liabilities to official institutions. But since CRU's will be used in partial settlement of future deficits, they will become a new international medium of exchange. If the surplus nations continue to be Continental Europeans, CRU's should reduce their anxiety about earning more dollars and pounds, and reduce their fixation on gold since CRU's carry gold guarantees and are presumably as good as gold.

But if the United States becomes a surplus nation in the years ahead, it is difficult to predict the effect on total reserves even with the CRU. Should the deficit countries be those who now hold large dollar balances, these balances are likely simply to be retired, thus reducing the aggregate amount of reserves. If, however, the new deficit nations hold few dollars now, then the United States would acquire CRU's and gold from them. In this case, the aggregate of reserves would not decline much, but the ownership of the reserves would shift to the United States.

The plan seems politically wise for it will reduce European complaints against sole reliance on the dollar and pound as reserves since the new unit, backed by their currencies as well, has reserve status. It is perhaps for this reason that the plan has been espoused by M. d'Estaing, who also sees in it a way to head off the more extreme plans for returning to gold brewed in his country.

But there are a number of criticisms of this proposal. The most obvious one is that the "growth" figure, $1 billion per year for five years, is quite arbitrary. It may or may not fit the world's needs. A decline of world trade or a dishoarding of gold would render it too large; a decline of other reserves—e.g., a U.S. surplus which removes dollars, could make it too small. But some flexibility in the determination of the amount of CRU creation to suit changing conditions is not beyond the collective ingenuity of the money managers, if it is not put beyond their power to use. In any event, the *idea* of increased liquidity is certain to shift attention away from improvement in the adjustment mechanism.

Perhaps the major criticism is that even with CRU's added to the existing system in the magnitudes currently planned, major reliance on the reserve currencies will continue with many of the attendant problems.[40] For example, if the United States achieves a surplus, the total supply of reserves would probably still diminish. A U.S. surplus realistically implies that one or more of the European countries incur deficits. In such an event, the deficit countries in keeping their currencies from falling on the foreign exchange markets, would probably sell their existing dollar holdings first, rather than use their CRU's and gold reserves. As these foreign-held (reserve) dollars are liquidated, world reserves decline equally. On the other hand, should the United States continue to run a deficit, the current surplus countries could either demand CRU's and gold or hold the dollars, and the problem remains. If the United States should lose gold and CRU's in fixed proportions rather than finance part of the U.S. deficit by having others accumulate dollar balances, the existing situation will remain. The American quota of the $1 billion per year CRU creation would hardly exceed $400 million, which is less than the recent annual U.S. deficits and much less than those in the early 1960s and late 1950s. Thus CRU creation will not forestall for long the necessity for the United States to eliminate its deficit.

The latest addition to CRU advocates is ex-Under Secretary Roosa.[41] His "Fund Unit Account" is similar to the Bernstein

---

[40] D. Daane, "The Report of the Group of Ten," *American Economic Review*, May 1965, p. 155, has criticized the CRU plan differently. If all imbalances are settled in CRU's and gold, then the world will come alarmingly close "to a slightly modified gold standard." Daane correctly notes that this would happen if CRU's replace rather than supplement existing reserve currencies. At the presently proposed level of CRU creation, however, this appears a remote possibility.

[41] *Monetary Reform for the World Economy, op. cit.*, pp. 75–100.

version of CRU's and holds a central position in his eclectic plan, which includes the long term loans and multiple reserve currencies provisions previously discussed. The Roosa version deviates from the CRU plan outlined above in two basic respects.

First, the participation of any country in the purchase of CRU's would be voluntary. Each year, once the aggregate amount of CRU's to create is decided upon and allocated among the potential participants, any unpurchased allocation of a particular country would be redistributed among the remaining participants on the agreed basis. Thus the plan would rely on the inherent attractiveness of CRU's and not on universal negotiated obligation of the participants.

Second, Roosa's version would also allow wide national discretion in the acceptance of CRU's in settlement of international imbalances. The only *requirement* would be that each participant accept CRU's in an amount which would make its holdings equal to its original purchase. Thus, there would be no required ratio of CRU holdings to gold holdings for each country. In fact, a country which refuses to buy CRU's at the outset would evidently not have to hold *any* CRU's, and could opt to remain outside the plan.

With these major exceptions, the CRU component of Roosa's proposal retains most of the other major facets of the Bernstein version. The national currencies paid to the IMF in return for CRU's would carry a gold guarantee and would be invested by the IMF in government securities—presumably, special note issues—in each country. But Roosa would require each country participating in CRU creation to buy and sell gold for its own currency at a price equivalent to $35 per ounce, thus eliminating the U.S. monopoly in pegging the gold price. And Roosa's plan differs somewhat on the basis for allocation of the CRU purchases. Whereas Bernstein would base this allocation on IMF quotas and gold holdings, Roosa's basis would be the use made of the nation's currency as other nation's reserves and the use made of the currency by the IMF in its drawings. This would heavily weight CRU creation toward the United States. Under 1965 conditions, this means that, depending on which criterion is used, between 40 and 70 per cent of the new CRU's would be purchased by the United States.

All the CRU proposals can be criticized for limiting the participation to the Group of Ten and Switzerland and for excluding the developing nations who need reserves so badly. Even in Roosa's voluntary system, while any nation could create its own currency to buy CRU's, developing nations should not be encouraged to do so. The gold guarantee from less developed nations would be considered of lesser quality so that the real value of the CRU's would be debased and the liquidity of the IMF could be impaired. Nations would be loathe to accept CRU's whose gold guarantee is of doubtful value.

Finally, the CRU system may increase the rigidity of exchange rates. Since the national currencies transferred to the IMF for CRU's must carry a gold guarantee, the reluctance of any country to devalue, even with a fundamental disequilibrium in its balance of payments, may increase. Again, the CRU system, like all its counterparts which focus on liquidity, tends to worsen the system's flexibility and the use of the available mechanism of adjustment via exchange rate changes.

SUMMARY

One undeniable fact which emerges from the preceding discussion is that no one plan for reforming the international monetary system is perfect. Each plan in solving some problems leaves untouched other fundamental difficulties. To serve equally and at the same time two such diverse masters as domestic growth and full employment on the one hand, and international liberalism with fixed exchange rates on the other, is a demand impossible to meet. The world wants a system which will eliminate balance-of-payments problems, but not at the cost of imposing domestic adjustments which are antithetical to modern domestic economic goals. The advanced countries are not willing to pay the price of an automatic and efficient adjustment mechanism (unless some miracle makes "incomes policies" effective)—which would eliminate the liquidity problem.

The proposals which seem to have the most support in official circles are primarily oriented toward creating a greater supply of reserves and liquidity and tend to ignore adjustment efficiency, hoping that more *time* for adjustment will allow even an inefficient mechanism to operate, without, somehow, making the cost in income lost and unemployment too high. The undeniable fact remains that adjustment *must* still occur, or any form of monetary and reserve arrangement will eventually collapse.

The concern for liquidity increasing measures have received added urgency in the first half of 1965. World reserves, defined as gold, official pound and dollar holdings, and IMF gold tranche positions, declined from the end of 1964. The decline of the U.S. deficit which had fed the increase in world reserves for a considerable number of years was the primary factor in this decline.

Even with this new sense of urgency, the world's monetary officials remained in substantial disagreement. This is well evidenced by the report of the Ossola Committee of the Group of Ten, which was established to study ways to increase world liquidity. The Committee, after reaching unanimous agreement that reserves needed to be increased, were in total disagreement as to how this increase should be accomplished.

The concentration on the "liquidity problem" in official circles might imply that they are satisfied with the way the adjustment mechanism has worked. But it probably implies a desire to bear those ills we know rather than risk new ones. And in large measure, the burden of proof falls on the reformers. The postwar period has indeed seen extremely favorable economic performance among the developed countries. International trade has expanded, actually more rapidly than output; currency convertibility has largely been restored in all countries; tariffs and quota restrictions have been reduced; all within the confines of the IMF-reserve currency system of which the reformers are so critical. Why, then, rock the boat with a major change, the effects of which cannot be completely predicted by the most informed observer?

Yet the doubt nags on reinforced by academic criticism which will not be stilled. The system has not worked perfectly. The deficit nations, the United States and the United Kingdom, have paid a sizable price in lost income, unemployment, and growth to sustain the system. Furthermore, there is trouble on the horizon in the form of liquidity scarcity when the U.S. deficit is eliminated. And the present system has been made viable only by various alterations in exchange rates at not infrequent intervals throughout the period. The major cause for concern appears to be that the current "significant" plans, focusing as they do on liquidity alone, tend to omit, or to make more difficult, this very basic mode of adjustment, as though a reformed system will not need it.

But it seems a safe prediction that this problem will rise again elsewhere in the future to plague the system, even though conferences are held and solutions compromised out which attempt to ignore it.

Epilogue

This book has attempted to explain the workings of the international monetary order. Certain flaws in the system have been enumerated, stemming both from its original architecture in 1944 and from the unwillingness of the participants to use all of the mechanisms of adjustment provided in the original blueprint, including exchange rate variations. In this system, the major and costly burdens of adjustment fall on the deficit countries. The special problems of the United States and the United Kingdom, the major deficit nations, have been documented. Some of the plans of reform have been outlined.

An epilogue allows assessment of future trends with some degree of freedom of insight. The quality of debate now seems to be more evolutionary, more open-minded, more compromising, more gradualistic than it has been in the past. There exists in many of the older plans for reform an apocalyptic streak, an unfulfilled and foreboding prophecy, to be cured by extreme measures. Doubling the price of gold, establishing a world superbank, freeing all exchange rates—all have given way to more moderate substitutes. The attacks and counterattacks on the system have awakened in many observers, heretofore silent, a desire for marginal changes in preference either to grand redesign or to inaction while the system breaks down. After all, with this system the Western world as a whole has grown more and been far more successful than even the optimists dared hope in 1945. The tendency to reason together may have been enhanced by the confluence of several factors tending to reduce extreme positions; by America's modification of its views toward accepting the CRU plan, once espoused by France in its desire to humble the dollar in its reserve currency status; by the amelioration of Britain's international position so that the threat of her currency's collapse no longer broods over all discussion; by the shift from surplus to deficit status in some European countries; by capital market and liquidity developments in Europe; and by other factors.

This epilogue will assess the prospects for reform of the system in terms of what is not likely to be done, what is being done, and, what ought to be done.

1966–1967

Before assessing these prospects, a few key developments likely in 1966 and 1967 bear brief analysis, for these developments are likely to influence the course of reform.

In the United States the over-all deficit on the balance of payments appears to have been cut by over half to an estimated $1.3 billion for 1965. But the gold outflow totaled $1,664 million in 1965, a figure exceeded only by 1960 and 1958, the major crisis years. To those who equate gold outflow with crisis, therefore, crisis continues unabated. To those who are not bemused by mercantilist beliefs in large gold hoards, the gold outflow appears to have bought bargains. It has permitted the export of investment capital, with which U.S. corporations and individuals over the years have bought most of the world's oil industry, some 80 per cent of its computers, about 50 per cent of its automobile output, and significant sections of other industries as well. The investments stimulate exports and produce perpetual income, while gold only takes space and earns nothing. But because this view is—to put it mildly—highly unofficial, continued government effort to stanch the gold outflow is certain.

In 1966, the United States is placing its major reliance for balance-of-payments improvement on the "voluntary" control of investment capital outflow, which it seeks to reduce by about $1 billion. This program has been criticized on several scores: It represents a further drift to controls in lieu of a basic corrective mechanism; it discriminates against newcomers to the investment field whose 1962–1964 basis is low; investment and exports are interdependent so that the restriction on investment will also reduce exports even in the short run and in the longer run, the balance-of-payments position is weakened by virtue of the restrictions.[1]

Because of the controls, many American companies, with restricted access to funds at home, have attempted to raise funds for their expansion in European capital markets, raising interest rates and borrowing costs in Europe and creating certain interesting feedbacks.[2]

The question remains, however, if equilibrium (defined in government parlance now as $250 million of a zero "over-all" balance) is achieved in 1966 or 1967 through controls, then what? If the controls are later lifted, private U.S. investment capital will surely flow out again; for the several motives which inspire capital investment, including the desire to be within the Common Market tariff wall which the "Kennedy round" might have lowered, will not have vanished. Controls can contain a disequilibrium, but not cure it. Does this evoke renewed controls? The definition of temporary begins to give. Actually, some private economists now estimate an increased deficit for 1966. Government sources appear sanguine about attaining the newly defined equilibrium; if all other conditions remain the same and investment is cut $1 billion, they will be right. But all other conditions rarely remain the same. The superiority of a viable mechanism of adjustment over controls is that the former can take changing conditions into account, the latter cannot. Changing conditions which work against the controller's forecast will either defeat the intent of the control, or provoke more controls, or, worse, do both.

THE PROSPECTS FOR REFORM

What is not likely to be done by way of reform may be summarized in two major ways: first, a further sharing of military and

[1] See the *Washington Post* editorial "Folly Compounded," December 6, 1965; and J.N. Behrman, "Foreign Investment Muddle: The Perils of Ad Hoccery," *Columbia Journal of World Business*, Fall 1965, pp. 51–59.
[2] See Ira O. Scott, Jr., *Financing U.S. Business in the Common Market*, Manufacturers Hanover Trust, November–December, 1965.

aid burdens among nations, at least in the visible future; and, second, a resumption of further acquisitions of dollar deficits by the surplus countries (without conversions to gold).

Chapter V notes that in both trade and capital movements, the United States is not far from equilibrium with the surplus Europeans. But the "leaks" from American aid and military expenditure have accounted largely for American deficits and European surpluses. For this reason, commentators as diverse as Professor Galbraith, the National Association of Business Economists, and the Republican National Committee have suggested reductions of expenditures in these areas, or at least a more equitable sharing of these burdens among nations, to help reduce American deficits.

With respect to the military burdens, sharing would involve important realignments of the structure of world power. Not only are such moves significantly under way, but indeed in Vietnam and elsewhere, the United States stands increasingly alone, and these added costs must exacerbate the balance-of-payments position. Because of its balance-of-payments position and National Plan, the United Kingdom's proposed "military review" can only mean, realistically, additional burdens for the United States. Nor is any resharing of aid burdens in sight, despite the increasing need for aid in the world. It has been noted that the American contribution to aid, as a per cent of its GNP, is not as great as its relative military burden nor superior to the Western average. Nevertheless, it remains desirable that all industrialized nations should contribute a like share of GNP to aid, and possibly a larger per cent than even the most liberal now do.

On the second way, an interesting, if minority, view of the overall problem has recently appeared in association with Kindleberger and Despres and Dr. Walter Salant. This approach, which might be called the "capital market view" holds that the United States has become the bank, i.e., the financial intermediary for the Western world. By borrowing short and lending on intermediate or long-term, the United States supplies loans and investment funds to foreign enterprises, and it also supplies liquidity to foreign asset holders. To inhibit this function, even by requiring equilibrium at any given time period, is damaging not only for the United States but—perhaps more so—for the rest of the world's economic growth.

Therefore, this position would ask that the Europeans recognize the value of the American financial intermediacy and be content to hold continuing American dollar deficits.

To counter the obvious argument that the very origins of the current crisis lie in the European unwillingness to do so (as reflected in vast exchanges of dollars for gold), this view holds that the lack of confidence in the dollar has been generated by the *attitudes* of government officials, journalists, and economists, and reflects their failure to understand the implications of the American intermediary function; but the private market does not lack confidence, as the increase in *private* holdings of liquid dollar assets shows.

However, this capital market view seems to ignore, at least in its initial form, one key power relationship which lies at the heart of the European objection; that is, that American long-term funds, particularly private investment, often buy *ownership* of industry in exchange for the provision of capital. Thus, the Europeans argue that their official holdings of dollars provide the wherewithal for American corporations to "expropriate" their European counterparts "with our own money"; the objection is particularly anguished when applied to the high-technology sectors of industry. The Europeans might be more prone to accept the capital market view if their industries were simply borrowing or even selling shares (but not control) in American capital markets. But, the Europeans point out, the interest equalization tax was designed to preclude them from precisely this sector of the American capital market; direct investment was inhibited later, and then voluntarily. The argument is not wholly fair—the world is more complicated—but it is persuasive in Europe.

The ownership objection of the European aside, there is no doubt of the fundamental validity of the capital market view. In the present state of European capital markets, the United States should continue to act as a supplier of capital, particularly long-term. But the very fact that the European authorities are not persuaded to hold what they consider an excess supply of dollars means in fact, that another way must be found to continue to permit the United States to export capital. One method is by earning sufficient foreign exchange on private account to do so. The argument between the capital market view and the preference for some form of exchange rate flexibility is one of means and not ends. If sufficient surpluses could be earned on private account, the American capital market function could continue uninhibited. The penchant of private holders to continue to want dollars as short-term investments—to use dollars for what Robert Roosa has called "vehicle status"—indicates that the depreciation of the dollar under flexible exchanges would be less than it would otherwise be. At the same time, the disappearance or minimization of American deficits would take away from official institutions those doubts which they now seem to hold about the dollar.

CRU

What is being done by way of reform seems to be the establishment of a new reverse unit, to be used in addition to gold, pounds, and dollars. The new unit will likely be some variant of the Composite Reserve Unit (CRU). The United States has now proposed such a reform; details of the American proposal are included in the President's *Economic Report* to Congress issued in January 1966. Simultaneously, a proposal to establish a form of CRU has resulted from discussions of the Common Market's Monetary Commission, excluding France. These views—to which may be added French and perhaps British views—will be submitted to the Group of Ten for debate, for modification, and for ultimate adoption in some form, presumably during 1966.

The initial Anglo-American position regarding reform favored superimposing on the current system methods to create new liquidity, but no specific form to do so had been selected. This idea was resisted by many Europeans, chiefly the French, whose finance minister, M. Giscard d'Estaing, told the 1965 IMF meeting: "Everyone . . . agrees . . . that the problem remaining to be dealt with in the immediate future is one of too much liquidity rather than too little."

That the Europeans tended to reject the original Anglo-American idea of additional reserve creation is hardly surprising. As surplus nations in the throes of varying degrees of inflation, the Europeans fear additional liquidity. They reduce the system to a basic formula:

Surpluses = Deficits + X. The unknown X can be the supply of new gold which is very small, or can be a substitute acceptable to all, such as the proposed new liquidity. If the new X is sizable it simply permits higher levels of deficits and surpluses to be accrued without any adjustment, and the Europeans do not wish to hold larger deficits. They tended to view the Anglo-American approach to liquidity as self-serving, and to reject it.

The ministers of the Group of Ten issued a communiqué in the course of the 1965 IMF meeting which attempted to reconcile the differences to some extent. The communiqué created the inevitable new committee (deputies of the Ten) whose task was

to resume on an intensified basis discussions to determine what basis of agreement can be reached on improvements . . . in the system, including arrangements for the future creation of reserve assets as and when needed. . . .

The contingency aspect of the foregoing quote, "as and when needed," may prove as important as the quest for agreement. For clearly this implies that whatever proposed new arrangement is accepted—including some variation of the CRU plan—likely will be significant only when Anglo-American deficits have been reduced so that liquidity is indeed threatened.

Thus the move toward a CRU plan represents compromises all around, including a shift in American sentiment. However, difficult questions remain: the relation of the new CRU to gold, the relative power of the Ten vs. the whole membership of the IMF, the question of majority rule vs. unanimity (meaning a one-nation veto power), the quantity and timing of CRU creation, indeed, the significance of the CRU itself if the United States does not eliminate its deficit. Many of these questions were discussed in Chapter VII. The answers in fact will depend upon the agreements reached in the future, in conferences at which political power is split, in contrast to the American power monopoly at Bretton Woods, and where therefore further compromise might have to prevail.

A functioning CRU plan will go a long way to solve the question of additional liquidity that might be needed if American deficits stop providing liquidity, so that world trade and investment can continue to expand. It also creates another method for lending to deficit nations, presumably with gold guarantees to the lender. Moreover, it reduces reliance on the dollar and pound as reserve units. This should not only please other nations which want reserve status for their currencies, but also relieve the United States and the United Kingdom to some extent from responsibility for the whole system, giving them more room or more time to adjust without unstabilizing runs on their currencies.

But the CRU plan does *not* provide an improved method of adjustment.

ADJUSTMENT

What ought to be included among the reforms of the system is an improved mechanism of adjustment. The lofty purposes of the monetary system established at Bretton Woods were three: to facilitate multilateral, and, hopefully, expanding, world trade without exchange controls; to achieve reasonable stability in exchange rates in the short run while leaving the way open for any nation to change its exchange rate in the longer run, if conditions such as fundamental disequilibrium warranted; and to allow governments to follow a policy of independence in their home economic policies, an independence which in effect meant—in the bitter aftermath of the depression—reasonably full employment, attainable targets of economic growth, and tolerable price stability. In many nations, including the United States, these goals in whole or part indeed become law. The loophole for exchange rate flexibility was thought to assume that these goals would not need to be disturbed periodically by crackdowns on economic activity in order to serve the needs of the balance-of-payments stability.

In short, the system was devised with a major eye to the ends to be served—free trade and capital movements in the international realm, and uninterrupted full employment and stable economic growth at home.

Since 1958, American and British experience has demonstrated that protection of the means—fixed exchange rates—threatens the very ends the means are meant to serve, at an unconscionable cost, as Chapters V and VI show.

At the same time, postwar experience shows that exchange rate

changes are a potent means of rectifying imbalances; the transition
of France after its 1958 devaluation from Europe's sick man to de-
fender of discipline is a dramatic case in point.

But it is also clear that the method of devaluing a currency
available under the existing system—jumping the peg to a new
value abruptly—has been determined to be virtually out of the
question for reserve currencies. Prospective par changes cause massive speculation and threaten to destroy international liquidity. Sen-
sible or not, it is now part of the rules of the game that a devaluation which expropriates part of the creditors' capital is not done,
even though part of that capital has been accrued from interest
payments which would not have been earned if invested in gold
or even in Swiss francs.

No monetary officials have stood more adamantly opposed to
the prospect of devaluation by peg-jumping than those of the
United States and, in practice, of the United Kingdom, even though
these deficit nations would have benefited. The central bankers
of surplus Europe have, of course, been equally opposed.

To the proposals—analyzed in Chapter VII—for completely free
exchange rates, these officials have been cold to the point of contempt. Neither peg-moving nor free exchange rates, although valuable and attractive intellectually, are likely to be relevant to policy
formation in the near future. The real or imagined disruptions to
world trade and investment and to the whole delicately interre-
lated system which the officials think would ensue from devaluation
by peg-jumping, let alone floating rates by the linchpin currencies,
have and do effectively block serious consideration of this type of
exchange rate adjustments. If a CRU plan is introduced, the limitation to peg-jump devaluations formerly imposed on the pound
and dollar may well be extended to the currencies of all major trading nations.

Having conceded the effectiveness of official resistance to these
types of exchange rate variation, the fact remains that it is a key
and presently missing link in the whole system, and that the system
cannot fulfill its diverse ends without it or some palatable substitute.

Between the obvious need for some type of exchange rate flexibility and the current crippling antipathy to it, some interesting
new approaches, compromising and evolutionary in nature, have

begun to emerge. Not surprisingly, they have developed in the United States and the United Kingdom, where the pinch has been felt hardest. Since the Europeans are neither immune from deficit status in the future, nor blind to the disrupting consequences of the type of adjustments the Anglo-Americans are forced to make, some support for further study of these ideas has come from those quarters in Europe formerly most adamantly opposed to devaluation—from some, but by no means all, of the central bankers who raised vast loans to Britain to prevent devaluation.

Dr. Marius W. Holtrop, president of the Netherlands Central Bank, who is regarded as one of the more conservative of European central bankers, told an economic forum in Frankfurt, that "the question should be studied as to whether it would not perhaps be possible to introduce greater flexibility into the rigid system of fixed parities [par values].

"As recently proposed by Dr. [Reinhard A.] Kamitz, the president of the Austrian National Bank, the advantages and drawbacks of a wider margin of permissable fluctuation of exchange rates around the official parity, which is at present limited to one per cent on either side, merit thorough examination; at the same time, the question should be studied whether a wider margin might perhaps help to facilitate limited changes of parity within the chosen range," Dr. Holtrop said.[3]

While the Group of Ten is studying the question of increased liquidity, the OECD has been studying the question of improved adjustment. Though its final deliberations will doubtless be influential, the Group has not yet made its findings or recommendations public.

One of the new approaches is to widen the support bands so that governments would use their hoards of liquidity to support their currencies at, say, plus or minus 5 per cent of par value, rather than at 1 per cent as current IMF rules provide. This approach has been implicitly endorsed by the Joint Economic Committee of the Congress. It is discussed, in conjunction with steps for greater harmonization of capital flows and monetary and fiscal policies among

[3] "Support Seen Building Quietly for Shift in Foreign Exchange," *New York Times*, January 9, 1966, p. F-1.

nations, in Chapter V. It is to this proposal, too, that Dr. Holtrop alludes.

Another approach, possibly usable in conjunction with widened support bands, would—in brief—permit movement of the peg, i.e., of the par value of currency, not in abrupt jumps or in free float, but in fixed, small, and gradual movements over a long time period. Originated by Professor Meade, and rather inelegantly labeled the "crawling peg" proposal, this plan destroys the incentive for massive shifts in liquid funds implicit in peg-jump devaluations, and with it the shocks imposed on the system by such shifts. It would permit the money managers to devalue (or revalue) a currency at a maximum rate of some 2 per cent per year, or 10 per cent—the maximum estimated overvaluation of both pound and dollar—in a period of five years, about the period in which these currencies have clearly been in disequilibrium. As a currency is devalued, interest rates must rise to hold capital; thus major reliance would fall on fiscal policy for internal manipulation of the level of growth and employment, a technique which the United States has in fact pioneered in its expansion since 1961.[4]

Probably not even the originators of these ideas would claim for them theoretical completeness in their present state. More thinking, research, and analysis will be necessary to test whether these ideas or some variant are usable in practice. And this type of further study is what both the Joint Economic Committee in the United States and Dr. Holtrop in Europe have requested, in an attempt to find new methods of adjustment, to avoid the old, costly and ironically ineffective techniques of devaluation and/or controls.

It has been said that every statesman in power is guided by the academic scribblings of a past generation. It behooves those in charge of the world's monetary system to heed the newer scribblings as well, before they condemn workers, taxpayers, and investors of any nation to the rigors of controls or discipline, which the lack of more sophisticated techniques will force them to use.

[4] For a fuller account of this proposal, see J. Meade's contribution to *International Payments Problems* (Washington: American Enterprise Institute, 1965), a later version of his plan. Able and brief analyses are J. Carter Murphy, "Moderated Exchange Rate Variability," *National Banking Review*, December, 1965; and John Williamson, *The Crawling Peg*, Essays in International Finance, No. 50 (Princeton: International Finance Section, 1965).

In international monetary arrangements in the past, closed minds which smugly refused to consider a new idea have often short-changed themselves. For example, the conservatives in the American Congress in 1944 refused to consider Lord Keynes's Bancor plan because it did not meet their needs as a surplus nation at the time, and they confused today with always. Had the United States used the Bancor plan, its Marshall Plan aid to Europe would have been offset by some $15 to $30 billion of Bancor deposits, which doubtless would have appeared useless paper at the time. But this Bancor later would have financed America's own deficits with Europe well into the 1960s, obviating the need for the gold outflow, the "classical medicine," restriction of investments, and recriminations. But the scene changes, and today's creditors are almost surely tomorrow's debtors. The same narrowness which gripped congressional minds in the 1940s still grips too many central bankers, American and European, and monetary officials in the matter of exchange rate flexibility today.

Unless some solution is found to the problem of equilibrating surpluses and deficits, the prospects are worse than more further gold outflow or bad feelings. The prospects are actually—in the absence of reform—for an increasing drift to controls, for an increasing move to autarky, toward nationalistic self-reliance and restriction of international trade and capital movements—toward all of the idiocies of the 1930s. It would be tragic indeed if these movements were permitted to take place when experience has shown how much is to be gained from international freedom and when the world more than ever needs growth.

Selected Bibliography

ALIBER, ROBERT Z. *The Management of the Dollar in International Finance*. Studies in International Finance, No. 13. Princeton: International Finance Section, 1964.

———. "The Cost and Benefits of the U.S. Role as a Reserve Currency," *Quarterly Journal of Economics*, August 1964, 442–456.

AMERICAN ENTERPRISE INSTITUTE. *International Payments Problems*. Washington, D.C.: American Enterprise Institute, 1965.

ANGELL, JAMES W. "The Reorganization of the International Monetary System," *Economic Journal*, December 1961, 691–708.

AUBREY, H. G. *The Dollar in World Affairs*. New York: Harper & Row (for the Council on Foreign Relations), 1964.

AUFRICHT, HANS. *The International Monetary Fund: Legal Bases, Structure, Functions*. New York: Praeger, 1964.

BAREAU, PAUL. *The Future of the Sterling System*. London: Institute of Economic Affairs, 1958.

BERNSTEIN, E. M. "Further Evolution of the International Monetary System," *Moorgate and Wall Street*, Summer 1965, 59–65.

———, et al. *The Balance of Payments Statistics of the United States: A Review and Appraisal*. Report of the Review Committee for the Balance of Payments Statistics to the Bureau of the Budget. Washington, D.C.: U.S.G.P.O., 1965.

BLOOMFIELD, ARTHUR I. *Short-term Capital Movements under the Pre-1914 Gold Standard*. Studies in International Finance, No. 11. Princeton: International Finance Section, 1963.

BRITTAN, S. *The Treasury under the Tories, 1951–1964*. London: Penguin, 1964.

CAVES, R. E. "Flexible Exchange Rates," American Economic Association *Papers and Proceedings*, May 1963, 120–129.

COMMITEE FOR ECONOMIC DEVELOPMENT. *National Objectives and the Balance of Payments Problem*. New York, 1960.

COUNCIL OF ECONOMIC ADVISERS. *Annual Report*. Published in the *Economic Report of the President*. Washington: U.S.G.P.O., annually.

DOW, J. C. R. *The Management of the British Economy, 1945–1960*. Cambridge, England: Cambridge University Press, 1964.

FLOYD, JOHN. "The Overvaluation of the Dollar: A Note on the International Price Mechanism," *American Economic Review*, March 1965, 95–106.

FORD, A. G. "The Truth about Gold," *Lloyds Bank Review*, July 1965, 1–18.

FRIEDMAN, MILTON. "The Case for Flexible Exchange Rates," *Essays in Positive Economics*. Chicago: University of Chicago Press, 1953.

GALBRAITH, J. K. "The Balance of Payments: A Political and Administrative View, *Review of Economics and Statistics*, May 1964, 115–122.

GARDNER, RICHARD N. *Sterling-Dollar Diplomacy*. London: Oxford University Press, 1956.

GILBERT, M., et al. "Domestic Implications of the Evolving International Monetary Mechanism," American Economic Association *Papers and Proceedings*, May 1965, 189–220.

GROUP OF TEN. *Report of the Study Group on the Creation of Reserve Assets*. (To the Deputies of the Group of Ten.) May 1965.

GRUBEL, HERBERT G., ed. *World Monetary Reform: Plans and Issues*. Stanford: Stanford University Press, 1963.

HABERLER, G. *Money in the International Economy*. London: Institute of Economic Affairs, 1965.

HALM, GEORGE. *The "Band" Proposal: The Limits of Permissible Exchange Rate Variations*. Special Papers in International Economics, No. 6. Princeton: International Finance Section, 1965.

HARRIS, SEYMOUR, ed. *The Dollar in Crisis*. New York: Harcourt, Brace and World, 1961.

HIRSCH, FRED. *The Pound Sterling: A Polemic*. London: Gollancz, 1965.

HORIE, SHIGEO. *The International Monetary Fund: Retrospect and Prospect*. New York: St. Martin's Press, 1964.

INTERNATIONAL MONETARY FUND. *Annual Report*. Washington, D.C., annually.

————. *International Reserves and Liquidity.* Washington, D.C., 1958.

JOINT ECONOMIC COMMITTEE. (U.S. Congress.) *Factors Affecting the United States Balance of Payments* (Compendium of Papers). Washington, D.C.: U.S.G.P.O., 1961.

————. *Guidelines for International Monetary Reform* (Report of the Subcommittee on Exchange and Payments). Washington, D.C.: U.S. G.P.O., 1965.

KENEN, P. B. "International Liquidity and the Balance of Payments of a Reserve-Currency Country," *Quarterly Journal of Economics*, November 1960, 572–586.

————. "Measuring the United States Balance of Payments," *Review of Economics and Statistics*, May 1964, 139–144.

KINDLEBERGER, C. P. *Balance-of-Payments Deficits and the International Market for Liquidity.* Essays in International Finance, No. 46. Princeton: International Finance Section, 1965.

LAMFALUSSY, A. *Investment and Growth in Mature Economies: The Case of Belgium.* London: Macmillan, 1961.

————. *The United Kingdom and the Six.* Homewood, Ill.: Richard A. Irwin, 1963.

LARY, HAL B. *Problems of the United States as World Trader and Banker.* Princeton: Princeton University Press (for the National Bureau of Economic Research), 1963.

LUTZ, FRIEDRICH A. *International Monetary Mechanisms: The Keynes and White Proposals.* Essays in International Finance, No. 1. Princeton: International Finance Section, 1943.

————. *The Problem of International Liquidity and the Multiple-Currency Standard.* Essays in International Finance, No. 41. Princeton: International Finance Section, 1963.

MACHLUP, FRITZ. *Plans for Reform of the International Monetary System.* Special Papers in International Economics, No. 3, Rev. Princeton: International Finance Section, 1964.

————, and MALKIEL, B. G., eds. *International Monetary Arrangements: The Problem of Choice.* Report on the Deliberations of an International Study Group of 32 Economists. Princeton: International Finance Section, 1964.

MEADE, JAMES E. *The Theory of International Economic Policy,* I, *The Balance of Payments.* New York: Oxford University Press, 1952.

————. "The International Monetary Mechanism," *Three Banks Review*, September 1964.

METZLER, LLOYD. "The Theory of International Trade," *A Survey of Contemporary Economics.* Philadelphia: Blakiston, 1949.

MUNDELL, R. A. "The Appropriate Use of Monetary and Fiscal Policy for International and External Stability," *IMF Staff Papers*, March 1962, 70–79.

National Plan, The. Cmnd. 2764. London: H.M.S.O., 1965.

NURKSE, RAGNER. *International Currency Experience: Lessons of the Interwar Period.* Geneva: League of Nations, 1944.

———. "Conditions of International Monetary Equilibrium," Reprinted in American Economic Association *Readings in the Theory of International Trade.* Philadelphia: Blakiston, 1950.

PAISH, F. W. "The Management of the British Economy," *Lloyds Bank Review*, April 1965, 1–17.

———. *Studies in an Inflationary Economy.* London: Macmillan, 1962.

PHILLIPS, A. W. "The Relation Between Unemployment and the Rate of Change in Money Wage Rates in the U. K., 1862–1957," *Economica*, November 1958.

POLK, J. "British Crisis and Response," National Industrial Conference Board *Record*, March 1964.

ROBERTS, B. C. *National Wages Policy.* London: Allen & Unwin, 1959.

ROLFE, S. E. "Trade Unions and Central Planning," Reprinted in W. A. Leeman, ed., *Capitalism, Market Socialism and Central Planning.* Boston: Houghton Mifflin, 1963.

ROOSA, ROBERT V. *Monetary Reform for the World Economy.* New York: Harper & Row (for the Council on Foreign Relations), 1965.

———. "Assuring the Free World's Liquidity," Federal Reserve Bank of Philadelphia *Business Review Supplement*, September 1962.

RUEFF, JACQUES, and HIRSH, FRED. *The Role and the Rule of Gold: An Argument.* Essays in International Finance, No. 47. Princeton: International Finance Section, 1965.

SALANT, WALTER, et al. *The United States Balance of Payments in 1968.* Washington, D.C.: The Brookings Institution, 1963.

SALANT, WILLIAM A. "The Reserve Currency Role of the Dollar: Blessing or Burden to the United States?" *Review of Economics and Statistics*, May 1964, 165–172.

SAMUELSON, PAUL A. "Theoretical Notes on Trade Problems," *Review of Economics and Statistics*, May 1964, 145–54.

SCAMMELL, W. M. *International Monetary Policy.* London: Macmillan, 1957.

SMITHIES, ARTHUR. "The Balance of Payments and Classical Medicine," *Review* of Economics and Statistics, May 1964, 111–114.

SOHMEN, EGON. *Flexible Exchange Rates: Theory and Controversy.* Chicago: University of Chicago Press, 1961.

STAMP, MAXWELL. "The Stamp Plan—1962 Version," *Moorgate and Wall Street*, Autumn 1962, 5–17.

TOBIN, JAMES. "Europe and the Dollar," *Review of Economics and Statistics,* May 1964, 123–126.

TRIFFIN, ROBERT. *Gold and the Dollar Crisis.* New Haven: Yale University Press, 1961.

————. *The Evolution of the International Monetary System: Historical Reappraisal and Future Perspectives.* Studies in International Finance, No. 12. Princeton: International Finance Section, 1964.

————. "The International Monetary System," *Moorgate and Wall Street,* Summer 1965, 17–50.

ZOLOTAS, XENOPHON. *The Problem of International Liquidity.* Athens: Bank of Greece, 1961.

————. *Towards a Reinforced Gold-Exchange Standard.* Athens: Bank of Greece, 1961.

Index

Accounting concepts of balance of payments, 17–36

Adjustments in balance of payments, 37–57; anti-gold reforms, 203–208; capital outflow restriction in, 56, 176–185, 188; currency devaluation and, 48–50, 88, 96–103; 153, 155–164; deflation in, 50–54, 69, 83–84, 88, 96–103, 108–115, 141, 143, 146–147, 155, 158, 165–170; equilibrium concept and, 37–38; flexible exchange rates and, 208–223; foreign exchange rates and, 39–42, 48–50, 164, 188, 194; gold-exchange standard and, 65, 194–195; gold standard and, 60–61, 198, 199–203; IMF system and, 82–86, 195–199; incomes policy in, 54–55, 88–89, 97–98, 103–108; inflation in, 50–54, 83–84; liquidity and, 38–47, 223–234; mechanisms, 47–57; monetary-fiscal policy and, 170–175; multireserve currency plans and, 234–249; price changing methods, 48–55; trade regulation in, 55–56; Triffin Plan and, 228; wage-price guidelines and, 54–55, 169–170; war and, 63; White Plan and, 72–75

Aldcroft, D. H., 115

Aliber, Robert Z., 161n

Altman, Oscar L., 230n

Angell, James W., 231

Angell Plan, 231–232

Antitrust laws: Common Market, 182, 183; competition and, 132, 133

Balance concepts, in balance-of-payments accounting, 28–32

Balance of payments: accounting, 17–28; balance concepts in, 28–32; capital outflow and, 19, 21; currency transfers and, 19–20, 21;

debits and credits in, 22–28; debt settlement and, 24–26, 32; deficit and surplus concepts, 28–34; defined, 17; economic factors in, 8–9; financing items in, 32–34; foreign exchange market and, 20, 22; foreign investment position and, 34–36; gold sales and, 6, 19–20, 21, 148, 149; payment and receipts categories in, 17–20, 21; war and, 63; see also Adjustments in balance of payments; United Kingdom—balance of payments; United States—balance of payments

Balogh, Thomas, 132

Bancor, 76–77, 78, 225–226, 227

"Band" exchange rate proposal, 213, 219, 220–223

Basic balance, in balance-of-payments accounting, 28, 31

Behrman, J., 156n

Belgium, 122, 183

Bell, Philip, 220n

Bernstein, Edward M., 30, 233n, 244, 245n

Bernstein Plan, 189, 244–249

Bimetallism, 44

Bloc flexible exchange rates, 219–220

Bloomfield, Arthur I., 61n, 62n

Bretton Woods agreement, 51, 78–82, 194–199

Bretton Woods Conference, 14, 40, 58, 71–82, 259

Brookings analysis, 146–147, 157n, 219n

Business, British: attitudes toward, 131–132; management qualities, 126–132, 135

Canada: floating dollar, 209, 212, 216

Capital: currency speculation and, 33–34; long- vs. short-term, 26; per-capita growth, 120–121; see also

[269]

SIDNEY E. ROLFE, an economic consultant to business and government, was chief economist for the CIT Financial Corporation in New York City from 1954 to 1960. He is currently president of two private investment companies which he founded in 1960.

Born in Gary, Indiana, Mr. Rolfe received his Ph.D. from the University of Chicago, and has taught at Princeton and Columbia Universities. In the early fifties he served as head of the manpower section of the Wage Stabilization Board.

He has contributed a number of articles to popular and professional journals, including the *Harvard Business Review*, *Review of Economics and Statistics*, and the *American Economic Review*.

Mr. Rolfe lives in New York City with his wife, Maria.

ROBERT G. HAWKINS is a Ph.D. candidate at New York University where he is an instructor of economics at the Graduate School of Business Administration.

DATE DUE

| 5.2ᴏ '82. | |
| 11.25 | |